Resurface

life

Resurface

A GUIDE TO NAVIGATING
LIFE'S BIGGEST TRANSITIONS

Cassidy Krug

PENGUIN LIFE

VIKING
An imprint of Penguin Random House LLC
1745 Broadway, New York, NY 10019
penguinrandomhouse.com

A Penguin Life Book

Designed by Alexis Farabaugh

LIBRARY OF CONGRESS CONTROL NUMBER: 2024048472
ISBN 9780593833117 (hardcover)
ISBN 9780593833124 (ebook)

Printed in the United States of America
1st Printing

The authorized representative in the EU for product safety and compliance is
Penguin Random House Ireland, Morrison Chambers, 32 Nassau Street,
Dublin D02 YH68, Ireland, https://eu-contact.penguin.ie.

Some names and identifying characteristics have been
changed to protect the privacy of the individuals involved.

To Nicholas and Ocean, my favorite turning points

Contents

How We Got Here and What to Do with This Book

On August 5, 2012, I was in a place few people have ever been or will ever be: standing on a diving board in an Olympic final, billions of eyes on me, as I prepared to see if I was the best diver in the world.

On August 6, 2012, my diving career was over. My parents are both diving coaches, and I grew up on the pool deck. Aside from one nine-month break, I had never spent more than a few weeks away from the pool in a row. Now diving, which had been the center of my life for twenty-seven years, was no longer my home.

The change was as sudden as turning off the lights.

No more practicing through gusting wind or sideways rain. No more protein bar meals. No more steadfast coach. No more waking up in the morning, knowing exactly what my goals were for the day, week, month, and quadrennium. No more training to be the best in the world at something. The Speedo tan lines that seemed indelibly tattooed on my hips faded. My chlorine-bleached hair grew in black-brown. I was no longer an athlete.

Immediately after returning from the 2012 London Olympics, I quit my job, my boyfriend, and my apartment. I changed cities four times. I tried and failed to be a writer, worked on a one-season celebreality TV show, developed an obsession with the flying trapeze, started a new career at the bottom of the advertising ladder, and spent the next seven years working my way up the rungs. All the while, I fully expected that a new passion would fall out of a tree and hit me on the head, another all-in-one pursuit that would deepen my friendships, fulfill my ambitions, and headline my identity. It did not.

Instead, whenever I was doubtful or uncertain, my mind would drift back to diving.

That moment of stasis between rising and falling, my body suspended in the air, full of potential, waiting for orders.

The water stinging my hands as I ripped a jagged, bubbling hole for my body to enter.

The dull, vast, post-dive oasis, alone underwater with my triumph or despair. My body always knew before my brain did.

I'd feel these memories with all my senses and wonder:

Did I choose the right path?

What could I have done differently?

Have I peaked?

It's been years, why haven't I moved on yet?

Seven years into my advertising and brand strategy career, these questions overcame me. I left my job and went searching for answers, first from other Olympians, then from people of all walks of life who had experienced major transitions. I spoke with people who've been in and out of prison and the military. People who have quit marriages, religions, careers, sports, and alcohol. People putting the pieces back together after deaths and diagnoses. People who have thrived through transitions, and people who have struggled, and mostly, people who have done both.

I wanted to learn: Is anyone else grieving the road not traveled? Is anyone else struggling to adapt to a new world? Is anyone else trying to figure out when to make their next leap and where to go? Who out there has navigated life transitions with grace, and what can I learn from them?

While I worked to include stories that represented a range of experiences, I didn't search exhaustively for the subjects in this book. A few are close friends. A bunch are second-degree connections who came my way when word got out that I was writing a book on transitions. The only person in this book that I cold-messaged was Stanley, the formerly incarcerated PhD candidate in chapter 3, because I read about him and couldn't stop thinking about his story.

Three takeaways from that: One, don't be surprised to find more thirtysomethings, more trapeze hobbyists, and more Olympians than you might in a perfectly representative sample.

Two, don't expect journalistic impartiality. I've become such a nerd-fan of the people I've included in this book, whether we were already close or they came to me as a friend-of-a-friend-of-a-friend-of-a-friend. My goal was to convey, with as much perspective and empathy as possible, each subject's take on their own experience. Most of the work of transitions happens between our own ears, and my priority was to understand and share these thought processes.

Three, I didn't have to cast my net far to find great stories, which leads me to believe that great stories are literally everywhere. This book was a marvelous excuse to reach out to people, grill them for an hour or two on their most interesting experiences, and ask them the meaning of life. I hope that, after reading this book, you are inspired to reach out to your own friends, grill *them* about their most interesting experience, and ask *them* the meaning of life. I expect you will find that the people around you are even cooler than you thought they were.

A final caveat: Some scenes and conversations—particularly ones that happened outside the realm of "book research"—have been recreated as best as possible. Some exchanges have been tightened or edited for clarity. Some unnamed characters in my own story are a mashup of several people. Blame the process of turning memories into memoir and inter-views into narrative.

Now, what have I learned?

If our lives are constellations, transitions are the stars. The moments that send us off in different directions, altering the shape of our existence. The liminal spaces of transitions are scary and often out of our control. But that's where we stage our personal revolutions.

Unfortunately, the prevailing advice on life transitions is not particularly helpful.

"Time heals all wounds," they say. Right, but how do you avoid just sitting around feeling sad?

"You're experiencing growing pains," they say. Okay, but how do I make them stop?

"This is an opportunity to find your passion," they say. Thanks, but that's quite a lot of pressure.

Maybe the prevailing advice misses the mark because the prevailing view of what a transition actually *is* is not very accurate. I used to think of transitions as events with a beginning, a middle, and an end—but my conversations have shown me most never really end. I used to think of transitions as Times Square milestones, but often, they're so subtle that we don't even know they're happening until after they've happened. I used to expect transitions to result in a new permanent state, a happily or sadly or purposefully-ever-after, but really, life is just a set of shifts.

I'm no psychologist—that ship sailed freshman year when Psych 1 overlapped with diving practice—just someone who's curious about people, fascinated by pivots, and working to handle transitions better in my own life. This book is an ode to the beauty and uniqueness of each individual and also the unexpected and telling ways that our dreams, fears, and instincts intersect.

I've based each chapter around one of those intersection points: places where my transition and many others all seemed to pass through the same stage or type of challenge. Each time I heard similar words come from the mouths of people with vastly different experiences, my ears perked up—like, for example, when Shelby, an ex-Mormon relationship therapist, and Obhāsī, a Buddhist monk, both told me how thrilled they were to discover a different philosophy than the one they were raised with, but how difficult it was to unlearn the thought patterns engrained by their former lives. I'm not saying Shelby and Obhāsī shared the same experience. Just that their individual experiences shared a challenge, and that challenge merited further exploration.

At each intersection point I've sought answers and advice from therapists, life coaches, business leaders, and academics, along with wisdom from transitioners themselves. Ultimately this amounts to a blueprint for a better transition: how to make the tough parts suck a little less and the good parts bring a little more joy.

Each chapter ends with a set of suggestions, including at least one "tell your story" prompt. In the process of researching this book, I asked a lot of people to share a lot of stories. Afterward they said things like, "What a great opportunity for reflection" and "I've never thought about my life like that before." Telling your story in writing has similar value. Writing the murky swirl of thoughts in your head gives them some order. It helps you figure out what's what and see your own life from a variety of angles. If you want to get the most out of this book, pick up your journal (or if you're like me and your hand cramps after a page, open your laptop), and give these exercises a spin.

It's worth noting that many of these exercises come from trained therapists who have devoted their lives to helping people navigate change. Our troubles with transitions often stem from biases, ruts, and traps in our own brains; therefore, it's hugely beneficial to find an outside observer to help you identify those biases, ruts, and traps, particularly if your transition is causing a lot of angst. In other words, this book is not a substitute for a trained therapist.

I hope that the stories in this book will serve the same purpose for you as they have for me: to help you feel a little bit less alone. The people I've met have taught me a lot about big changes: how to let go of my old life, navigate the aftermath, and embrace what comes next. My wish is that these pages will offer you insight and encouragement as you navigate the space between one dream and the next.

Resurface

1.

Recognize the End

Life doesn't lend itself to neat beginnings and endings. But there's value in acknowledging turning points. How do we recognize a major shift if we didn't see it coming or even notice it happening? How do we ground ourselves when faced with a change that feels entirely out of our control?

On August 5, 2012, I was standing thirteen feet from the springy end of a green Duraflex diving board, waiting for the referee to blow the whistle that said it was time for the very last dive of my life. I'd spent the past five minutes dunking into and out of the hot tub, jumping under a hot shower, drying my legs with my shammy, and then wetting them with the same shammy, and now I was the perfect temperature and the perfect level of dry. The London Olympic natatorium was a low buzz of water filtering and bright lights humming and hushed faraway voices. I was in the best shape of my life, physically and mentally, and the excitement of this moment elevated me to the top of the anxiety peak without pushing me over. My skin was electric without feeling shocked, and my heart beat like a tom-tom, not a crash cymbal. I was in the zone. The bronze was mine to win or lose, and damn, I was ready to win it.

I was born a pool brat, the daughter of two diving coaches, and attended my first meet at one week old. Growing up, the training and competition cycles guided my life as reliably as the seasons. There was our annual family road trip from Pittsburgh to the Ft. Lauderdale International Meet in May, the opening of the outdoor pool and start of two-a-day practices in June, and the two weeks of no diving in late August when I got to see my California cousins at the annual Krug family reunion. And then, of course, every four years, the Summer Olympics, the mythical mountaintop when everyone around the country stopped what they were doing and actually paid attention, for once, to the weird niche sport my family built our lives around.

In Olympic sports like diving, athletes plan in four-year increments. More than years, my life was punctuated by quadrennia.

Seoul, 1988: Three-year-old me stared in rapture at the Olympic gymnasts on TV, then began mimicking everything I saw, bouncing on the couch and teetering on lines on the floor. My parents begrudgingly enrolled me in a beginner gymnastics class, hoping my love for gymnastics would soon transfer to diving. It took a decade longer than they'd hoped. For my first twelve years of organized sports, diving was Mom and Dad's world; gymnastics was mine.

Atlanta, 1996: Eleven-year-old me stayed with my cousins in Santa Rosa while Mom and Dad worked for NBC at the Atlanta Olympics, spotting divers from the production truck and gathering intel to feed the commentators. I can tell you every single thing about the gymnastics that year: Dominique Moceanu's ponytail bobbing as she pranced and shimmied to "The Devil Went Down to Georgia," Kerri Strug's heroic second vault, and the inevitable grace of Amy Chow's bar routine, the hardest in the world. Most of the girls in my fifth-grade yearbook wanted to be either artists or marine biologists. My future goals were "be in the Olympics and own three dogs."

Sydney, 2000: At some point, I decided that doing gymnastics flips off a diving board into water was fun, and diving gradually worked its way into my schedule. By the summer of 2000, I was fifteen and powering through two pool workouts in the morning followed by four hours of gymnastics at night. It was too much. I saw the teenagers on the Sydney Olympic gymnastics team and knew I'd run out of time. I quit gymnastics to focus on diving.

Athens, 2004: The Athens Olympics took place the summer after my freshman year at Stanford. I entered the season big on talent and short on finesse. Decades of rigorous gymnastics training meant I was strong enough to do the hard dives but wild enough to land so flat on some of them I practically bounced off the water. But that fall my new Stanford coach, Rick, refused to let me even practice the hard dives, revealing that in my haste to prove how strong I was, I'd never really learned the easy ones. Rick introduced me to a new way to train, breaking each dive down into its elements—takeoff, somersault, kickout, entry—and drilling those until they were perfect. Before I got to Stanford, I approached a training session like a game of darts, celebrating wildly when I hit the bull's-eye, but expecting to miss most of the time. Rick turned practice into more of a road race: I learned each step so well that it would have been inconceivable to trip and fall.

Near the end of my freshman year, I surprised myself by qualifying for the Olympic Trials. Then I surprised myself even more by making the finals. I didn't make the team, but I did get a summer dream job with NBC as a production assistant for their Olympic broadcast. When I wasn't restocking the drink fridge or driving a golf cart across the dusty production lot, I snuck into the stands to watch the divers practice. Some were not much better than me. Since I was a toddler, the Olympics had been a distant dream. In 2004, they became a possibility.

Beijing, 2008: My first retirement. After graduating from college in 2007, I'd resolved to try to make the 2008 Olympic team and then go start my "real" life. I'd gotten good—good enough to be a contender. But a pinched nerve in February and too much recovery time in March, April, and May set me up for a dismal Trials in June, and I watched the Beijing Olympics that August alone on my couch.

Retirement had always been on the horizon. I'd watched countless divers enter the mysterious beyond. Some petered out in high school, others made it through college, and only a few continued past college graduation. Despite being coaches, my parents raised me to believe that you give a certain amount of time to sports and then let them go. When I was young, my dad would put me to bed with a string of possibilities: Good night my writer, my diver, my gymnast, my mathematician, my scientist, my artist. Rick, in his way, had also instilled the idea that sports should be a finite part of a larger life. During our daily warm-up time, he'd grill us on our academic areas of expertise. I was an English major, so he'd send me David Brooks's latest column before practice and expect a thoughtful analysis between sets of lunge jumps. Rick made sure I was dreaming not only of the Olympics but of the future after them.

So when I didn't qualify for Beijing, I followed through on my decision to retire from diving and start real life. I got off the couch, boxed up my swimsuits, and got a job at the Stanford Alumni Association. I was out of diving for a full nine months before the smell of chlorine and unfinished business lured me back in the spring of 2009. But I was conflicted, holding two narratives in my head. The first narrative: that I had left diving only to realize how much I loved it and came back determined to make an Olympic team. The second: that I had left diving, failed at building a fulfilling post-athlete life, and returned because it was my comfort zone.

London, 2012: My first, last, and only Olympics. August 2012 had been circled on my calendar since my return to diving in 2009. I had decided, long before qualifying for the London Olympics, that afterward I would finally, truly retire from diving. The end. Win or lose, Olympics or no.

By this time, Rick was adamant about this. At meets, he'd mutter to me about the other divers who'd stayed on past their primes, who lounged in the hot tub, dove a little, and played phone games while trainers wrapped ice bags around their shoulders. Once a month, we'd grab dinner at a local Italian restaurant. "You can keep diving if you want," he'd say. "But I won't coach you. You should move on with your life." A few gin and tonics in and the hyperbole would come out in full force. "When are you going to write the next great American novel?" he'd say, pounding on the table for emphasis.

Rick was right, diving had stopped filling my cup. I was twenty-seven and had graduated from Stanford half a decade earlier. While my friends were backpacking around Europe, planning weddings, and starting master's degrees and PhDs, I was still spending every day practicing the same five dives. While they were joining companies with free lunches and ping pong and working their way toward leadership positions, I was accumulating hundreds and thousands of repetitions, moving in slivers of centimeters toward perfection. I was antsy to get on with it. The 2012 Olympics would be the funeral for my athlete self.

· · ·

On the day of my Olympic final, I was a study in well-earned confidence. The nerves I'd been fighting my whole life were gone, magically replaced with an exuberant joy I never thought competition could bring me. I had practiced this dive at least ten thousand times and it was part of me, etched deeply into my muscle memory. I was about to show billions of people what I could do. I knew, with certainty, that I was about to have the highest board ride, the best form, and the cleanest entry I had ever had—perhaps the best the world had ever seen.

I took four measured steps and a hurdle jump, shooting my left knee to my chest. This approach landed me exactly on the end of the board, the springiest part, impeccably balanced. I felt it in the way the fiberglass bent with my weight and then sent me skyward, our efforts combined to beat gravity. I heard it in the sound the board made, deep and echoing and hopeful, no dissonant thuds. At the very last moment before my feet went airborne, I threw my arms down, starting a dazzlingly fast somersault.

But amid this unexpected confidence, I forgot a basic step. I eased into the twist rather than starting it in one sharp, smooth movement, meaning it took a split second longer than it should have. I was still twisting when I should have been getting my body into position for the entry. The dive moved like a word with the emphasis on the wrong syllable, and its final motions were awkward: a stalled rotation, a panicked bend, an ungainly last-ditch effort to enter the water with my dignity.

I stayed under an extra moment to delay the inevitable. When I came to the surface, I heard fives, not eights, eventually putting me in seventh, not third, at my first, last, and only Olympic Games.

I emerged from the water an automaton version of myself, my arms and legs robotically shepherding me out of the pool. The weight of the moment made my ears ring. I heard my teammates hooting and hollering and thought, *they're lying.* The entire seventeen-thousand-person arena couldn't have cheered loud enough to make the judges forget how bad that dive was.

I looked at Rick in time to see him with his head in his hands. Since my freshman year in college, his face had been my barometer. It had always shown me, deliberately, what I needed to see. When he was angry, he lowered his aviators, revealing his blue eyes glaring and the vein jutting out of his forehead, which meant "you're seconds away from getting kicked out of practice and so help me *gawd*, you'd better fix this." When he was happy, he'd be on his feet, fists in the air, yelling superlatives, which meant "you made the change!" When he was calm, he'd recline in his chair, his hand gesturing lazily, which meant "good enough, just go do another one, we need to get a lot of numbers in." But now he looked at me and I didn't recognize his face. I saw traces of . . . sadness? Anger? Love? I went to him and he gave me a long hug and said, "I can't talk to you right now. Find me later." I was relieved. Normally we'd talk for hours after meets about what I did right, what I did wrong, and what I should do next, but now neither of us knew what to say. By the time I got to the locker room, my cheeks shook with exertion. Then I sat on a bench, wearing a towel with all the drying power of a wet sock, and sobbed. How could I be done?

After minutes or hours—I don't know—I pulled on damp sweats, heaved my soggy backpack over my shoulder, and went to search for Rick.

I found him on the pool deck, watching the practice session for the next day's events.

"What happened?" he asked.

I knew it was coming, but I still wasn't ready for it. "I don't know," I said.

"I've *never* seen you make that mistake."

"I know," I said, and struggled to explain. My brain was hazy. "I think I just . . . got so excited to rip the entry that I forgot to do the dive."

We sat in silence for a beat, watching the other divers practice.

"You were really in the hunt," he said finally. "Did you have fun?"

It was a question he asked after nearly every meet, and one I usually answered with uncertainty. I always *wanted* to have fun competing. Between the affirmations, breathing exercises, and visualization, I'd spent a decade working very hard to convince myself that the wild feelings in my chest were "fun."

But this had been different. I'd just done five dives in a row, surfing a high I'd only read about in books. I wasn't ignoring the crowds or fighting back imagined disasters or trying in vain to pretend I was alone with Rick at Stanford and this was just another practice. Before each dive, I stared down the crowd, from the $800 tickets at eye level up to the top of the rafters where I could barely make out bodies. I smiled. And I said to myself, "Let me show them what I can do." Not because I wanted it to be true, but because it was.

"It was the most fun I've ever had," I said.

"You have to keep going," he said. "You could really do it, buddy. What do you think—four more years where all we do is try to beat the Chinese?"

"Maybe," I said. "Ask me again tomorrow." But I knew it was too late. The world was too big, and the pool was too small. He had built up retirement so carefully, and with such principle, that it was a foregone conclusion.

. . .

In the eighties, a psychologist named Nancy K. Schlossberg identified four categories of transitions, a framework that many therapists use today.

- **Anticipated transitions.** These are the transitions you see coming, like my retirement after the London Olympics or graduating from college.

- **Unanticipated transitions.** These are the transitions that blindside you, like a sudden, career-ending injury or winning the lottery.

- **Nonevents.** These are things that you've planned for and expect but don't occur, like not making it on a particular team or not having kids when you always thought you would.

- **Sleepers.** These are the shifts you don't recognize until after they've already happened, like falling out of love or becoming an addict.

My friend Ryan, one of the most successful American distance runners ever, had a sleeper retirement. It started with a host of athletic plagues. In 2011, he got plantar fasciitis in his left foot, causing him to favor his right foot, like a tire inflated a little more than its twin. That overcompensation eventually led to him straining his right hamstring in the middle of the 2012 Olympic marathon in London and walking off the course just past the ten-mile mark. A gnarly strain in his left quad in late 2012 was followed in 2013 by a tear in his right quad, which was followed by a stress fracture on his sacrum. While all this was happening, his energy was also starting to fail. His injuries gave him months of time off, but it still wasn't enough. Waves of fatigue would hit him so strongly that the man who had been running one-hundred-mile weeks since high school couldn't make it through a thirty-minute jog. The tests said low testosterone. The doctors said that was the price you pay for all those one-hundred-mile weeks.

He didn't accept this fate lightly. Starting in 2012, he spent three years entering races he was mostly too fatigued or too injured to finish. His retirement crept up on him, a classic sleeper transition, slowly sapping his strength until he had a moment of painful clarity: "I was never gonna run faster than I had before." By that time, his last great race was years behind him.

When we think of transitions, we usually think of them as either anticipated or unanticipated. Moments you see coming. Moments you don't. The plot twist is that not all transitions are moments. Who knows the last time you'll speak to a faraway friend or rock your child to sleep in your arms? Sleeper transitions start with quiet milestones that only appear in the rearview mirror.

* * *

When we look back at something we've experienced, we tend to judge it based not on our overall emotional state throughout the experience, but on two specific moments: one, the most intense point or points, and two, the end. This is a phenomenon called the peak-end rule, and it's been observed in a wide range of creative (and possibly sadistic) experiments. In one study, researchers compared a group of patients who received a standard colonoscopy with a group who underwent the same standard procedure plus three extra minutes at the end in which the scope remained in place, motionless.[1] The pain of a colonoscopy, I'm told, is mainly caused by the movement of the instrument, so those in the extra-time group spent that time feeling discomfort, but not pain. Afterward, those who had had the unnecessarily longer procedure rated the overall experience more positively and were more likely to come back for future colonoscopies than the standard group, ostensibly because the end of their procedure—those three bonus minutes—was less painful. Many social scientists believe that this effect holds true for more complex experiences. Take, for example, past romantic relationships. The peak-end rule predicts that your perspective on your ex is driven by a few intense memories in the middle and the breakup, rather than your average emotional state while you were together.

The nature of a transition—aka the end of an experience—makes a big difference in how we feel about the life that preceded it, as well as the life that follows.

So what do we do if, like Ryan, that transition is out of our control?

"I've always envied wrestlers," Ryan said. Then he told me about shoes on the mat, one of the few great athletic retirement rituals.

Picture this: Rulon Gardner, a gentle giant of a man, has just won the bronze in the 2004 Athens Olympics at what he has decided will be his final match. He gives an awkward bear hug to his much-taller opponent and walks to the edge of the stage to shake hands with his coaches. He gestures to a team official, who brings him an American flag, and returns, one last time, to the center of the mat. He's wearing the flag now and sits down right on the edge of that center circle, right in the middle of the arena. He fumbles to loosen the laces on his shin-high, ankle-stabilizing wrestling shoes, stopping once to wipe tears out of his eye with his palm. As he removes his right shoe, the camera pans to his face, and this giant, buzz-cut, heavy-browed man is sniffling with as much strength as he used to pin Sajad Barzi, the six-foot-five Iranian he just trounced. As the announcer rattles off his accomplishments, Rulon puts his shoes side by side in the dead center of the mat, stands up, and holds up his arms to the crowd. Everyone—coaches, crowd, and competitors—stand as well, and they roar as one, an outpouring of support. He has set his shoes down; he is finished.

For wrestlers, shoes on the mat flies at the level of weddings and funerals. It means "no regrets"—that an athlete has left all the sweat, heart, and muscle that they have on the mat. At the press conference afterward,

Rulon remained tearful: "I put the shoes on as a four- or five-year-old kid, and I took them off as a thirty-three-year-old kid." Like weddings, not all retirements last forever—Rulon himself has attempted a comeback several times since that day—but at least in the moment, it gives respect where respect is due and provides a chance at closure.

Shortly after Ryan retired, his friend Pastor Matthew texted that he was planning to run seven marathons on seven continents in seven days to raise money for his church. It was probably akin to texting someone to let them know that you're passing through their hometown—not to hang out, just to acknowledge that you're spending time on their turf. But in this case, something compelled Ryan to text back, not with "Good luck!" or "Godspeed," but a request: "Mind if I join you?"

When he retired at the end of 2015, Ryan had started weightlifting, building a gym in his garage and devouring fifty grams of protein every three hours. In his running days, he was stork-like: a few inches taller than the other men at the start line, his body weight seemed mostly made up of joints. By the time he decided to take on the World Marathon Challenge with Pastor Matthew, he'd put on forty pounds of muscle, filling in the concavities between his shoulders and elbows, his knees and ankles, his cheekbones and chin. He tried to get into distance training again, but the fatigue came back and he quickly found himself unable to keep up with the mileage required to prepare for a single marathon. So he stopped training and trusted that his greatest ability was one that low testosterone couldn't take away: his ability to suffer.

In his first three races of the World Marathon Challenge, Ryan hovered around a seven-to-eight-minute mile: nowhere near his heyday, but fast enough to make me question what the word "fatigue" meant to him. Marathon four, which took place in Spain, was a "sufferfest"—a mysteriously painful slog that felt like running through molasses. One flight and four hours of sleep later, Ryan got his redemption racing in Morocco: It was his best time yet, and he mused in a video blog that he had trained so little leading up to the event that he was probably gaining fitness as he went. On marathon six, in Dubai, Ryan started with "five-out-of-ten" hip pain, and by the end of the race, he was hobbling.

The first time Ryan tried to stand after the flight from Dubai to Sydney he nearly collapsed in the aisle. The race—seven of seven—started at 1:30 a.m. The moon lit the runners' path along the beach. Waves crashed as Ryan hobbled, mostly alone, along the grassy stretch next to the shore. Near dawn, Ryan ran into Pastor Matthew, who had started the race late after spending an hour at the hospital dealing with an anxiety attack and a torn patella. The two walk-ran together—Pastor Matthew pulling everything he had out of himself to inspire his church; Ryan doing the same, but for closure. They hobbled for miles toward the dawn.

After crossing the finish line, Ryan eased himself down to the ground, pulled off his shoes, and left them on the line. It was early in the morning and already humid, and only a handful of fans and fellow runners were there to witness the finish. He got up and limped away from his last marathon, feeling the concrete through his socks and the satisfaction through his pain. In a way it was fitting to have a rough day, he said in a video blog: "High highs and low lows, and that's what happens when you dream big, train hard, and go for everything." Then he thanked the marathon itself: his most worthy opponent, his archnemesis, his old friend.

Ryan had created a closing ritual that helped him reinterpret his retirement not as a sad, slow decline, but as a triumph.

There are a lot of definitions out there for a ritual, but here's one I like from anthropologist Robbie Davis-Floyd: "a patterned, repetitive, and symbolic enactment of cultural (or individual) beliefs and values." *Patterned and repetitive*: Ryan chose a series of races for his ritual, marked by the rules, courses, and finish lines he knew so well. They connected him not just to his own past as a runner, but to a shared experience with all runners. *Symbolic*: It's not a direct cause-and-effect situation. He wasn't running for rational reasons: time, fitness, ranking. There was some magic and mystery involved. *An enactment of cultural or individual beliefs and values*: Ryan's running career was about transcending doubt, exhaustion, and pain. The World Marathon Challenge—on no training, little sleep, and increasing levels of pain—was a pure enactment of the values that drove his career.

Rituals mark many of the anticipated and unanticipated milestones of our lives. Wedding ceremonies, graduation ceremonies, and funerals are all rituals to help us close one door and open another. But for many transitions, our culture doesn't provide rituals or templates to help us share loss and make meaning. I reached out to Ezra Bookman, a professional ritual designer who develops secular rituals for companies, civic organizations, and individuals, to learn why rituals are valuable. He looks at rituals as "punctuation for the run-on sentences of our lives." Often, we experience massive changes without pausing to reflect on them. Rituals help us to insert commas, periods, and exclamation points to mark our most important moments.

"Can a ritual really help you move on?" I asked. "Or is that more a job for therapy?"

He laughed. "It absolutely can. But maybe try both."

Ezra described the experience of transition as making the conscious decision to let go—over and over again. A ritual helps you strengthen the behavior of letting go. "I'm creating that new neural pathway to see [my transition] differently," he said. "And allow myself to let go more easily." For Ryan, the World Marathon Challenge helped him see his retirement differently—as something he ended on his terms. It also helped him to let go of the running season of his life.

. . .

Rituals don't need to involve running over 180 miles around the world, and Olympians aren't the only ones who participate in them. My friend

Karie was a salon owner before she retired last year. I called intending to ask her about the transition to retirement, but instead she told me about an even more impactful transition—a nonevent that shifted the entire course of her life: not being able to have children.

From childhood, the only thing she knew irrevocably about her future was that she would someday be a mother. All her early jobs involved kids. She started babysitting young. As a teenager she worked as a camp counselor, and as a young adult, she was a summer camp director. "This was something I always—*always*—wanted to do," she said. It was predestined, a single path with no cross streets.

When she was thirty, she married her husband and they started trying to have a baby. Two years later, they were still trying. A series of tests revealed that Karie was missing one of two fallopian tubes and half her uterus, and that her only chance at motherhood was IVF.

Successful IVF results in tremendous joy, but the process, whether successful or not, is torturous. Most insurances still don't cover it, and a single cycle can cost $10,000 to $50,000. You pay those dollars for the privilege of injecting yourself with hormones using long thin needles multiple times a day for weeks. Eggs are ripened, extracted, grown, and fertilized, and the subsequent embryos are tested for genetic disorder and transferred back into you. For Karie, the chance of all this resulting in a child was around 20 percent.

Doctors do what they can to keep expectations at bay, but their efforts pale in comparison to the emotional flywheel of the process itself. Ultrasounds show ovaries full of follicles, and hope paints a tiny face on each dark bubble. But say fifteen follicles grow. Maybe eleven mature into eggs that survive the extraction surgery. Of those, nine are able to be fertilized. Three develop into embryos. Two are genetically okay. And it still takes a good deal of luck for either of those to be successfully implanted. The hope and disappointment cycle through so quickly that they sometimes crash into each other. But IVF feels like your only shot, *so it has to work.*

Karie's first round of IVF resulted in an abundance of embryos: seven! Each was implanted. None took. She did not get pregnant.

Karie had never really dealt with failure—not in high school, not in college, not in beauty school, not as a young hairstylist. But in the IVF years, failure permeated her life. "My own body betrayed me," she said. She and her husband were failing to have the child they both desperately wanted. The IVF was failing, which meant her doctor was failing. After the first round, they found a new doctor and took a second chance on IVF—but that, too, failed. "Each time, it was like losing a dream," she said.

After her second round, Karie was drained—of energy, of money, of belief. She was tired to the bone of losing. "You know, I really respect somebody like Brooke Shields who went through six rounds of IVF," she said. "I'm like, God bless you, baby. I just couldn't." She and her husband considered adoption, but they realized that that, too, was a long journey with a high probability of loss. "You just can't live in that failed and negative place for so long," she said. "I stopped because I wanted success."

Transitions create voids. It's the moment of weightlessness at the top of an arc, the canyon between two cliffs. With hindsight, we know that we always end up somewhere. But in the midst of it, that void can feel permanent. We don't yet know that gravity will bring us back down, or that there's another cliff across the chasm. Once kids were off the table, Karie's future was a blank fog. It was hard to talk about what she'd been through. People stopped inviting her to baby showers because they didn't know what to say. Friends knew she was grieving but didn't know how to offer comfort. Her expectations for the present and future were shattered.

Intuition told her she needed to find something else to pour herself into, a place for all that hope and energy to go. A conversation with her husband revealed the other side of the canyon. "I said, 'What am I going to do with my life now that I'm not gonna be a mom?' and he said, 'Why don't you open your own salon?'"

Up until that moment, Karie had expected to just work as a stylist. The pressure and responsibility of salon ownership didn't fit with her picture of motherhood. But the nonevent that shaped her life, the transition to a future without children, created space for goals that she hadn't considered before.

Last year, Karie retired, two decades after opening her salon. She has a devoted following of staff and former trainees. She used to host fashion shows for her trainees when they graduated, where she sat in the front row with a box of Kleenex crying tears of pride. In the first COVID Christmas, when the quarantine shuttered most of her industry, she spent five days driving over five hundred miles around the Bay Area to hand-deliver hundred-dollar bills to her forty-seven employees. "If I would have had a kid," she said, "I probably would have stayed home and just poured everything I had into this child. But now I've trained a hundred or so hairstylists, they all have careers today, and they all are taking care of their own families because of my salon. And I feel really, really fulfilled about that."

A nonevent is a special kind of devastating. It doesn't just blindside you; it patiently waits while you nurture your dream and weave it into your life, then pulls the thread, unraveling not just your present but your picture of the future. For Karie, recognizing the end was inextricably linked with identifying a new beginning. She couldn't control her ovaries and uterus, the seven embryos that resulted from her first round of IVF, or the sole embryo that resulted from her second round of IVF, which she named Velcro because she just wanted it to stick. But she did choose when to stop trying for one future and start building another. Recognizing the end of her dream of having children made space for her to build an entirely different dream—one that has brought her more pride than she could have imagined.

Karie's story includes a ritual as well.

A few years after her last round of IVF, at forty-five, Karie began experiencing excruciating pain in her abdomen. Doctors discovered fibroids—muscular tumors in the walls of her uterus—and ended up removing both her uterus and her ovary. "I never got a baby shower," she said. "So I decided to have a hysterectomy shower."

She called it a "Goodbye Aunt Flo" party, invited her girlfriends, and served Bloody Marys. Everyone sat in her living room and shared stories of their first periods, then left with bundles of tampons tied with curled ribbon as party favors. It couldn't erase the physical or emotional pain she'd experienced, but it did give her the chance to associate at least one happy memory with the organs that had brought her so much sadness. "People get really sentimental and sad at menopause because it's like, oh, my uterus did so much for me," she said. "Well, mine did nothing for me. It had caused me pain for so many years. I really enjoyed celebrating that particular transition." The party helped to bring a taboo topic out into the open and made the transition less lonely. It also gave Karie the last word. It changed how she told her story, and how she thought about it in the years that followed.

Anthropologist William Bridges said change is something that happens to you, and transition is how you choose to react to that change. But I think there's a third step: interpretation. There's incredible power in getting our own story right—in interpreting our endings in a way that helps us move forward feeling good about them. I've realized how lucky I was to have been able to *anticipate* my retirement from diving. I saw it coming. I knew, in my very last moment as a diver, that it *was*, in fact, my very last moment as a diver, and I was able to prepare my heart, at least a little bit, for the aftermath. But I was also lucky to have a mentor like Rick to help me interpret it.

Is the story of my life as a diver a story about the agony of defeat or the pride of accomplishment? Is it about leaving too soon or about going out on my terms? That conversation that Rick and I had in the hours after my last dive reminded me that I'd succeeded in something more important than points and placings. Rick helped me see the best version of myself, the one to carry me through the rest of my life. And now, more than a decade later, when I talk about my experience being a diver, pride and joy outweigh disappointment. I walked away because the pool was small and the world was large. I may have messed up my last dive, but while doing so, I proved that I could master the shaky dread of competition and embrace my adrenaline. And I had fun doing it. Interpretation isn't about blacking out the bits I don't want to remember. It's about highlighting the bits I do.

· · ·

Economist Nick Powdthavee studies life satisfaction after big transitions like divorce, death, and job loss. He's spent his career devising ways to quantify the intangible. For example, his work has explored whether it's possible to assign a cash value to the happiness of having a baby or the unhappiness of a spouse's death. In his book, *The Happiness Equation*, Powdthavee describes how he and a team of academic collaborators explored the popular belief known as set point theory: the idea that every human has a baseline level of happiness that they tend to return to even after major life changes.[2] Following set point theory, someone who wins the lottery may be happier for a period of time, but will eventually return to their previous, pre-lottery-win state of mind. Similarly, someone who experiences a major injury may be less happy for a period of time but will eventually return to their previous, pre-injury state of mind.

Powdthavee and his team studied people going through an assortment of life transitions. They found that for many types of transitions, the set point theory seemed to hold true. For divorcées, life satisfaction began declining a few years before their separation, dropped steeply the year of the separation, and within five years post-break was higher than it was in

the marriage. For people who experienced the death of a partner, life satisfaction bounced back to baseline in two to four years.

Other types of transitions, like job loss, seemed to test the set point theory. Researchers noted a steep drop in life satisfaction in the year people
lost their jobs. For those who remained unemployed, particularly men,
satisfaction did not return to baseline even five years later—a point
against set point theory. But while their happiness did not return to baseline, it did show signs of improvement over time. One might think that
the longer you're unemployed, the more of a drag it is, but it appears that
people do habituate *somewhat*. One thing people never seem to adapt to
is a long work commute: when your commute lengthens, your life satisfaction decreases and stays at that decreased level until the commute
shrinks.

Put simply, it's harder to adapt to negative forces that continue—the
ongoing time suck of a long commute, or the lingering *nonevent* of sustained unemployment—than ones that force (or enable) you to move past
the change.

That made me wonder: How do you recognize an end that never actually seems to end?

· · ·

Five years ago, Nora, a friend in my writing group, was diagnosed with
Hodgkin's lymphoma.

Before Nora got sick, she was chronically overcommitted, attacking all
the world's problems at once. She was a social worker in a level I trauma
center, comforting families while their sons and daughters lived or died
in the room next door. At the same time, she was completing her third
and final year of a part-time master's program and consulting for an immigration organization in Washington, DC, that regularly flew her from

Chicago to DC for meetings. Her longtime boss called her a henchman because when things went wrong, he could count on her to take care of them. Other nicknames included the Wild Pony and Hurricane Nora for her tendency to both stir up and solve trouble. "I felt at my most alive, most electric, when I was figuring things out, solving problems, continuing to move through the world at a headlong pace," she wrote in an essay she shared with our writing group. The trait at the center of all her various nicknames was energy, both focused and frenetic. No matter how fast life moved, Nora moved faster.

She handled her diagnosis in her signature problem-solving mode. "I was like, I'm gonna be so good at this," she said. "I'm going to do all the things that my oncologist tells me to do, and then this is going to be over with." She expected her disease would follow the path set by pop culture. As she wrote in a column for *Catapult* online magazine, "Those are the options: you are either the dead chemo friend or the inspirational cancer character. After you finish treatment, you get a scan that says you're okay. I have yet to see a show where treatment doesn't work the first time, a frequent occurrence in cancer world. Magically, you move on unscathed by treatment, with no obvious lingering issues."[3]

Chemotherapy scrambled her brain like eggs. Each infusion was "a whisk stirring things up and making words, lights, sounds, and objects around me confused and slow." The brain fog got so bad that she could hardly read. But ultimately, it worked. After nine months of treatment, she was cancer-free. It was time to close the book on cancer and enter the "moving on unscathed" phase of her transition. After three more months of rest and recovery, she and her husband moved to New York City, where Nora attempted normalcy: work, walks, drinks with friends. But her brain still felt scrambled, and navigating a wild new city continuously depleted her mental and physical reserves. "Mostly, my attempts at playing normal kept me in a cycle of fatigue, pain, and cognitive overwhelm, ending with me in bed, an ice pack on my pounding head and earplugs in while the construction downstairs echoed through our tiny Brooklyn bedroom," she wrote.

Eight months after moving to New York, about a year after treatment ended, a friend invited Nora on a trip to Mexico City and she said yes, hoping it would force her out of her convalescence. But on a short walk from lunch to her Airbnb, she became so fatigued and disoriented she got lost, blindly crossing streets, barely avoiding the cars zooming past. The trip marked a turning point, but not the one she'd hoped for. It was in Mexico City that she first internalized that she might never come back to normal. "I kept thinking I would get better, but I didn't," she told me. "That was really jarring. It's been five years, and it's still jarring."

As a trained social worker, Nora's more than familiar with the importance of interpretation. At every milestone since her diagnosis, she has tried to recognize the end and make meaning of her experience. And she has amassed a lot of tools with which to do so: therapy, writing, an openness to talking about her experiences with loved ones and friends going through their own diagnoses. As part of our writing group, she's shared drafts upon drafts of stories attempting to put a bow on her health experience and move on. "I have a high need for meaning-making," she told me recently. "But I kept trying to do it without really understanding that the changes were still happening. When the hits keep coming, you keep needing to adjust." In the past few years, she moved to New York City, then out to Connecticut to escape the sensory overload of city life. She was a freelance nonprofit consultant, then worked at a farm, then at the local bookstore. She experienced the abrupt start, anxious middle, and dragging continuation of the COVID pandemic as an immunocompromised person. Each event has seemed like a fitting moment to end her current chapter. "I keep kind of hoping that one of these things will make it feel like this transition is over," she said. "And it's not."

Nora's story shows both the value and limitations of recognizing the end. Her work to make meaning of her experience hasn't been in vain.

She learned a critical lesson in Mexico City—that she couldn't "mind over matter" her lingering symptoms away, and that she would need to change her expectations for her body and her life moving forward. She recognized the end of her pre-cancer way of life, and that has helped her manage both the pain of overexertion and the sting of failure.

But recognition hasn't brought assurance. She's in remission, but her recovery is so full of stops and starts, good days and bad days, misdiagnoses and symptoms that defy any logic or pattern, that she feels trapped in this phase. "The thing about Olympic athlete retirement is that it's all so official, and so structured," she said. "But there's no structure for me." Some endings are not as clear-cut as retiring from sports or removing a uterus. Grand rituals like marathon sufferfests and even smaller ones like menopause parties may not fit the situation. The meaning you make— how you interpret your story—may change as life goes on.

"Rather than seeing it as, 'Oh, I'm trying and failing to be healthy,' I'm just living with the body that I have and trying to show up in ways that make me happy, or that help me connect with other people, or that involve work that I care about," Nora said. "Whether it's on a smaller or large scale." In situations where the hits keep coming, maybe it's more useful to live meaningfully than to make meaning—to focus more on incorporating what you've learned about yourself into your days than to tie a bow around your years.

Another of Dr. Schlossberg's contributions to the psychology of transitions was to recommend that therapists stop referring to them as having a beginning, middle, and end, and instead use the words, "moving in," "moving through," and "moving out." It's a better way to communicate the fluidity of the phases: they're not milestones, but active states that overlap and continue. It isn't always possible to recognize an end, but you can still recognize a change.

Tools for Recognizing the End

Often, our greatest transitions are out of our control. We can, however, choose how we react to and remember what we experienced. By changing our interpretation of what happened, we are able to redefine our story, even long after the events have passed.

How to Guide Your Interpretation

Tell Your Story: Twenty-Minute Life Story

The way you tell the story of your transitions can have a positive (or negative) impact on how you move into, through, and out of them. In narrative therapy, practitioners work with clients to examine, deconstruct, and reshape their stories. Even if none of the facts change, there is always more than one way to view a transition, and seeing yourself as a story character can give you a new perspective on your life.

Here's one exercise to help you organize your story (plus gain emotional distance from your past, make meaning of your challenges and choices, and feel control over your narrative). The goal is to get down the skeleton without delving deep into the details.

- Write your book title and subtitle.

- Write five to ten life chapter titles representing the biggest transitions in your life so far. Write one sentence to describe each chapter. Did you overcome any challenges? What strengths did it show or develop?

- Write one (or more, if you're inspired) chapter title and description for your ideal future: What would you like your life to look like? Who would you like to be?

How to Make Change Conscious

Express Change

Is change making you feel uptight, overwhelmed, or out of control? Release some of that stress by externalizing what you're thinking and feeling. There are lots of ways to do this, depending on your favorite methods of expression. In any case, the point is not to craft a coherent narrative or create art for the refrigerator—it's to create an escape valve for pent-up anxieties and emotions.

- **Words:** Put your fears, thoughts, and emotions on paper, stream-of-consciousness style. Type or write two pages as steadily as possible, without judging or editing yourself. Start with what worries, excites, or troubles you about this change and go in whatever direction your mind takes you.

- **Pictures:** Draw or paint the change, again, without judgment. This can be specific, like a cartoon, or symbolic, with colors or shapes that represent your feelings.

- **Movement:** Perform a familiar movement from your everyday life like pacing back and forth or sitting and standing up again. Now, do it again, but infuse your feelings about this change into your movement. Notice what changes about how you move.

How to Make a Milestone

Consider a Ritual

Many anticipated and unanticipated transitions have built-in rituals (think graduations, weddings, and funerals) that inspire us to make meaning of our transitions, set intentions for what comes next, and connect with other humans (past and present) to share in the joys and hardships of change. If you want to mark a change, consider creating your own ritual. Here are four questions inspired by my conversation with Ezra Bookman, the ritual designer:

- What shift do you wish to make? What are you letting go of (e.g., a running career; dreams of having children) or moving toward (e.g., a period of exploration and freedom)?

- What traditions and stories inspire you (e.g., marathons as a catalyst for self-growth; baby showers to communally welcome new parents to a new season)? What traditions or stories do you wish to differentiate from (e.g., the value of winning above all else; the mindset that loss is taboo)?

- What values do you want to symbolize (e.g., perseverance, humor, togetherness), and how might they inform this experience?

- How will you create a shared experience with others (e.g., invite other people to witness, participate, or share their own stories)?

Don't Forget

Moving On Is a Dynamic Process

In the words of Walt Whitman, you are large, you contain multitudes. As you work to make meaning of your experience, you may find you contradict yourself. Your emotions don't fit into tidy boxes. Closed doors reopen. That's not just okay . . . it's life.

Many Transitions Don't Wrap Up Neatly

They stubbornly refuse to end. The meaning of a transition and the self-understanding that comes with it aren't always clear until decades later. In those cases, give yourself a pass on interpretation. Not everything needs to be put into the perfect frame. Sometimes, you just need to put one foot in front of the other.

2.

Honor Grief

With every transition, we leave something behind. How do we pay our respects to what we've lost? How do we cope without it?

When I was a sophomore in 2004, I spent every morning—before seven until after eight—with the diving team in the gymnastics gym at Ford Center. We divers packed a lot into that bulging hour. We did an active stretch in the still-dark gym, followed by a set of smooth, tai chi–esque movements that mimicked the positions of each of our dives, followed by a series of jumps and tumbles that crisscrossed the spring floor, gaining difficulty as the sun rose. Then it was over to the in-ground foam pits for fifty standing somersaults. We worked in silence, punctuated by cheers when someone did something well. Every once in a while, whispers of a hangover traveled down the somersault line, accompanied by pitying glances and quiet, secretive snorts of laughter. Once, in the middle of an arch-up, I let out a roaring fart that earned me some real laughs and the nickname Gassy Cass. But we rarely talked. We were athletes at work. Chatter would have ruined the mood.

Our grand finale was a conditioning circuit, including squat jumps, muscle-ups, arms-only climbs up the floor-to-ceiling rope, and the final ab extravaganza. We did crunches until we flopped like fish, then seal-stretched our seizing cores. At long last, we settled into rag doll heaps, where we savored a brief escape from our bodies before peeling one another off the floor. Then, we walked our bikes the half mile to the pool. Practice started at eight forty-five.

. . .

My retirement from diving, at twenty-seven years old, left a gaping hole in my life. How should I fill my days, if not with somersaults and conditioning sets? And even though I found other ways to fill the days, I couldn't fully fill that hole. For a decade after I stopped diving, one of the things that bothered me most was that I still thought about it. I assumed a transition followed the laws of physics. Like the arc of a dive, you rise, you shift, you fall. Or like the entry, you're above the water, you're breaking the surface, you're under the water. I couldn't understand why the yearning kept rising back up long after I'd left my sport behind.

It wasn't just the epic moments I longed for. I missed the sand between the rocks of my diving life. The creaks and cracks of ten bodies powering up in a dark gym, the view from the top of the rope, the rubbery feeling of being peeled off the floor by a teammate with no more strength left than I had. Diving really sucked sometimes. Back spasms and wrist strains and dislocated toes too minor to be rested and too painful to be ignored. Entire months of Rick yelling like a madman while I made the same mistakes over and over again. But—call it morbid nostalgia—I missed that too. A goal that was worth yelling about. A coach that cared enough to yell.

I don't believe in ghosts, but I've witnessed the ghost of my athlete self. She comes out when I try to do the same conditioning sets I trained my body for ten years ago. I do the first rep well. By the third, my legs have failed completely. There's no struggle in the interim—I go from can to can't, and then the ghost is gone. Put me on a diving board today and the board thuds, the water harrumphs, and the energy rebels. I can't do what

I could before. But in my imagination I can still make my body feel the way it did when I was an athlete. The magic lives in my memory.

Today, my dreams about diving follow the same basic theme: It's years later and I'm making a comeback that I am extremely ill-prepared for. The last one was in a cavernous, skylit pool somewhere in Europe, where US officials had decided I was to test my mettle after a decade out. I'd somehow made it from prelims to semifinals. But now I was warming up for semis and coming to terms with the fact that my body no longer knew what it was doing. Rick yelled from the pool deck, "What do you expect, buddy? You haven't put in the work!" These dreams drudge up the worst feelings of my diving days: never prepared enough, always disappointing someone. But they still make me miss it. Very few things make me *feel* like diving did.

I expected this longing to fade over time. Instead, it has ebbed and flowed. I retired at twenty-seven still feeling like my body worked the same as it had when I was twenty-two. Maybe that was one of the things that made it so easy, at that time, to give it up—I was in my invincible twenties, the future stretched out in front of me like a never-ending promised land. But by my mid-thirties, I was feeling quite *vincible*. An old friend, Olympic gold medalist Laura Wilkinson, retired in 2008, took nine years off, and came back as a mom of four to train for a spot on the Tokyo 2020 team. She didn't make it, but watching her on TV, at forty-three and a half, competing at the Trials made me ache for the life I had allowed to slide past me. The sane part of me said, *Let it go. That was a different time. You were a different person.* The wild part said, *Well maybe I've still got it.*

These feelings made me angry. After nearly a decade away, I was sitting at a desk, pining away over the same damned sport. I'd traveled, moved cities, taken up new hobbies, built a new career. But those things felt dull by comparison, with memories of the pool coming back in vivid color.

. . .

Do other people feel this complicated sense of longing? Ghosts of selves they've left behind? Irrational dreams of running back to where they started? I began asking around.

At my friend Elie's naturalization party, we spent the weekend in a house by the beach to officially welcome him to Club America. Elie's family wasn't there to celebrate—they were still in Lebanon—but the rest of us brought babies, parents, grandparents, and two dogs, Lady and Norman, who prowled the kitchen for fried fish scraps. Everyone dressed in clothes that represented America to them, and our outfits spanned a range of viewpoints from earnest pride (my friend's grandfather, Pepito, wore a military hat and solemnly saluted us) to outright critique (one friend wore an orange jumpsuit with "Guantánamo" written in Sharpie across the back). No one in attendance, including Elie's wife, had known him for longer than nine years.

It was fitting to have a range of ideologies at the party. It matched my perception of Elie himself: deeply earnest, with a propensity for both idealistic poetry and dad jokes. His moral compass always points toward freedom, and it's led him to question all of the assumed "rights and wrongs" of his childhood—where he should live, the politicians and causes he should support, and whom he should marry (not a Lebanese girl, but a Jewish girl from Chevy Chase, Maryland).

Lebanon is at the center of many overlapping cultures. It's a geographical stone's throw from Europe and Africa, a half-day road trip to Gaza and Jerusalem, home to roughly seven thousand years of human civilization and familiar settings in the Bible, the Torah, and the Quran. As "the highway between Europe and the Middle East" (Elie's words), Lebanon has often found itself in the path of invading empires and the cross fire of competing nations. Elie was born in 1988, near the end of a fifteen-year civil war. The year he was born, the children of Beirut were a mainstay of global newscasts, playing soccer and holding baby siblings against a backdrop of smoke and rubble. The war ended in 1990 and the gunshots were sparse by the time he was old enough to remember them. But the economy never fully recovered.

Elie's greatest transition, his decision to immigrate to the US, took years—another blow to my assumption that transitions happen in a blink. "I didn't wake up on some random Tuesday and say, 'That's it, I'm emigrating forever,'" he said.

The possibility of leaving Lebanon was always on Elie's radar. But his teens and early twenties were driven by hope that he could change his country from within. For most of his life, Lebanon had been occupied by Syria, but in 2005, Elie's generation stormed the streets and pulled off a peaceful revolution to reclaim their country. He was just a high school kid, sixteen and lanky, and his parents kept the family locked indoors for the first few days of protests. It was only when the Lebanese military that had been keeping the crowds at bay turned on their leaders and joined their fellow citizens that Elie and his family—parents, aunts, uncles, his brother, his cousin, and his grandfather—wrapped themselves in red and white scarves, piled into the car, and drove to the heart of Beirut. The drive was a march on wheels, everyone hanging out of their windows and yelling, some leaving their cars entirely to walk among the bumper-to-bumper jubilation.

When Elie and his family got to Martyr's Square they joined a sea of somewhere between five hundred thousand and 1.2 million people, a quarter of Lebanon's population. Elie was surrounded by waving Lebanese flags and cedar trees painted on bridges of noses. His body vibrated and his voice became one with the air yelling, "Hurriyye, siyede, istiqulel"—freedom, sovereignty, independence. It was hard to make out individuals in the crowd. Every once in a while he'd see a friend he knew, but then they'd slip back into the mass of red and white like drops in the ocean. It didn't scare him to lose sight of them. As a country, Lebanon had always been a conglomerate of uneasy truces, but for the two months of the revolution, everyone was a friend.

"That was the first day where it felt like we were all Lebanese," he said. The chanting crowd, the ocean of red and white, the heat of a million hearts longing for the same thing performed a sort of alchemy on him. "It was anger sublimating into hope," he said.

Elie entered college still believing in his country's rebirth. But by graduation, the government had devolved. Many of the pro-Syrian politicians that had been in power before the revolution were maneuvering their way back. Hezbollah, a militant political group driven by opposition to Israel and the West, was ascending in the government and successfully taking aim at Lebanon's religious and cultural freedoms. He could feel the fatal shakes of the country's fledgling economy, which would, by 2020, totally collapse. The words that he and his peers had invoked—freedom, sovereignty, independence—shriveled like old balloons. "It went from 'maybe I can stay and have a good future here,'" he said, "to fuck this, this place is never getting better." He boarded a one-way flight to America in August of 2012.

But for Elie, all this was just the first half of his transition. Point B can look so close from the starting line, but as we live, it keeps moving. Time and space stretch out; the goalposts run away. Though he was physically on American soil, it would be another decade before he could call America home. He attended business school and got a work visa that allowed him to stay in the country only as long as he was employed. He worked eighty hours a week, but executives still threatened to deport him at the slightest mistake. He managed to switch jobs, but desperation forced him to accept a lowball salary. He got married to his wife and they bought a house together, but he didn't allow himself to think of it as a permanent residence until he became a citizen.

Deep in Elie's core is an instinct to question authority. This is also one of the hallmarks of being American: We can support who we want to support, love who we want to love, and say what we want to say. But those rights did not materialize when he flew to San Francisco. They were doled out begrudgingly, one by one, by his student visa, his temporary employer sponsorship, his H-1B specialty occupation visa, and his marriage to an American citizen. Even his green card, which allowed him to live permanently in the United States, wasn't enough to make him feel whole. He tried to be socially and politically active, volunteering with the Trevor Project, phone banking for candidates, and debating issues, politely and earnestly, within his social circle. But he couldn't even vote. He was afraid to go to demonstrations because one misstep could get him deported. He was in America but had no cushion.

. . .

Transitioners grieve what has been lost—a sport, a country, a connection. But I think we also grieve a version of ourselves. The ghost of my athlete self rose from the purity of my diving life, the mission-honed camaraderie of my teammates, the shared goals with my coach, the things my body could do. This ghost exists in a parallel universe, one that becomes less realistic by the day. My teammates have long since moved on, my coach has retired, my body has aged. But the ghost lives on, arising when the gaps are largest between my past and my present, when I lack the sense of purpose that diving brought.

Elie's ghost is the version of himself that stood shoulder to shoulder with friends and cousins, flag-clad and chanting "freedom," to reclaim his country. He called it "the most powerful moment I've been part of." But of all of us who have known and loved Elie in his decade in the United States, no one was part of that moment with him.

"Everyone in my life today is there because I've chosen them," he told me. "But you can't replicate being surrounded by people who've known you for twenty years." We were not there with him at his most idealistic.

And those who were have continued to grow and bond without him. He told me about a wedding he'd recently gone home for, to see his favorite cousin, who was like a sister to him, marry an old friend from his Scout troop. He hadn't seen them in ten years. "I'm used to feeling like a foreigner in the US," he said. "But it hits me hard when I feel like a foreigner in Lebanon."

"Has the way you've missed home changed over time?" I asked.

"I think I miss it more now," he said. "I feel intensely guilty that my parents are aging without me, or that I made it here, but my closest friend is still stuck there. It's a sense of survivor's guilt. And that's intensified over time."

Though our losses were different, I felt a kinship with Elie. I had assumed that my own sense of loss should fade as the years went on, but it didn't. Here was someone else who had felt it grow stronger. Some grieve the dead. Some, like me and Elie, grieve the living—a sport or a community that we loved, moving out and away from us on a vector. There's a great blessing and a small curse to grieving something that isn't dead.

I asked him if grief was an appropriate word for what he felt.

"I don't grieve the life that I had in Lebanon," he said. "I grieve the reality that never existed. I wish that I could have had the same life that I have here without leaving Lebanon, found the same type of love, the same kind of career growth, or the same kind of freedom. I wish they were even a possibility in Lebanon, but they never were."

When I followed up with Elie a few weeks after the beach house party, he told me about a protest he'd attended in San Francisco, marching for another beleaguered Middle Eastern state. For the first time since his immigration, he did not fear deportation. It was almost that same bodily feeling of togetherness—of "something larger than myself," of a sea of strangers becoming family. We tend to intellectualize grief, making it a mental exercise. But for both of us, it materialized as a very physical ache for a very physical feeling. Love isn't just in our heads. It's encoded into our lungs and hearts as well.

"I had this capacity for help and support that I didn't apply back there," he said. "I didn't do that for the country I was raised in. But I can do that for the community I choose now."

. . .

We normally associate grief with death, but psychologists define it more broadly as the natural response to a great loss. "Loss of any type can be a grief experience," said Dr. Megan Neyer, a family friend and practicing therapist. "A death. A change in lifestyle. A breakup. All of these things are losses." Loss is, by definition, part of every transition. Even if the transition was something you chose, as it was for me and for Elie, when you change you leave something behind. But the more significant the loss, the more intensely we feel the grief. It's a word that shrinks to a pebble in your shoe and expands to the size of the earth.

A lot of Dr. Neyer's work is helping people to simply acknowledge this feeling. "You either avoid it or you experience it. Experiencing it is what I want people to do. If you process it and let it be what it is, it doesn't paralyze you." It reminded me of a Buddhist perspective on the difference between pain and suffering: the idea that pain is inevitable, but suffering is optional.

On the Ten Percent Happier website, Sebene Selassie wrote about this concept:[1]

> Pain is all the things I can't necessarily control about life: illness, old age, construction work on my block, the slow guy in line in front of me at the grocery store. . . . Suffering is the tension I create around the pain: lamenting that I have the flu, hating my gray

hair, complaining incessantly about the noise of the jackhammer outside my apartment window, shooting imaginary laser daggers at the guy unloading his shopping cart one . . . orange . . . at . . . a . . . time.

We can't avoid pain, and that pain deserves to be acknowledged without anyone trying to solve it. But a lot of our suffering comes from wishing that things were different than they are. When I get angry with myself for still missing diving, or when I feel frustrated that I can't just bury the longing and move on, that's suffering, and I might as well avoid it if I can.

Just as there are different types of transitions, there are different types of grief. Sometimes anticipated transitions cause *anticipated grief*—grief for something you're expecting, but hasn't yet happened, like the grief you might feel if you find out a loved one is diagnosed with a serious illness. On the flip side, there's also *delayed grief*, which happens when you're not cognizant of the magnitude of your loss until later. This rings true for my experience. I did not fully understand what I was giving up until I'd moved farther away from it. There's *complicated grief*, which arises from strong conflicting feelings, like leaving an abusive partner or quitting an addiction. And *cumulative grief*, which builds from a series of losses, reminding me of Nora—her illness set off a series of hits that just kept coming.

There are many more types of grief—collective, disenfranchised, abbreviated, inhibited—a dark rainbow of terms. I find these definitions comforting. Understanding that there was a thing called delayed grief made me feel more okay about missing something long after it's gone. My abnormality felt normal.

Dr. Mary-Frances O'Connor, a psychologist who studies the lasting physical and mental effects of grief, explained it as an emotion that never truly disappears, though we often expect it to. This expectation can be counterproductive: "If we expect that we're not going to feel grief in the future . . . then we'll be disappointed if years later, even decades later, we come across something and suddenly we get all teared up and have that wave of grief," she said in an interview on the American Psychological Association's podcast.[2] Her words helped me see my relationship to diving not as a pitiful attachment to a long-gone ex but rather as a result of leaving behind something that meant something to me. I loved diving, and as long as that love remains—which I hope it always will—I will grieve it sometimes.

In varying ratios, most of us transitioners experience adulterated sorrow: the mixed emotions that accompany change. Clouds with silver linings, bittersweet milestones, eulogizing the road not traveled. In situations like these, the old adage comes to mind: Both things can be true. We can miss our past lives *and* be thankful for our present. But I wondered how my "yes, but" mourning compared to grief with a capital G: the grief of definitively unchosen transition.

. . .

The great *before* and *after* of my friend Dawn's life was her mother's death. Four years ago, Dawn's mother, Karen, was diagnosed with stage 4 colon cancer. For the next nine months, Dawn split her time between her home in LA and her parents' home in Naples, Florida, cobbling together freelance work as a design director and artist manager while she, her dad, and her aunt divvied up 24-7 care. They watched Karen lose ninety pounds, watched her hair go brittle and break, watched her face go gray and her voice go quiet and her body go stiff. Dawn started seeing a therapist who specialized in anticipatory grief. "You hear about it all the time," Dawn told me over coffee in a too-hot coffee shop. "The cancer just taking people away before they die."

Dawn is half Trinidadian and half Chinese, with an eye for fashion and a heart that draws people to her. She's good at articulating the more amorphous things in life—beauty, art, philosophy. She speaks softly, and I had to struggle to hear her over the aughts pop blaring in the coffee shop. As she told me about her mother, she stared up into the light, and it seemed more like she was channeling than talking.

Dawn's mom was a devout Catholic, and in the months preceding her death, she cocooned herself in faith. She traded in her beloved videos of old Rodgers and Hammerstein musicals for religious texts so she could "stay focused." Each day a priest came to the house to give her communion. At 3 p.m. she prayed the Divine Mercy, her frail fingers piecing through worn rosary beads, repeating her Hail Marys and Holy Gods and the final intonation: . . . *that in difficult moments we might not despair nor become despondent, but with great confidence submit ourselves to your holy will, which is Love and Mercy itself. Amen.* Dawn had left the Catholic church in her twenties, but now she read prayers aloud from a worn book, *Spirituality and the Gentle Life,* while her mother mouthed the words.

In one of her last journeys outside the house before her final trip to the hospital, Karen asked Dawn to go with her to see the cemetery she'd chosen. Her colon had already failed, and she'd been on a feeding tube for months. She slept most of the day. No one thought it was a good idea to pack her into the car and drive an hour from Naples to Immokalee. But she was adamant that her daughter see the place where she would be buried. "She wanted to take me there so I wouldn't be going there for the first time, so scared, after she died," said Dawn. So she, her dad, and her partner wheeled Karen from the house to the car and loaded her in. Dawn noticed Karen shifting in pain at every bump and turn.

When they got to the cemetery, Dawn saw a small lawn of gravestones strewn with fake flowers bright and faded. Gaudy arbors, trees in pots, solar lights, trellises, and plastic angels marked each plot. Pinwheels danced in the breeze. "The tackiest shit," she said. "But it was so vibrant. Everyone was doing what they could to make it a little bit colorful and a little bit happy, and it was one of the most beautiful places I've ever been." She smiled as her voice broke. "How did that even occur to her that that would be helpful to me? And it was. Because I was able to go there after she died and know my mom was not afraid."

All Karen wanted was to die at home. But when the doctor told her she had one day left at home or two to three in the hospital, she went. Her sons were away and she needed to buy them time to come and say good-bye. Two days later, surrounded by nearly her entire family, she said the 3 p.m. Divine Mercy and then looked at each person in the room—her sons, daughters, and grandchildren—and called them all by name, "Dawn, my joy . . . Christopher, my joy . . ." Soon after that, she was in-tubated. Twenty-four hours later, she was struggling through pain for each breath. It seemed clear she'd never sit up, breathe alone, or speak again. They asked the doctor what they could do. "If it was my mom, I think I'd take the oxygen away," he said. But his opinion wasn't what really mattered. Dawn called her mother's most Catholic friend while Dawn's dad called the priest. Both said her soul would be safe.

It was Dawn who handled the conversation with the nurses. Dawn who whispered into her mother's ear what they were going to do. Dawn who told her that the priest had okayed it. And Dawn who, surrounded by her dad, her aunt, and her brothers, gently pulled the oxygen mask away. Karen took three wheezing breaths. They felt her soul fill the room as it left her body.

· · ·

"What was your grieving process like?" I asked.

She laughed. "It's rich you refer to 'grieving' in the past tense," she said, and I immediately felt the coffee shop window magnifying the sun on my neck. "But no . . . I mean, it took a year to really understand she was gone."

Dawn stopped doing all but the bare minimum to take care of herself.

Every day she woke up with fresh grief and had to remember again that her mother was gone. "It was too overwhelming to think about not having her anymore forever," Dawn said. "So I just had to keep saying, 'she's not here in this moment.' And then the next moment, I'd say it again." It can take years before we're ready to process an experience. In the interim, life is about getting from today to tomorrow.

Dawn sat at her computer for hours, trying to find some text or note or bit of advice that might help. She'd quit Catholicism because she was stifled by its rigidness and frustrated by its dogma, but it left behind a void: no belief system to help her make sense of her loss. In the lowest point of her depression, she discovered a book by a Vietnamese Buddhist monk, Thich Nhat Hanh, called *No Death, No Fear*. It was a tiny star in a black night. "If the wave bends down and touches her true nature she will see that she is water," she read. "Water is free from the birth and death of a wave." He put words to a feeling she'd been struggling to define, that some part of her mother lived on.

"Energy can't be created or destroyed," she said, now fully present in the coffee shop time and place, not channeling a story but helping me see a way of being. "Well, love is an energy, and the love that she gave to me, was given to her."

Normally, a piece of me closes off when people start using phrases like "love is an energy." But this time, I got it. I felt it.

"Being aware that that energy is always gonna be alive and active, that was the real transition for me," said Dawn.

That realization has changed Dawn's relationship with herself and those around her. She walks down the street knowing that those she passes—a homeless person, a grandmother, a toddler—could so easily be her, and she them. It has also given her something to do with all the love and grief—at this point, it's hard to differentiate those feelings—of her mom's death. Karen received love. Karen gave that love to Dawn. And now Dawn passes that love forward to others.

I see it in our friendship. When I moved to Los Angeles, Dawn was one of the only people I knew, and I didn't know her well. She took it upon herself to introduce me to the hidden heart of this spread-out city. Every few weekends she and her partner invited me to family dinners, home cooked meals with friends from all the spokes of their lives. Though she's on the shy side, it felt like she was the mama of all of these friends, not just the organizer but the one who wrapped everyone up, brought them together, and made them feel seen. "We're all connected," she said when I asked her about it. "Friendship strengthens and connects us and I think about how much more we could do to be aware of that while we're all still here."

I felt traces of connection between my story and hers. The surreality of the moments, days, and weeks after. The memories coming back in vibrant color. The woven strands of love and mourning. But I also wondered if they were actually comparable. I pictured my grief buzzing like a gnat around her colossal loss.

"Was there anything someone like me could have said to help?" I asked.

Her answer was decisive. "No."

I thought about all the times I'd tried to find the words to comfort a grieving friend or googled "what to say in a sympathy card" and blushed. I remembered a conversation with a coworker who had lost her dad. Every word I tried to utter felt hollow, yet somehow I uttered them anyway, trite sayings and sideways attempts at comparing my past sadnesses with her present ones. I came out of that conversation with my teeth gritted at my own awkwardness. I want to believe that even in the furthest-apart experiences, there's a relatable thread or two. I am, after all, writing a book about those threads. But when it comes to grief, it has always felt very hard to put that empathetic philosophy into practice.

While I was spiraling in doubt, Dawn had been continuing to mull over my question. "There's nothing you can do or say that's going to make it better," she repeated. "But I think I just appreciated people try-ing. Like, if someone has an intention of support and showing love, I don't think you can go wrong from that place."

But what about all the awkward things people said? The things that triggered the wrong memories of her mother in the wrong moments? The uneven comparisons that must have made her think, *you actually have no idea what I'm feeling right now?*

"I remember the people who reached out," she said. "I have no idea what they said."

We put pressure on ourselves to have exactly the right words to make a difference. I found something comforting in the idea that one can say ex-actly the right words and they *still won't make a difference.* The greatest things you have to offer when a friend is grieving are your intention and your ear. Let them know you care and listen when they want to share. Your voice is secondary.

Recently Dawn's partner lost his dad, and she found herself in the po-sition of trying to offer solace. It's helped to have a shared language for grief, but it hasn't erased the helplessness of trying to share someone else's burden. "His relationship with his dad is so different than my relation-ship with my mom," she said. "He's a different person than I am." It's trite and it's true: everyone grieves differently.

Physically, grief can make you feel both drained and restless. Mentally, it can prompt apathy or anger. Socially, it can lead to withdrawing from friends or being unusually dependent on them. The most well-known model for grieving is the Kübler-Ross five stages: denial, anger, bargain-ing, depression, and acceptance. But even "stages" is a misnomer—they're more like colors in a Jackson Pollock painting. "I would have a few months of being at peace with everything and then all of a sudden I'm going through the shed and I find something that my mom sent years ago and it's like a knife through the heart," said Dawn. Furthermore, acute grief means constantly shifting between the past and the future:

between facing the pain of what you've lost and the uncertainty of life in a changed world. To minimize suffering, sometimes you need to ignore the future. To rebuild your life, sometimes you need to ignore the past.

· · ·

Ultimately, there's no solving grief. But, as Dr. Neyer advised, if you process it and let it be what it is, it doesn't paralyze you. That said, what does it actually mean to "unpack" or "process" your grief?

Psychologist and grief expert Dr. Robert Neimeyer has written thirty books and authored more than five hundred chapters and articles on the subject. At the core of all those millions of words are "three Rs."

First, *retelling.* This means telling the story of what you've lost, over and over, in different ways, to yourself and others, so that you can see new possibilities that you didn't before. Some call that insanity—"doing the same thing over and over and expecting different results." But as a writer, I get it. "The first draft is a skeleton . . . just bare bones. The rest of the story comes later with revising," said one of my literary heroes, Judy Blume. Ernest Hemingway was blunter. "The first draft of anything is shit," he reportedly told a young mentee. "I rewrote the first part of *A Farewell to Arms* at least fifty times." Grievers retell their stories for similar reasons: to make them more coherent and less overwhelming. The chapter you're reading has been rewritten *a lot,* particularly the parts about my own love and loss of diving. As I have been writing and revising, I have also been grieving.

Second, *rebuilding.* This is about recreating your relationship with whatever beloved thing you've lost, which I find kind of radical. I'd always assumed that the goal of grief was to forget so you could move forward. But according to Dr. Neimeyer, it's quite the opposite. "Grieving isn't a process of letting go," he said at the Association for Death Education and Counseling's annual conference. "It's a process of finding a new way to hold on."[3] For Dawn, this has involved reimagining her mother's love as something that's constant and alive. It's also been about butterflies. After her mother's death, Dawn started seeing butterflies everywhere: on postcards, in boxes of old keepsakes, in a "thinking of you" text from a distant friend. That year, monarch butterflies laid eggs in her garden. And every time she sees a butterfly, she knows that her mother is still with her. "We need the dead in order to grieve them well," Dr. Neimeyer wrote.[4] Symbols and rituals can help reaffirm an ongoing relationship.

Third, *reinventing*. We are never the same after a great loss as we were before it. But by acknowledging that, we can appreciate our own growth and be intentional about how we change. Part of reinventing involves asking yourself questions about the opportunities your grief has opened. How have you changed as a result of this loss? What can you do now that you couldn't do before? These questions remind me of how free I felt when I no longer had to make every decision based on how fresh my legs would feel at the next practice or how many training days I'd get before the next competition. I do grieve diving, but I don't regret the life I've lived instead. What's the opposite of grief? Joy, pride, laughter? I've experienced them plenty on the path I chose.

Dr. Neimeyer talks about reinventing as a process that "mines the lessons of loss, but puts them to use in the construction of a changed life."[5] Dawn's loss has inspired her to live her life with greater empathy for strangers and a more urgent appreciation of her friendships. Elie's loss of his home country has driven him to fight for freedom in his new one. And I've experienced far more of the world than I would have if I was diving forever.

It's important to note that all three of these "R" processes tend to take a better course with guidance from a therapist or trusted audience. Constant retelling of a sad story can be a downward spiral or a restorative one. Rebuilding a relationship can be an unhealthy obsession or a comforting source of stability. And the process of reinvention is made richer with outside perspective on you and your grief.

There is no magic way to move through a great loss any faster. No matter how diligently you retell, rebuild, and reinvent, loss hurts, which brings me back to the difference between pain and suffering—how can you acknowledge pain but not suffer? I asked someone who, for decades, experienced pain on the daily: Ryan the Olympic marathoner.

He told me about his motivation for choosing sports—first distance running, then weightlifting—that pushed him so hard. "There are those moments where you are in the crucible," he said. "Either you're gonna make it or you're not. And my body, my mind, my spirit, my emotion, my whole being is in that moment. I'm searching within myself to answer the question, how deep can I go? How much strength can I draw from within myself?" To him, pain wasn't a hell to be avoided. It was an opportunity to learn what he was capable of. An opportunity for transcendence.

Elite distance running and the death of a loved one are not the same. But that idea of transcendence—of hard-earned wisdom, of coming out of the fire stronger and wiser than you went in—echoed between Dawn's story and Ryan's. Dawn came to her realization about love energy. Ryan grew ever more assured in his capacity for challenge. Pain honed them both, as surely as pressure and heat make diamonds. No one would ever choose grief the way Ryan chose to run. But know that however bad it gets, the process of grieving will show you a new side of the world—and yourself.

Tools for Honoring Grief

By definition, a transition means leaving something behind. If you've lost something important to you, you may continue to grieve it for your entire life. But by recognizing that feeling, you can learn how to live with the absence of what you've lost. And learning to live with this pain will give you a deeper understanding of yourself.

How to Keep the Bond Active

Tell Your Story: Discover New Things About Your Loss

A great loss isn't just something to box up and send to the basement. Tell the story of your grief over and over. Seek out new ways to open up about your loss. Journal about your story. Say it out loud. Ask someone you trust, who makes you feel seen and safe, to interview you about it. Keep asking fresh questions and exploring fresh ways to tell it so it's not a recitation—it's an active process of discovery.

- What memories make you smile, laugh, or cry?

- What are the times when grief knocks you over? What do you think triggers those moments?

- What's one thing you learned from the person or experience you're grieving, and how did they/it teach you that lesson?

- Why was that person or thing special? What were their/its superpowers? What did you love about them/it?

How to Carry Forward the Legacy of What You've Lost

Reinvent Yourself

Think about how you've changed internally as a result of this loss and what impact that has had—or what impact you would like it to have—on your actions, habits, or ways of interacting with the world.

- How have my values changed?

- What can I do as a result of this loss? What can't I do?

- What has this loss taught me about myself?

- What baggage am I holding that no longer serves me?

How to Support a Friend

Check In on Grieving Friends, Even if You Don't Know What to Say

You don't have to have experienced the exact same thing in the same way to be supportive. Even if you have, they are likely not processing their grief in exactly the same way you did. Text just to let them know you're thinking about them. Send small gifts (like Goldfish crackers) or lighthearted content (like cat videos) you know they like. Pay attention, listen actively, and show them they're in your thoughts. Remember, your ear is often more valuable than your voice.

How to Feel Less Alone

Keep Learning

Embracing grief, mitigating suffering, and making meaning of our stories is a long and multifaceted process. There are a million ways to grieve and about as many ways to offer comfort and growth. These four books span wildly different perspectives, but all have taught me something new about grief.

- Read *No Death, No Fear: Comforting Wisdom for Life* by Thich Nhat Hanh for a set of meditative chapters weaving personal and universal anecdotes with Buddhist philosophy.

- Read *It's OK That You're Not OK: Meeting Grief and Loss in a Culture That Doesn't Understand* by Megan Devine for a practical and empathetic guide to grieving and supporting others.

- Read *The Grieving Brain: The Surprising Science of How We Learn from Love and Loss* by Mary-Frances O'Connor for a science-y exploration of what happens to our brains and bodies when we experience grief.

- Read *The Art of Losing: Poems of Grief and Healing*, edited by Kevin Young, for beautiful, heart-wrenching words.

Don't Forget

Accept Your Grief and All Its Colors

Don't push it away or try to forget. Don't expect it to end tomorrow, next month, or next year. Allow yourself to feel it, wrestle with it, and deal with it. You loved, you lost, and you are changed. Remove the grief timer from your process. There is no timeline for grief, and no expectations for how you ought to feel after a great loss. Save yourself the suffering of "should."

Seek Support

It can feel like nobody gets it or could possibly get it. But try anyway. If you are grieving, consider seeing a therapist or counselor as they'll have a trained ear, experience with grief, and a range of tools and ideas to help you cope with and make meaning of your loss. Also, know that there's a vast network of free organizations that support grievers. A quick Google search for grief support will help you find local groups, digital communities, hotlines, textlines, and other resources for those who have experienced similar types of loss. Choose an organization that feels safe and comfortable for you, whether that's a church, YMCA, or other community space. If joining a group out of the blue feels daunting, don't be afraid to ask for more information. You can call an organization with questions like, "What does a session look like?" or "How do you handle big emotional reactions?" or "What type of experience or training does the moderator have?" to decide if it feels like a good fit.

3.

Embrace the Murk

*Transitions bring on the murk: a liminal period when our
identities are in flux and the next step isn't yet clear. How do
we deal with that uncertainty? How do we regain our sense of
self? How do we figure out what to do next?*

From 2009 to 2012, my life was a tripod of crystalline structure.
At any given moment, three things mattered: (a) work—an ambition that existed outside my body; (b) relationships—people
who I cared about and who cared about me; and (c) diving. But diving
mattered most.

After I graduated from college in 2007, I worked a part-time job in
marketing at the Stanford Alumni Association, where I relished the
Clark Kent–like feeling of changing from Speedo to Banana Republic
and going to an office building every afternoon. My days were packed
full: gym somersaults as the sun rose, a quick hour of diving basics at the
pool, three hours at work, a longer afternoon practice, a few more hours
of work, and finally a cardio, Pilates, or sports psychology session before
dinner. I lunched on apples and energy bars as I walked the six minutes
from work to the pool. Back at the Alumni Center I surveyed alums
about their experiences at class dinners and speaker events, diligently
categorizing complaints about the noise level in the reception room
and the political biases of the panelists. I was proud to be buttering
my own bread, paying the rent without relying on diving. The gentle,

no-emergencies pace of the Alumni Association gave me a welcome re-spite from the physical and mental intensity of practice, and the fact that I was fairly good at summarizing survey remarks helped even out my self-esteem on days when my body rebelled. My job was just enough: enough work to pay rent, enough mental stimulation to keep me from fixating on shoulder angles all day, enough writing to make me feel like I was paving the way for some sort of future career, enough validation to make me feel like I mattered for more than just my athletic ability.

On the relationship front, I spent those Olympic training years dating a charismatic polymath who avoided structure as aggressively as I sought it. He was an over-the-top extrovert with an ability to build intense friendships based on spontaneous airplane conversations, chance en-counters at Lucky Strike bowling alley, or (in my case) accidentally get-ting my political junk mail addressed to his frat house. After bringing me a heap of mail shortly before the end of the school year, he wrote me long emails all summer and sent me a care package of mix CDs and board games. Our first date the next fall was a meandering tour around cam-pus that ended with him pulling a guitar out of his trunk and making up a love song on the spot.

Novelty lit him up like a Christmas tree. Every new friend he made, new band he loved, or new philosophy he tried was the best one ever, a universal source of truth, a catalyst for Version 2.0, 3.0, 4.0. His life was driven by wild bursts of obsession: obsession for the famous start-up founder he met at the bowling alley and immediately moved in with, ob-session with the "energy" of the start-up founder's seven-story party house built into a hillside in San Francisco, obsession for La Victoria burritos and their signature orange sauce. "I love hard and hate hard," he said often. That may have been one of the things that brought us together: my passion for diving and his for all sorts of things. But my passion was steady and consistent. His was not. He left the San Francisco party house after a falling-out with the tech bro. He had to go to the hospital when he damaged his stomach from all the orange sauce. Meanwhile, I sat on my steady tripod, practicing, practicing, practicing, and patiently trying to get just a little bit better.

In some sports, practice is a weak shadow of competition. But in sports like diving, where your greatest opponent is yourself, practice *is* the game. I competed the same dives, from the same height, into the same water. The only difference was the amount of adrenaline in my body. In diving, perfect is the end-all-be-all, that ten on the mountaintop. Perfect all the pieces, and you perfect the dive. Do it perfectly once, twice, ten times in a row. Do it perfectly in sideways rain or after dusk. Do it perfectly when Rick is lounging in his chair or when he's standing with his fists clenched. Do every piece perfectly—the hurdle, somersault, come-out, and entry— separately, then put them together and do that perfectly too. Did you pound the board? Did you rush your arm swing? Did your feet flex on the way into the pike? Were you a few inches too far out? Did you finish your rotations too low to the water? Did you enter at an angle a few degrees short of vertical? Did you brace for impact a little too loosely or a little too late? Did you make a splash? It wasn't perfect. Do it again.

While my boyfriend was diving into new obsessions every other night, I was practicing the same five dives. We dated off and on for seven years. He was the relief valve in my engine, the sway in my skyscraper. He was a window to life without diving, without hangups, without rules. I'd built such solid walls around my existence, and he provided just enough chaos to keep me content in my structure.

In my last year of diving—the penultimate year of our relationship— I'd often drive the hour from Palo Alto to San Francisco after practice on Saturdays to spend the night with him at the house of seven stories. It was a fantasy castle where, at any given day, at any given hour, one might find a guitarist from Korn and a cashier from Guitar Center jamming together on the third floor while someone's girlfriend sprinkled gold dust on a batch of raspberry cake pops in the kitchen and a teenage Russian start-up founder wearing headphones the size of his face coded something complicated on a projector screen. I watched all this while sipping my beer, nursing a strange mix of wonder and dread. Around midnight, my boyfriend would put me to bed with a kiss and head down to the basement recording studio to make music. I'd lie awake, my body vibrating slightly from the bass pummeling through the floor, asking myself: Will I ever be open-minded enough to appreciate this? More importantly, will I be ready for practice on Monday?

I had a growing sense of differences too great to graft together. But I had no idea who I would be once diving ended. Maybe without the sense of duty protecting diving as the most important thing in my life, I would become someone who could appreciate his magic. In any case, I didn't have the energy to figure it out. The go-no-go decision on the boyfriend would have to wait until after I retired.

. . .

I had decided long before I got to the London Olympics that I would retire from diving immediately afterward. I was committed to the plan.

In September of 2012, the month I got back from London, I went to the White House to meet the president, got my Olympic rings tattoo, and did a Tough Mudder. I said my final goodbye to my coworkers at the Alumni Association, moved out of my apartment in Palo Alto, and brought a few big suitcases to my boyfriend's house in San Francisco. Now that I was done with diving I was finally free to live his uninhibited life but found I was still unable. Years of watching various things happen to his brain while mine remained sober and predictable had left me with a deep fear of mind-altering substances and a not-unrelated difficulty in experiencing the house's shared euphoria. I had planned to move in with him, but instead we decided we both needed "some space to grow."

By October I had no diving, no job, no apartment, and a relationship on the rocks. But I still wasn't worried. I knew exactly what I was sup-posed to do next: become a writer.

Long before I wanted to be a diver, I wanted to be a writer. I was a pre-cocious kid, speaking in full sentences before I had hair on my head. In grainy family videos I sat on the couch, reciting every word from a Wiz-ard of Oz book larger than I was. *"I'm mewwwwting,"* I'd screech, face crinkled in agony. In fifth grade I started a poetry club in home room, writing rhyming couplets about dancing animals and how much I hated math and giving them, unprompted, to the teacher. In high school I took all the English classes available, even taking some classes twice. In my mandatory Stanford Intro to the Humanities class, the teaching fellow would ask an open-ended question about symbolism and I'd get that ex-ploding feeling, my erudite comment threatening to burn through my chest. I loved college writing workshops. I basked in the glow of the "compliment sandwich" feedback we'd all been trained to give, two good things sandwiching one opportunity for improvement, all worded to make the writer feel truly great about herself. I graduated with a set of warm fuzzies and the belief that launching a writing career would be as easy as getting an A in a workshop.

After college, there was no room in my tripod of diving, work, and re-lationship for another pursuit. I torch journaled after bad competitions or fights with my boyfriend, but there was no craft to my rants. But after the Olympics, with a clean slate and a clear schedule, it was time to re-sume my original destiny. I boarded a one-way flight to Pittsburgh and set up shop in my childhood bedroom, still carpeted in bubblegum pink, at my childhood desk, still full of the notes I'd passed in middle school. Living at home meant no expenses and no distractions: I was away from all the baggage and old diving juju of the Bay Area. I wasn't paying rent. My mom was making my meals. It was the ideal environment to finally focus on writing. I opened my laptop and . . .

Not a word came out.

I spent two months at home, and during that time I napped every day. I got a Groupon membership to a local gym and took weekly Zumba, cardio core, and African dance classes. I started lists of interesting details to include in future stories. I tweeted dutifully, once or twice a week, not because I enjoyed Twitter, but because I wanted to retain the smattering of followers I'd gained during my fifteen minutes of Olympic fame in case I ever published something. I drove forty-five minutes to a hip Pittsburgh coffee shop, sat in a dumpy armchair, and wrote about how much of an impostor I felt like sitting in a dumpy armchair in a coffee shop, pretending to be a writer. I read *I'm an English Major—Now What?* from cover to cover, twice.

Every day I sat down dutifully to write. But my brain was empty. In school, I'd clip-clop away at my laptop with no real concern for who my audience was and why they might care what I had to say. Now I was stupefied by the realization that instead of paying tuition so that people would read my work, others would need to pay me.

In his book on time management, *Four Thousand Weeks*, writer Oliver Burkeman describes procrastination: "Suddenly, the thing you'd resolved to do, because it mattered to you to do it, feels so staggeringly tedious that you can't bear to focus on it for one moment more." He diagnoses this malady as "attempting to flee a painful encounter with our finitude." The moment I sat down to actually write, the naive conviction I'd felt about it being my calling evaporated. I was too scared to put the work in to find out.

For the previous twenty-seven years of my life, I'd climbed the structure of organized schooling like a jungle gym. This structure provided certainty about my motivation (impressing my classmates and teacher), subject matter (whatever was assigned), cadence (built around semesters and deadlines), and performance (As). Diving was built on the same scaffolding: my coach, my competitors, my competition schedule, and the scoring system gave me all I needed to keep climbing. In a world without the comforting confines of school and sports, I was lost.

When it became clear that "just writing" wasn't working, I pored through Craigslist for writing gigs and got myself added to the freelance roster of a reputation management website. I made something like eleven dollars an article ghostwriting bogus blog posts and SEO-juiced bios designed to push unflattering news and mugshots lower in Google search results. Over the next few months, I wrote fifteen or so blog posts and bios, for a total of $165. That was the extent of my post-Olympic writing career.

I was in the murk: the mess of doubt, ambiguity, and emotional confusion that comes with change.

At times, the Pittsburgh period of my life felt like wading through tar. Other times, I felt like I was in a popcorn machine, possibilities whizzing by me faster than I could catch or take advantage of them. Everything was new. I didn't know where I was going. It was an uneasy blend of stuck and chaotic.

The murk is a breakdown of the structures we use to understand our world: the people we see, the places we navigate, the expectations we rely on, and the habits we form. The hallmark of the murk is uncertainty. For smaller transitions, a handful of dominoes go down: A new college semester might bring new teachers and a new class schedule without fundamentally changing your world. But for larger ones, it can feel like the transition knocks down the entire set. For me, the first domino was retiring from diving, but it knocked over others: my city, my boyfriend, my job, my body, my schedule, my sense of purpose.

Diving was a dam, and when the dam broke, my life roared through. I was excited, hopeful, and free. I was also sad, scared, and overloaded.

· · ·

Humans have always bounced between the desire for certainty (and therefore control, structure, and security) and the desire for newness (and therefore adventure, freedom, and choice). Too much certainty and most of us end up eventually feeling stifled, every day stretching out in front of us like a highway with no exits. But too much newness feels like chaos, like an intersection I once navigated in India with no lanes, no rules; cars, tuk-tuks, bicycles, and pedestrians stopping and speeding in every direction; and a giant steer sitting right in the middle. Every move required 100 percent mental, physical, and emotional attention. The self-help author Mark Manson wrote, "In life, we have a limited amount of fucks to give. So you must choose your fucks wisely."[1] Unlike the steer, I gave all my fucks to navigating that intersection. The overwhelming newness of the situation kept me from being able to make reasoned choices about where to focus.

Embracing uncertainty requires certain muscles, and I hypothesize that ours are atrophying. Picture meeting someone for coffee on a first date. Dating apps give you certainty that you've selected the "right" person from a sea of contenders. Yelp reviews give you certainty that you're choosing the best coffee shop on the block. Texting provides certainty about why your date is running late and when they'll be there. You can even share your location with a friend, giving you certainty that you'll be okay, even if your date turns out to be an axe murderer. In many of these cases, "certainty" is more of an illusion than the truth: people don't live up to their dating profiles, ghosting is rampant, and 30–40 percent of Yelp reviews are fake. But even the illusion of certainty is addictive, and we now expect it in many aspects of our lives.

The desire for certainty is even stronger for kids these days (I lament that I'm old enough to use that phrase) than for me and my fellow millennials. When I was a high school senior in 2003, my Nokia phone could barely send a text. Today, twenty years later, one in nine American families uses Life360, an app that enables parents to track their teens' location history, battery life, and how fast they're driving. It's not shocking to me that parents want to keep an eye on their kids. What's more surprising is that their kids, according to a survey by the company, want to be surveilled. The survey found that 74 percent of teens and early twentysome-things agree that the increased physical safety and convenience is usually worth the cost of having less privacy.[2] The transition to adulthood is defined by a push for independence, but today's teens are delaying all kinds of independence-related milestones: getting their driver's licenses, starting their first jobs, drinking alcohol, having sex, and moving out of the house. Meanwhile, mental health is suffering. In 2004, my freshman year of college, 55 percent of young adults aged eighteen to twenty-six reported excellent mental health. By 2023, only 15 percent of that age group said the same.[3] Pundits blame everything from toxic media culture to rising housing prices, but I'll throw another explanation into the ring: We've become less comfortable with uncertainty. The digital cocoon is too cozy, new experiences are too risky, and the uncertainty of life is too scary.

In the murk, the structures we use to navigate life disappear. At first I only saw the external breakdowns in structure, the activities and habits surrounding my job, my relationship, and my sport. But a conversation with my friend Emma reminded me that the most difficult loss is the internal structure we build to contain ourselves: our identity.

· · ·

When I started writing this book, I put out a call on Instagram for people to share their most impactful transitions. "This is kind of a morbid answer and potential trigger warning, I guess? But not killing myself," wrote Emma about hers.

Emma and I met through our shared passion for trapeze, a hobby I've discovered in recent years (more on this later in the book). The Emma I know is artsy, earnest, and kind, her hair a perpetually luminous shade of fuchsia, aquamarine, or pink. I never realized how much work it had taken her to become the person I know.

It's hard to trace the roots of depression. Growing up, Emma identified as "the weird kid"—close with a few other oddballs, but self-conscious around everyone else. But weird was fine; all of the heroes of the fantasy books she devoured were "weird." What really got to her was that they were all so skinny. Emma's discomfort with her body, combined with social anxiety, created what she called "a cloud around my brain."

In middle school, when she tentatively opened up about feeling sad, her mom made a joking remark about how she had everything she could ever want, so she might as well just kill herself. "My parents loved me a lot and did so much, so well. But creating an environment where you talk about emotions was not one of those things," she said. It was a single conversation, one inattentive reaction, a drop in a bucket—but those few words fundamentally shaped Emma's worldview. In the case of her mental health, her takeaway was: there's no real problem here, so it's my responsibility to hide it.

Throughout high school, anxiety snowballed into depression, self-harm, and disordered eating. When the future felt overwhelming, she clung to the idea that if her life ever got too hard, she'd end it.

College exacerbated her mental health issues. In high school, Emma's niche was being the lonely-but-talented theater kid. But in college, everyone had been raised on the loner hero fantasy. Everyone was talented. And everyone seemed to be struggling with the same things. When she confided in an older classmate about her eating disorder, he responded that he'd had an ex-girlfriend who had thrown up like fourteen times a day. "All I took from that reaction was that my problem was not bad enough," she said. Being away from her family also gave her illness space to expand. She did more damage to herself and felt more guilt and shame for doing it. Near the end of her freshman year, a teacher noticed she seemed down and asked her after class if she needed help. He persuaded her to speak with a guidance counselor, who persuaded her to go to the hospital, where she spent a week in the psychiatric unit.

If this were a movie, this hospital stay would have been the climax. Emma would have started seeing a therapist, gotten on the right medications, and figured out her real passion. Her depression and suicidal thoughts would have screeched to a halt in the span of a jump cut. But this was real life. She was in the murk. Her hospital visit *did* give her permission to start prioritizing her mental health. But it took years to believe she was a person with a future. "The hardest part about deciding to work on getting better is that you're losing this very reliable part of yourself," she said. "When you grow up feeling very depressed all the time, that kind of becomes your identity."

Identity is the answer to the question, "Who am I?" and for many of us, it is a slippery fish to pin down. According to the American Psychological Association, your identity is a sense of self defined by a set of physical, psychological, and interpersonal characteristics, affiliations (e.g., ethnicity, politics, hometown), and social roles.[4] It's healthy to feel like your constellation of traits is special and unique, and it's also healthy to feel that, while parts of you may change, you still remain *yourself.*

Though we're often forced to boil it down to quick answers at dinner parties ("What do you do?" "Oh, I'm a diver training for the Olympics") our true identities might take the full night to describe. They bridge who we are and who we want to be (a diver and a wannabe Olympian), the groups we're part of and how we're different from others in those groups (an elite athlete who's a lot more balanced than other elite athletes), traits we're proud of and traits we're ashamed of (chill enough to hang with the denizens of a seven-story party mansion, but not chill enough to partake in the partying), cold hard facts and matters of perspective (I messed up my last dive at the Olympics, but not because I couldn't handle the pressure). These characteristics influence our actions, perceptions, social interactions, needs, wants, and ideas.

Mental health practitioners often use a pie metaphor for identity. The OG example of this is the Wheel of Life, an exercise popularized by the godfather of the life-coaching industry, Paul J. Meyer, back in the sixties. The Wheel has eight slices: career, finance, health, significant other, family and friends, fun and leisure, personal development, and contribution to society. You recognize the areas that you are currently spending the most time on, and separately, the areas that you would like to prioritize in your ideal life. It becomes a helpful visual of who you are and who you want to be. Exercises like these are useful in a variety of contexts—everything from promoting inclusion in middle school classrooms to a therapeutic aid for making tough decisions. I once had a boss who made each of her direct reports fill out a Wheel of Life so she could help us find work-life balance. A pie with many slices helps us navigate change. As some pieces grow, shrink, or change flavor, the rest of the pie stays true to who we've always been.

Emma's depression had taken over a large portion of her pie. She'd grown used to attributing every interaction as evidence that people hated her. Who was she, if not hated? She never doubted that her life would end before she reached thirty. What were her goals, if not death? "I actually had a really solid sense of self," she said. "It was just really negative." Getting better meant chipping away at who she thought she was until there was very little pie left. "When I lost that very deep self-hatred all the time—that nonnegotiable way of thinking about myself—I was like, 'I have no idea who I am,'" she said.

. . .

Identity isn't just what you do. It's how you perceive yourself. In college, Emma had been *doing* a lot: taking classes, making friends, signing up for extracurriculars, just like a good, people-pleasing college kid should. But those things didn't figure highly into her perception of herself. There was a jagged dissonance between the veneer and the reality, which was that, beneath it all, she was deeply unhappy. While her week in the hospital didn't solve her problems, it did help her make space to start. "It was the first week where anyone said, 'You don't have to do anything but take care of yourself,'" she said.

"So what happened after the hospital?" I asked. "How did you manage to redefine yourself?"

Her response surprised me.

"For a while, it was like, 'I have some vague ideas about what to do. I'm not passionate about any of them. And we're just going to put off the killing ourself thing," she said.

In the midst of the murk, our first instinct is to find certainty as quickly as possible. We feel like we are drowning in chaos—we must flail to safety. We want clarity. But the only way to survive the murk is to embrace the uncertainty.

That's what worked for Emma. Getting better meant leaning into *not* knowing. "Instead of thinking about what comes next, I thought, 'I just have to get through today. I don't need to know who I am, or figure out an identity, I just need to not go back to that [old] one,'" she said. Getting through one day gave her a mote of confidence that she could get through the next. Slowly, she built a belief that she had what it took to survive life.

It's natural to want clarity. But when clarity eludes us, it's important to be okay with not knowing. People with a high tolerance for uncertainty are more likely to respond to the unknown in healthy ways, seeing it as an exciting challenge, rather than as a threat. Meanwhile, high intolerance for uncertainty has been associated with stress and anxiety, maladaptive coping responses, and vulnerability to eating disorders and depression. But by treating people's fears of the unknown, therapists have been able to treat these disorders.[5] You can shed light on the murk by rehearsing imagined scenarios or gathering intel on the "unknown" future. You can also emotionally reframe the unknown, breathing into the positives of the murk's soup: possibility, curiosity, excitement. A third approach is to bolster your belief in your own ability to handle whatever the murk sends your way.

. . .

It wasn't until three years after graduation that Emma was struck by a realization: she could see a future for herself. It was a classic sleeper transition. "I guess it snuck up on me at some point," she said. "There was never a point where I made that decision. It was just that enough things had changed in my life and my day-to-day operations to make me feel differently."

"Anything you've learned with hindsight?" I asked.

"I think I've gained a better sense of what to prioritize," she said. "I've learned that there is a basic level of 'okay' that you need to hit before you worry about anything else." She's learned to fight two harmful instincts: one, trying to solve everything all at once, and two, expecting a perfect recovery. "'Okay' didn't mean I stopped thinking about dying," she said. "'Okay' just meant a day when I didn't self-harm. It meant not getting so angry at myself for the way I felt."

Her response made me think again of the difference between pain and suffering. Thich Nhat Hanh describes this as two arrows: the first shot by an event that happens to you; the second—and far more painful—shot by yourself. "When an arrow strikes you, you feel pain. If a second arrow comes and strikes you in the same spot, the pain will be ten times worse," he writes. "If you stop to worry, to be fearful, to protest, to be angry about the pain, then you magnify the pain ten times or more. Your worry is the second arrow."[6] Emma recognized she couldn't stop her pain, but she could, to a certain extent, lessen the impact of the second arrow.

. . .

How long does the murk last? In some ways, forever. You may never be as certain after a transition as you were before. Growing up means learning that life is more complicated, and you contain more volumes than you'd originally thought. I wanted writing to be like diving—a straightforward path with formal markers of achievement and an assurance of my identity. But I didn't have that certainty—not about writing or about the career I chose later. And maybe that's just part of growing up. It's cliché to say there's nothing like your first love. Maybe there's nothing like your first identity.

Emma taught me that it's okay not to know what path you'll take out of the murk. In fact, sometimes the harder you try to find a way out of it, the longer you spend in it. Just coping with change is difficult enough without trying to envision where all this will bring you ten years down the road. I think this understanding could have brought me a lot of peace of mind when I was in my own murk. So what if writing didn't work (not then, anyway)? Just go one day at a time. Try things and eventually you'll find something that's a better fit for you.

. . .

The unknown takes on a different shape for each of us, so it's worth looking at several extremes. Emma's transition left her without a sense of who she was or what she wanted; for her to move through it she had to keep her head down and put one foot in front of the other. Others have the opposite problem. They know exactly what they want on the other side of a transition, but then the murk obliterates the path they expected to take to get there.

I first heard Stanley's story in a university donor-relations video for

Project Rebound—an organization that provides mentorship, support, and community for formerly incarcerated people hoping to attend college. At age twenty-four, Stanley went to prison, where he stayed more than two decades until his release in 2019. His time behind bars ignited a hunger for education so powerful he made dog tags that said "PhD" on them. He earned his associate degree while incarcerated and vowed that if he ever got out, he'd get his doctorate. In the video, he'd been out on parole for three years and was about to graduate from CSU Northridge, meaning he was well on his way. Unlike Emma and me, Stanley seemed to have had a clear ambition throughout his transition out of prison. How did he stay strong and focused through all the setbacks that the murk can bring? Are there traits we can cultivate that help us weather uncertainty and lack of control? I reached out to him on LinkedIn, and a few days later he was sharing his perspective over Zoom, patiently and with exceedingly good humor correcting my assumptions about the US carceral system.

Two days before Thanksgiving in 2019, at age forty-five, Stanley changed out of his prison denims and into his dressouts and walked through the gates of the California State Prison at Corcoran, where his best friend picked him up. First they spent an inordinately long time trying to find a breakfast buffet. It had been twenty-two years since he'd had a say in what he ate. "I wanted a variety to choose from," he said with a staccato chuckle that rose as it got going. "But there aren't as many buffets as you think there are." His laugh rolled out past his words and kept rolling. "I'm like, man, no, where are all the buffets?"

Then, they went to a dollar store to get some toothpaste and deodorant, and Goodwill to buy a jacket. No one prepares for cold weather and rain on their release day. Then his friend drove him three hours to the coast so he could see the ocean again. After spending a night in a hotel room there, Stanley reported to his state-mandated transitional housing. But due to a mix-up, they weren't expecting him and had no free rooms.

He spent several days going back and forth between his parole agent and the housing manager (while learning to use a modern smartphone) until the housing manager acquiesced and took him in. He was one friend away from homelessness while he sorted it out.

His greatest impression of his release day wasn't joy so much as relief. In the later years of his sentence, he'd been denied parole twice. He was finally granted parole on his third try, in April of 2019, and expected to be released in July after the standard ninety-day confirmation process, but a bureaucratic issue kept him locked up for another four months. "You never know until you know," he said.

Like me, Stanley's transition led him through a murky crossroads, with no job, no housing, and no significant other. But unlike me, he didn't have the luxury of wallowing at home while he figured things out. And unlike me, he wasn't starting with a blank slate. Hiding in Stanley's murk was a gauntlet of obstacles. From prison, he had plotted out his path to self-sufficiency and the title of "doctor": spend a few years working in construction to save up the money for college, sprinkle in a couple community college classes to get himself into the swing of academia, enroll full time, graduate as soon as possible, and apply for PhD programs. But very little went according to plan.

He applied to the International Union of Operating Engineers, which would enable him to make the kind of money he needed to save for school, but before he could take the membership test, the pandemic hit and the union suspended testing. He looked for general construction work, but it was the early-pandemic construction doldrums. He spent eight months searching. He finally got a job with a sheet metal company but was soon laid off when the project he'd been hired for fell through. Eventually, he found work fulfilling Amazon grocery orders and detailing cars.

Amid his work slump, a guidance counselor at the community college where he'd started taking classes persuaded him to apply to CSU

Northridge, where he was accepted, enrolled full time, and took on a job as a student assistant. Instead of one union job that could pay his bills and help him save money to focus on future schooling, he found himself drowning in three minimum wage gigs and a full slate of classes. And even then, he wasn't doing enough. He earned good grades, but to be accepted to a PhD program, he needed to get exceptional grades, attend conferences, take on extracurriculars, meet the right people, and apply— a full-time job in itself.

He was also coping with changes to his psyche. "Having been in prison for so long, you don't realize that you get institutionalized. The environment becomes a part of you," he said. For more than two decades, Stanley had never experienced darkness—there was always a cool fluorescence overhead. At his transitional housing, when everyone went to bed and turned out the lights for the night, he had panic attacks.

On top of all of that, he was still grappling with ongoing dissonance in his identity. During his time in prison, Stanley came to terms with the violent crime he had committed and the childhood trauma that had contributed to him being a person who could commit such a crime. He strengthened his faith in God. He began leading therapy groups to help others cope with their own trauma. He found new purpose in lifting up the men around him. It was "not just a transition, but a transformation." But it's taken mental and emotional work to build his identity around the values at his core, rather than his past actions and the gaps they've made in his life: his crime, his sentence, and all the milestones they've kept at bay. "It's part of what I've struggled with. To a certain extent, I still struggle with it," he said. "Understanding that I am who I am, and that certain actions don't define me." This struggle made me think of Emma's battles to remember that her negative thoughts didn't define who she was.

Identity change isn't a one-and-done shift. It's a battle that's refought with every instinctive flash of frustration or anger or self-pity. Will you give in to the second arrow, allowing yourself to fixate and suffer from what you can't control? Identity shifts are as slow and as seismic as tectonic plates.

For Stanley, the murk also means a persistent fear that he'll wake up one morning and be sent back. He's still on parole. If all goes well, five years to the day after his release, he'll get to remove his ankle monitor, stay out past 11 p.m., and travel fifty miles without first receiving written permission. But until then, his parole agent has astounding power over his future. Roughly 25 percent of all state prison readmissions are due to technical parole or probation violations: actions that wouldn't otherwise be considered criminal, like missing appointments, breaking curfews, or failing alcohol tests. A parolee must abide by ten to twenty conditions a day, depending on their state, crime, and individual stipulations from their parole agents. It's the luck of the draw whether you're assigned to a parole agent who's stringent on rules or more forgiving. Will they accept the fact that you worked late or your car broke down as a reason to miss curfew? Will they send you to jail for a failed alcohol test, or note it in your record and give you a warning? This is one of the things Stanley wants to research for his PhD: How could the parole system be overhauled to be less arbitrary and better equipped to enable transitions, rather than hinder them?

It's a sad irony that parole itself is his latest obstacle. As he was finishing his undergrad degree, he applied to several PhD programs and was accepted to study criminal justice at Rutgers University in New Jersey. He was scheduled to start last fall but couldn't attend because, under the terms of his probation, he couldn't move out of the state of California. A frantic call to the dean earned him a one-year deferral for his admission. Now, that one year is almost up, and he's still awaiting the verdict on his request to transfer his parole from California to New Jersey. If his transfer is not granted—which could happen for a thousand arbitrary reasons—he risks losing his spot in the PhD program.

"How do you cope with having that little control over your life?" I asked.

"One thing I learned in prison was how to be flexible," he said. He described the night-and-day personalities of the guards who might be randomly assigned to his unit, the ever-present chance that his unit would go on lockdown for a few hours or the whole afternoon, and the constant possibility of an unexpected transfer to some other part of the prison. Whatever he had planned for his day, his week, his life, he had to be ready to change those expectations in a moment. "Any given day, there's a lot of unpredictability," he said. "So when I got out and things weren't exactly as I thought they'd be, that flexibility allowed me to navigate and adapt." Stanley had no expectations that life would hand him what he wanted, so when obstacles arose he found ways around them.

When I asked if he had any final bit of advice that might help others navigate the murk of transition, his words mirrored Emma's in a way I didn't expect. "Sometimes, you don't really know," he said. "You can only discover the answers as you go. I think that's part of the transition. Being okay with not having it all figured out."

His mantra is "trust the process"—it's the secret that has enabled him to stay flexible when nothing goes his way, either within or outside of prison walls. He has faith in his direction, which has allowed him to function in situations where each step is full of uncertainty.

I asked one more question, which brought us back to where we started—the reason I'd been drawn to Stanley's story in the first place. "Why, two years into your prison sentence, did you make dog tags that said 'PhD' on them?" I asked. "Of all the things you could have chosen, why was that your goal?"

"Because I wanted everyone to have to call me doctor," he said with that same staccato laugh, like a lawnmower starting. "That's really what it was at first. Just so I could put that title with my name."

He paused and thought for a moment. "Now since I've gotten out, what has really motivated me to get my PhD is recognizing the impact I can have. The PhD gives more credibility to the research I want to do, which will allow it to be more impactful on people in our society." I pictured Stanley in 2000, two years into his sentence. It was another type of murk, those early prison days. He needed a dream, and he chose one without thinking too much about it. The process of reaching it defined his path and added to its richness. And as he moved along that path, it grew in importance, gradually becoming part of his identity.

The murk is uncertain. Transitions break down our structures, both externally (our daily schedules, support systems, and habits) and internally (our ambitions and identities). Uncertainty is not inherently good or bad, though for many of us, the uncertainty in the midst of a transition is unsettling. We must resist the urge to fight it, fear it, or power through it.

Stay flexible. Try things. Fail and change course. The murk is full of opportunities for those who are willing to embrace it.

Tools for Embracing the Murk

You're stepping into the unknown. Keep moving, even if you've lost the path. Keep trying things, even if you make mistakes. Keep believing in yourself, even if nothing is going as planned. Give yourself the grace to coexist with uncertainty and the space to change your mind.

How to Get Comfy with Uncertainty

Tell Your Story: Spin Fears into Opportunities

Remind yourself that you don't have to accept your first reaction to uncertainty: You can choose excitement, curiosity, and potential over fear or anger.

- Draw a line down the center of a piece of paper.

- On the left side, write down the fears and anxieties related to your transition.

- On the right side, reframe them. What's the positive spin?

  - Here are some examples:

Fears and Anxieties	Positive Spin
I don't know what's next and I'm scared.	*It's freeing not to know what's next. There are so many possibilities ahead. What interests me?*

> *What if I apply to this job and I'm rejected?*

> *Even if I'm rejected, I will have gained experience through the application process, and I'll be better prepared for what's next.*

- Reflect on those positives. When you're feeling doubtful, reread them. Stick them on the wall by your desk.

How to Figure Out What's Next (By Doing)

Novelty Week

See all those possibilities whizzing by you like kernels in a popcorn machine? Grab 'em! Spend a week tuning into the things that pique your curiosity and trying at least one new thing a day. Go to an event, take a class, plan a coffee date with someone you admire to learn more about them. Take that first French lesson, try pottery, ask someone to teach you how to play pickleball. Every day, do something you haven't done before.

Commit . . . for a Bit

One thing a day is (hopefully) fun, but you'll only be able to scratch the surface. So commit . . . for a bit. Take a community college class, join a rec league, or get a beginner Arduino kit and block off a few evenings a week for a month to learn to build electronics. Stick with it long enough to feel some frustration and experience other downsides—and give yourself time and space to work through those. At the end of a month, assess: How much do you love it? Do you want to keep going? Proceed! Do you want to give that time and energy to something else? Proceed!

How to Figure Out What's Next (By Thinking)

Bake a Fresh Pie

We're all changing, gradually, throughout our lives. Transitions often enable us—or force us—to recognize the changes we've made and incorporate them into our perceptions of ourselves. See the murk as an opportunity to identify who you are and who you want to be.

Draw a circle and divide it into the eight Wheel of Life slices: career, finance, health, family and friends, romantic relationships/significant other, fun and leisure, personal development, and contribution to society. Feel free to amend these slices; for example, if family plays a major role in your life, separate friends and family, or if you happen, as I do, to get invested in hobbies to an extent where "fun and leisure" doesn't seem to apply, then add a slice for hobbies.

Rate your satisfaction with the slices by drawing a horizontal line across each one, placing it near the center of the circle for not satisfied or near the outside of the slice for very satisfied. Shade the inner portion of each slice.

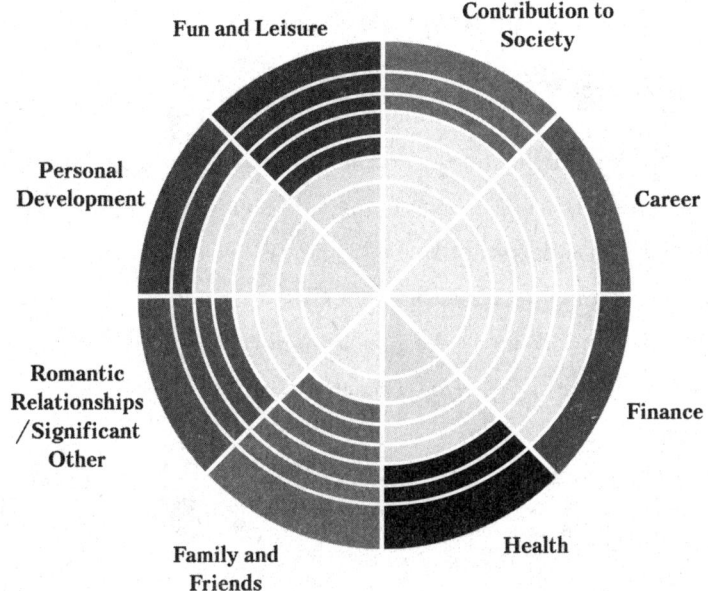

Fun and Leisure

Contribution to Society

Personal Development

Career

Romantic Relationships /Significant Other

Finance

Family and Friends

Health

Examine the slices where satisfaction is low. Is this an area you want to invest time and energy into improving? If the answer is yes, consider these areas as focuses for Novelty Week or Commit for a Bit exercises. Share the wheel with your friends, coworkers, or partner and ask them to fill it out. Compare notes. What are you struggling with? How can you better support one another?

Note: If this feels impossible, put the pie back in the oven. Some transitions are too fresh or too volatile or too lawless to wrangle our identities into neat slivers. There's a time and a place for pie. It's later. No biggie.

How to Keep Your $*@! Together

Ground Yourself in Your Comfort Zone

The murk is sticky and uncertain. Ground yourself in whatever makes you feel whole. What foods did you love as a child? What show or movie do you know by heart? Where do you feel most at ease in your skin? What friend can you talk to to make you feel most like you? Balance the novelty with weekly time to double down on the things you *are* certain about.

How to Neutralize the Controller

Define "Okay"

If you find yourself in quicksand, survivalists recommend no sudden movements. Similarly, when you're in the murk, don't flail or try to figure out your new life and identity all at once. Don't try to be perfect. Figure out what it means to you to be "okay"—just one or two things that you must feel or do—and prioritize around that. Allow yourself to appreciate an okay day. If it's not an okay day, drop whatever balls you need to make tomorrow better.

4.

Ask for Help and
Seek Community

We weren't built to go it alone. But sometimes, it's hard to know where to look for support. How do we ask for help moving into, through, and out of transitions? How can transitions be not a loss of community but an opportunity to build community?

After several months of writer's block and Zumba classes, it became clear that I was not about to launch a thriving career as a freelance short story writer. I needed to find a job—a real job, with tasks and structure and preferably close oversight by a kindly supervisor. The trouble was, I had no idea what else I wanted to do, much less how to maneuver my way into it. *I'm an English Major—Now What* had chapters like "Books," "Freelancing for a Living," and "Going Corporate." They all sounded vaguely like directions I might enjoy, but after reading through it, I still didn't feel particularly attached to anything.

I pored through LinkedIn, making lists of job descriptions, sorting them into groups, and typing the details into a spreadsheet. I ruminated for hours over whether each posting actually felt like something I wanted to do. I applied to the jobs that sounded like they might be a good fit, writing painfully formal cover letters of my expertise and career interests. I sent resumes out into the ether. I mostly didn't hear back.

There was only one thing I knew for certain: whatever I did, however I did it, I wanted to live in New York City. I'd been eying New York from a distance since the summer after my freshman year in college. That summer, a friend had gotten an internship in the city and he'd invited me to stay with him for a weekend. I took the bus from Pittsburgh two days after getting my wisdom teeth out. My friend was subletting a cramped third-floor walk-up off Fourteenth Street with a model named Candy. I slept on their couch. While he worked his internship, I explored the city by foot and subway, dodging the summer spit of window AC units and eavesdropping on whatever conversations poked through the car horns. After he was done with work, we weaved through Chinatown markets, drank margaritas at narrow bars, and watched the sun set from camp chairs on his unfinished rooftop. Everyone I met seemed to be hustling in a different direction. By the time I left, I knew that I would live there someday, once diving no longer tethered me to California.

That day was now. But go to New York and do . . . what? "You're a words and ideas person," said my mom. "There are plenty of jobs out there for people who are good with words and ideas." But it was hard to break through the vague sense of possibility.

I wasn't the first words and ideas person in the family. Mom had originally coined the term to describe her younger sister, Patty. Aunt Patty is an exhaustive researcher, likely to consult fifteen recipes before trying to cook a new dish, and a compulsive brainstormer, always there with a friendly "what if we tried this." When I started competing internationally as a diver, she sent photos of her black lab Lucy with paper "Good luck!" signs hung around her patient neck, thematically embellished with a sombrero if I was competing in Mexico or a set of shamrock beads if the competition was near Saint Patrick's Day. Her ideas, and the spoonful of sugar with which she always delivered them, enabled her to build an extremely successful career in marketing at a pharma company.

Back when I first toyed with retiring from diving in 2008, she had created, printed, and mailed me a PowerPoint presentation entitled "Life as a Continuum." An asterisk on the title page noted, "Some people start out life being able to write. Then they join corporate America and life becomes PowerPoint. So here's the PowerPoint guide to next steps in life." The PowerPoint was designed to help me figure out if I wanted to keep diving for four more years, take my talents to the workforce, or some hybrid of the two. Her advice that I didn't have to go 100 percent in either direction—that I could work and dive for two or three years before we really got into Olympic crunch time—was what had led to me taking the Stanford Alumni Association job in the first place, a choice that had been great for my self-esteem and bank account while I was training.

But my current transition felt like a different kind of pressure. In 2008, I was only twenty-three. Now I was twenty-seven and felt even further behind. In 2008, I'd been looking for any job that might give me a different frame of reference than the pool. Now I felt like my next career needed to also be my calling.

Somewhere between my overlapping phases of "trying to be a writer" and "trying to get a job," Patty flew through town and invited me to dinner. I complained to her, somewhat melodramatically, that nothing was going right and I didn't seem qualified to be anything other than a diver. "Would you be interested in talking to some of my advertising contacts?" she asked. I was aghast. I was steeped in the dual meritocracies of school and sports. If I needed help to get an A on a test, I didn't deserve it. If a judge scored me well because he was friends with my coach, I didn't deserve it. If I got an interview because Aunt Patty had put in a good word for me, I didn't deserve it. In school and sports, opportunities are based upon performance, not request. Making connections in any way but a cold email to a hiring manager seemed fundamentally unfair.

She must have seen the look on my face. "You're not asking for a job," she said. "You're just asking them what they do and what made them successful." My palms started sweating. I imagined myself standing in front of a solid oak desk while a Very Important Person in a two-thousand-dollar suit swiveled to face me.

"Just what is it that you're looking for?" they ask.

My ears buzz with the static chime of too much silence. "I have no idea," I answer.

"Well stop wasting my time," they say, and with a squeak of their chair leather, they turn back to their Very Important Work.

"I'm sure they'd be curious to talk with an Olympian," Aunt Patty said, reading my mind. "You could trade stories. You tell them about the Athletes' Village and they tell you about their job."

I was skeptical, but it was true that people were generally quite curious about the Olympic Athletes' Village. And when I pushed past my imagined awkwardness, I had to admit I was quite curious about what working people did all day. Also, I couldn't sit in my room in Pittsburgh forever.

"Okay," I said. "Let's try it."

A few days later she followed up, sending me a new PowerPoint slide: "8 Reasons Why Interviewing for Information Isn't That Bad." The list included words of wisdom like, "Number 4: It's really flattering to have someone think you're an expert," and "Number 8: Lots of studies show (too lazy to look it up but trust me it's big) that folks land their dream jobs via the informational interview approach."

She also shared seven names for me to email, all of whom worked in advertising, publishing, or market research. "This is a list of nice people who have kind of fun jobs that use creativity, writing, and leadership skills," she said. "All of them have said that they would love to talk to you."

Patty's help made me feel a lot of ways—most notably, lucky. Who else is lucky enough to have an Aunt Patty in their lives, someone who knows how to unlock all the doors and who cares enough to give you the keys? That luck made me a little uncomfortable, like I was sneaking into the building. Nevertheless, I put on my big girl pants and wrote each of them an email with a few sentences about myself, what I wanted to learn, and when I was planning to be in the city. Then I squeezed my eyes shut and hit send.

· · ·

I arrived in New York in November of 2012, late at night in the middle of a blizzard. A friend from high school had offered to let me crash on her couch during my visit. I was only staying a week but had packed for a month. Fat flakes got caught in my eyelashes while I shuffled around her sprawling Upper West Side apartment complex, dragging my suitcase like a snowplow. The next morning, the city shone bright from that fresh white layer of snow that lasts about ten minutes before being stomped and salted into slush. My first meeting was with a woman who Patty had introduced as "The nicest, smartest person I've met in a long time." Apparently they'd traveled the world together leading focus groups on pediatric nutritional supplements. She worked at an advertising agency and did something called strategic planning.

I'd left my friend's apartment with twenty minutes to spare based on the Google Maps estimate, but it wasn't enough. I clunked down the wrong subway stairs, pushed through the wrong turnstile, and hopped on a train going the wrong direction. When I got off, I was running so far behind schedule that I decided to spring for a cab. I then learned, amid the nausea of a driver navigating traffic with feet on both the brake and the accelerator, that it takes twice as long to get to midtown by car as by train. Despite the frigid weather, I had to open the window; I was sweating with panic.

When I finally arrived, the elevator door opened on a bright space with high ceilings, concrete floors, and a stunning view of the city. Patty's friend met me with a smile, answering my profuse apologies with a graceful, "No worries!" She walked me through the office, an open floor plan with rows of desks personalized with photos and neon sticky notes and swag from various brands. The atmosphere seemed cheerful. I'd always thought that if being a writer didn't work out, I wouldn't mind becoming a copywriter and dreaming up the next Doublemint gum jingle or Bud-weis-er frog commercial. I told Patty's friend as much and she smiled: "We can absolutely introduce you to some copywriters," she said. "Although to be honest, I don't think I'd enjoy it much. They spend most of their time making changes to keep all the rest of us happy."

I hadn't considered that.

She explained that ad agency teams are a trifecta of roles: the account team, who keeps the ship running; the creatives, who write and design the ads; and the strategic planners, or strategists—the link between dry business briefs and all the zany TV commercials I'd fallen in love with as a kid. That's what she did. The strategists were responsible for knowing everything there was to know about consumers and culture and then shining a light on how to connect with people. It was structured creativity: applying my words and ideas to very specific tasks. I wasn't sure if I could do it, but I wanted to be the type of person who could. Forty-five minutes later, I was heading back down the elevator, feeling for the first time like I had some semblance of what I wanted to do with my life.

I grabbed lunch at a deli in midtown then walked to my next meeting at a crisis PR firm. It was in an austere, rectangular skyscraper whose tenants included banks, hedge funds, and the American Institute of Certified Public Accountants. This time, the elevator doors opened on a gray office with marble floors. The woman who met me was as friendly as the strategic planner had been, but I felt ill at ease. This office was eerily calm, like Kansas before the next tornado. I only remember a few snippets from our conversation: "The team they call when a company gets in trouble." "Always on." It wasn't until I stepped out onto the sidewalk that I started taking full breaths again.

. . .

I started to get the hang of asking for help. A friend sent intros to a bevy of former colleagues. An old high school classmate, Jess, took me to the house party of someone in publishing and pointed out who worked at what magazine. In seven days, I did informational interviews with thirteen different people: advertisers, journalists, editorial assistants, marketers, crisis PR folks, researchers, and TV producers. "I feel like I've learned more in one week than I did in three months at home," I wrote to Aunt Patty. And it was true. Actually meeting people, seeing their offices, and hearing how they talked about their jobs gave my gut something to go on. By the end of the week, I had a solid set of yeses, noes, and maybes.

Meanwhile, my friends helped me try on city life, complete with the good (art, eavesdropping), the bad (tiny rooms in walk-up apartments, hangovers), and the ugly (rats!). They taught me to scan subway platforms for signs of a route change and keep my radar on for the magical express train. They told me about the adult rec leagues and book clubs they'd joined when they first arrived. The lives you witness give you some idea of what to expect for yourself—even more if you actively share your hopes and fears and ask your questions.

Once I was open to receiving support, I was shocked at how ready people were to give it to me. Everyone I met shared some version of the same message: Figuring out a career from scratch isn't easy. Moving to New York isn't easy. But we were all there too. My trip confirmed what I had long suspected: New York was a good place to be reborn.

. . .

Over time, I learned the two golden rules of support. One, if you don't ask for help, you're unlikely to get it. Organizational psychologist Adam

Grant suggests that up to 75–90 percent of "expanded role" assistance within organizations is only offered after a direct request—in other words, people generally only offer help beyond their stated job description when someone asks them for it directly.[1] It's quite rare to have an angel like Aunt Patty shooting exactly the right unsolicited PowerPoint slide at you at every fork in the road. And two, people are more likely to help than you think. Another organizational psychologist, Vanessa Bohns, has tasked research participants to make a variety of requests like asking strangers to borrow their phones, fill out questionnaires, provide detailed directions, raise funds for a charity run, and even commit a small act of vandalism (writing the word "pickle" on a page of a library book. Egad!). Across all her research, she's found that people helped at a rate 48 percent higher than participants predicted they would.[2]

Asking for help is just one part of a larger challenge: maintaining, building, and rebuilding *relationships*. Transitions—from retirements to immigrations to births to deaths—often sever our bonds. Sometimes the separation is physical: We're no longer in close proximity to our people. And sometimes it's emotional: Things change, and we no longer feel the same sense of connection. But humans weren't made to go it alone. Every single one of my conversations illustrated some aspect of this.

Relationships are an essential part of *moving into* a transition.

In the final years of his athletic career, Ryan the runner and his wife, Sara, adopted four girls from Ethiopia. While they were not a reason for his retirement, they helped him feel hopeful about the shift.

"One of the tiring things about being a professional athlete is that you have to be very self-focused and self-disciplined to perform at a high level," he said. "You can do things to try to get outside of yourself, but at the end of the day, your day revolves around you." The fight to be the best means putting your training, sleep, and daily schedule first. Steve Prefontaine, the first man to run a sub-four-minute mile and patron saint of pain sports, said this gem: "To give anything less than your best is to sacrifice the gift." The question I wonder about is: What must you sacrifice to avoid sacrificing the gift?

Ryan looked forward to retiring and shifting his focus to taking care of others. "That was one of the things that I was ready for and excited about moving to a new season," he said.

Relationships are an essential part of *moving through* a transition.

When Dawn told me about the experience of losing her mother to cancer, she'd made a point of sharing how much she'd appreciated the friends and family who had reached out to her. There were times when she just wanted to talk about her mom and have someone else listen. But she'd also shared how important it was to connect with people who got it. In her mom's last year, Dawn had come back to LA for a weekend to spend her birthday with her partner. That was the weekend that LA Lakers legend Kobe Bryant died, plunging the entire city into mourning. As reported in the *LA Times*, "Around the city and far beyond, people gasped and struggled to accept the news. Friends texted friends: 'Are you OK?' They cried in bars and churches, on street corners and golf courses and basketball courts. Restaurants closed Sunday night to honor his memory, and people placed basketballs outside their front doors, like flags at half staff."[3] For Dawn, it was a surreal moment of solidarity. "I saw that nobody escapes this," she said. "It made me feel like more people understood what I was going through than I knew."

An acquaintance also lost a loved one around the same time as Dawn's mom was dying. They held each other through their grief, and the two are now best friends. "We're alone in our grief a lot of times," she said. "You don't know which of your friends have lost someone unless you witness it." For Dawn, those three levels of community—friends who cared, strangers who shared the feeling, and the closest bond, someone who was also moving through a great loss—were all essential support.

But as Dawn mentioned—you don't always know who will be able to relate to your loss. Sometimes you need to teach people how to support you.

. . .

At thirty-six years old and three and a half years into a marriage she thought would last forever, my friend Sarah got divorced. Suddenly, Sarah was alone with a broken heart. She had a tight-knit circle of friends who loved her. But they didn't understand the depths of her grief. Most were like she had been: recently married, thinking about kids, settling in for fifty more years together. Divorce was not on anyone's radar. "It felt like a transition where I didn't have a lot of company," Sarah said.

She started going to a support group for recent divorcées, but most of those women were emerging from thirty-year marriages, talking about grown children and menopause in a way that made Sarah feel more alone. The women in Sarah's support group knew what it was like to be divorced, but they didn't know *her*. Meanwhile, her friends knew her, but had no idea what it was like to be divorced. They said things like, "You'll find someone new," or (I can distinctly remember uttering these words myself) "You're better off without him." Everyone was trying to refocus her attention on something other than loss, trying to shift Sarah's negative emotions to reassurance, confidence, or hope. But that wasn't the support she needed. "I think a lot of people have an inclination to try to fix things," she said. "But there wasn't anything people could do to fix what I was going through. I needed people who would just sit there and be sad, or angry, or hurt with me."

Luckily, Sarah had a great therapist. Together, they worked on how to ask for support. "I had to really learn to stop expecting people to be able to read my mind," she said. Sarah learned to notice the types of reactions that made her feel worse and head them off, saying, "I want to share something. I don't want you to try to come up with a solution for it. Please just let me say this and then tell me, 'Wow, that sucks.'"

She and two friends took a trip to Iceland on what would have been her wedding anniversary. Her friends made big plans, and she was worried that she wouldn't be able to appreciate them. Her therapist urged her to tell them that. It was hard to say out loud that they might fly three thousand miles to one of the most stunning places on Earth and she might not enjoy it, but she did it anyway. "You have an amazing day planned," she said. "But I need you to know that I might not be able to get out of bed." Just getting those words out lifted the burden of "should" from Sarah's back. And they ended up having a lovely day.

It was one thing to open up to her closest friends. But Sarah knew that she would need all the help she could get on the date of her divorce, eight months after her initial separation. So, she wrote an email and asked her parents to share it with anyone who asked about her. It is, in my opinion, an opus.

She started by thanking her parents, then laying out, clearly and compassionately, what she needed from them: lots of hugs ("Hold me and let me cry as long as I need to."), reassurance ("Tell me: 'This pain won't feel this way forever.'"), and validation ("Remind me: 'This situation is terrible.' 'You never wanted or asked for this.'"). She also included a section for others: "I want to be overwhelmed with happy texts! I'm enlisting as many people as possible to text me jokes, memes, GIFs and/or other positive messages throughout the day. If they're not sure what to say, suggest: 'I love you and you're going to be okay.' If even that feels like a lot, tell them they can *never* go wrong with a picture of a cat."

"I was getting cat GIFs from friends of my aunts," Sarah told me. "It was their way of saying I love you and I'm here for you, even if they didn't feel quite comfortable saying exactly that." It's hard to bridge the gap between good intentions and good support, and she did it so graciously.

While we're on the subject of building relationships, Sarah's story brings up another thing: vulnerability. That's the big kicker for professor and social worker Brené Brown, who's written six *New York Times* bestsellers on community, shame, and self-worth. In her viral 2010 talk on the power of vulnerability, she describes analyzing thousands of research conversations to learn the difference between people who felt worthy of care and belonging and those who didn't: "These folks had, very simply, the courage to be imperfect," she said. "They were willing to let go of who they thought they should be in order to be who they were."[4] Sarah could easily have melted into the shame of an early divorce, but instead, she asked her parents to share her story and request for help openly—and in doing so, she gave everyone from close family to distant acquaintances a way to support her.

. . .

Relationships are an essential part of *moving out* of a transition.

When Emma was a year or two past the worst of her depression, she discovered trapeze. "I don't think I've ever been as happy as I have been for the past two years," she said, "Just because I suddenly found a community of people who are weird and something that I want to work hard to be good at that's not tied to a career."

A community isn't just a group of friends. A community is made up of people who actively share something: a belief, an activity, a love. Talking together and being together are important, but *doing* together—that's what makes a community a community. There's something about what MIT philosophy professor Kieran Setiya calls "atelic activities," activities we love for their own sake, more for present enjoyment than achievement of a future goal, that bring people together.[5] If you want to find community—find an activity you're interested in. Friends will likely follow.

Beyond the shared joy of a specific activity, there's also something deeply fulfilling about sharing hard things with other people. In his book *Tribe*,

Sebastian Junger writes about how loyalty and belonging benefit us as individuals.[6] A war correspondent, Junger began his career covering the conflict in Kosovo, then spent more than a year embedded with an infantry platoon in Afghanistan. His book is devoted to answering questions that kept coming up: Why do many soldiers feel more at home in war than in peace? Why did British psychiatric patients' symptoms subside during the Blitz? Why did German cities that were bombed the hardest during World War II also have the highest morale? His research pulls observations from different eras and cultures and identifies a unified explanation: Each of these environments—harrowing, dangerous, and foreign as they may be—create ripe conditions for a tribe. Junger writes, "The beauty and the tragedy of the modern world is that it eliminates many situations that require people to demonstrate a commitment to the collective good." He goes on to argue that mankind needs this desperately—that we thrive on meaningful and urgent opportunities to contribute. I don't think it requires a war or close proximity to violence. I think that we can create those bonds by supporting one another through hard things.

While Emma was dragging herself out of her depression, it felt like too much pressure to figure out who she wanted to be or what she wanted to do. But her trapeze community helped her gain a more concrete sense of who she is. "I think that's helped me find more of an identity," she said. It reminded me of something Sarah had said, describing the friends she'd made in college, long before her divorce: "The better I got to know certain people, the more I felt like I had found my place. They were bringing out the parts of me that I felt best about." Our communities and our identities are symbiotic, feeding one another.

· · ·

If the anecdotes above make relationship building seem like an easy side-effect of finding a hobby, that's not my intention. Because it's not.

One-on-one relationships and communities alike require investment. The time you spend with someone or the act of doing hard things in close proximity is an important component. But bonds grow stronger when people take an active role in connection: checking in on your teammates, planning moments for support or celebration, asking questions, welcoming new people into the group. Transitions create community and transitions take it away. People leave, people move on, people find other things to care about. If a community is not actively living, it fades.

I spoke with a woman named Carolyn, a seventy-two-year-old former teacher who'd been forced into an early retirement back in the nineties by health issues and school system policies. Three decades later, she told me about the long-term consequences of her retirement. "If I was out there in the teaching world, the kids would be showing me different things," she told me. "Different games, different words, different dances, different everything. And the teachers would be teaching me different things." The issues and policies that kept her out of work had also closed a major channel for human interaction, support, and growth. She wasn't totally devoid of companionship—she had a steadfast relationship with her husband and had made other friends since her retirement—but that didn't make up for the volume of what she'd lost. When she was forced into retirement, Carolyn didn't just lose her job—she lost a connection to community.

. . .

Recently, scientists at Harvard University completed an eighty-year study tracking the health and happiness of 268 people. The study began in 1938, when all the original participants were college sophomores at Harvard. Over the years, additional groups have been added, including the spouses of the original participants and a cohort drawn from Boston public schools. Among all groups, the greatest predictor of long-term well-being wasn't money or fame or cholesterol levels, it was the quality of their relationships. "The people who were the most satisfied in their relationships at age fifty were the healthiest at age eighty," said Robert Waldinger, director of the study.[7]

Around the world, and especially in the United States, individualism has been on the rise for decades.[8] This trend is visible across a striking array of behaviors and tendencies, from our increased likelihood to live alone rather than in multigenerational households, to the words we read and write: analysis of published literature over time has revealed steep upticks in individualistic words (e.g., "unique," "individual," and "self") and downticks in collective words (e.g., "belong").[9] We reap some benefits from the freedom that individualism provides, which I'll explore in later chapters. But if the secret to lasting health and happiness is community, our culture is not doing a great job of prioritizing it.

Accepting support requires us to reveal our vulnerabilities. It runs counter to our sense of independence. It implies we can't go it alone. It runs the risk of rejection, of making people feel obligated, of wasting people's time. But we forget that humans are evolutionarily wired for the two-way street of relationships: giving and receiving. No one I spoke with landed that point more resolutely than Becca.

· · ·

The year she turned twenty-seven, Becca took a road trip from California to Wyoming. Along the way, she decided to stop into a skydiving drop zone in Utah for an afternoon. There, she received an impromptu offer to work at one of the most coveted skydiving schools in the country. She accepted. She couldn't shake the feeling that she was meant to be there.

At the time, Becca had been skydiving for years and still loved it just as much as she had when she'd started seven thousand or so jumps ago.

Still, she knew that moving from California to Utah—a place with real winters, which she'd never experienced—wouldn't be easy. "I knew that if winter came and I wasn't working and I didn't have people around me, I would not be okay," she said. "So I decided to be super purposeful about building relationships." She set an intention to say yes to every invitation, to be the person that shows up, even if it's just for twenty minutes.

She didn't know how much she'd need those relationships.

Becca doesn't remember July 6, 2021, or most of the following week—which she considers a blessing, because if she remembered, she'd be coping with PTSD right now on top of everything else.

She wasn't teaching that day, just playing. Her thing was "swooping"—coming in with enough speed to fly a couple feet from the ground for hundreds of yards. In my diving career, I always found it a little unfair that a foot of height or a sliver of angle could mean the difference between a five and a ten. In the precise physics of swooping, it's the difference between life and death.

On Becca's fifth jump that day, the wind switched directions as she was landing, and instead of gliding just above the ground, her body rolled like a boulder through the Utah dust, her tiny performance parachute whipping and twisting behind her. Luckily, one of her fellow instructors was a twenty-two-year-old kid with a fresh EMT certification. Her injuries had locked down the airway through her mouth, so he figured out how to open one through her nose. (Not easy. "My face was pretty mushy," she said.) He kept her alive until a helicopter arrived to bring her to a level I trauma unit (miraculously) only twenty-nine miles away. There, a neurosurgeon removed her crushed C3 vertebra, "stuck it in a blender with some growth hormones," and put it back into her back. The final tally: shattered C3 and C4 vertebrae, three lower lumbar fractures, two broken eye sockets, a broken nose, and a gnarly black eye.

"Ninety-nine percent of the people with my injuries don't even make it to the operating table," she told me over Zoom two and a half years later.

Today, there's no sign of the broken nose or eye sockets. No brain damage. No face damage. There was a little double vision in the beginning, but that went away. In fact, her head, both inside and out, works just as well as it did before hitting the ground.

Her body, not so much. Becca is paralyzed from the neck down. She can talk, swallow, shrug, turn her head, smile, frown, and make the most epically exaggerated eye roll I've ever seen. As of recently, she can also feel her body—nothing as precise as soft, hard, hot, or cold, but she can tell if something's uncomfortable or someone's touching her. But she can't move anything below her neck except for the occasional muscle spasm, which rips through her like a possession, sometimes tossing her body across the bed. With total concentration, she can manipulate her lung muscles enough to pull in a few minutes' worth of short, shallow breaths. Mostly, a ventilator does the breathing for her through a hole in her trachea. Doctors and scientists are working on sci-fi miracles for people like her; for example, clinical trials that may be able to bridge the gap from her brain over the injured area to the part of her spinal cord that isn't damaged. But she can't try any of that stuff while she's on the ventilator. Every day she does breathing workouts to strengthen her lungs with the goal of someday ditching the vent.

I stalked the hell out of Becca on social media in the days leading up to our conversation, which is a pretty standard part of my process. But once I started scrolling through her Instagram feed, I found it impossible to scroll away. There was too much action. She's swerving down a mountain in a snowstorm on an adaptive sled, sending up clouds of powder at the turns (I later learned that she's able to control it herself through a straw that makes the sled turn left if she sips and right if she puffs). She's being fed a tequila shot and a Michelob Ultra chaser in the parking lot of a Luke Bryan concert. She's on a stage doing stand-up comedy, saying things like, "The closest I've gotten to getting laid in the last year and a half is having someone scratch my inner ear," while her brother holds the mic in front of her face. And oh my God, she's jumping out of a plane again, her body strapped tightly to a friend who's stabilizing her neck as they free fall from the sky.

Just a few more posts back in time and it's July 29, 2021, the first picture of her new life, a few weeks after her accident. She's gazing serenely from a hospital bed, a shadow of a black eye on her cheekbone, her neck firmly lodged in a brace that goes from her chin to her shoulders, the breathing tubes poking through the front. The caption starts, "Life has a funny way of going in directions that you never saw coming . . ."

A month before that, it's an action shot of herself mid-swoop, frozen in flight, the tops of her toes just barely brushing the ground. She's smiling so big you can see all her teeth.

There's something about an Instagram feed that puts things into perspective. Before July of 2021, our posts struck me as similar. Her skydiving stills and my trapeze videos. Her visit to a Wyoming ranch and my camping trip to Los Padres. Our odes to friends and loved ones. The one-off selfies that made us feel fierce. It's hard not to ask the question: Who would I be if what happened to Becca had happened to me? How would I handle a transition like that?

. . .

One thing I was very sure of as I prepared for our conversation was that I should not, would not, could not use the "I" word. I suspected there was something deeply annoying about talking to a woman in a wheelchair I've never met and calling her inspirational. And yet, I couldn't help myself. I dropped the "I" word two and a half times in the first thirty minutes.

Becca told me that, as a kid, she'd been so scared of heights that she had a panic attack at the top of a staircase. Then, when she was seventeen, her mom had persuaded her to go skydiving. "It was the first time in my life that I ever recognized fear for what it was and made the very conscious decision that it wasn't going to own me," she said. "My mom said I walked different after that. My confidence was different. It changed everything for me."

As someone who's now worked at a circus school for ten years, I know that few people in this world overcome fear the way that Becca did. I've talked hundreds of students off the trapeze platform, reminding them that everyone feels fear (not just them), and that the feeling of flight is a magnificent high (which it is), and that they will be so proud of themselves if they jump right now (they will). And most of them do jump and do get to experience the adrenaline rush afterward, the satisfaction of having done something hard. But it's rare for someone with Becca-grade fear—her mind blanking at the top of a set of stairs—to fall so deeply in love that she comes back for another class, much less becomes a teacher and makes it her life. Most of us try to test and dull and cope with our fears, but Becca truly owned hers. She had been in the process of becoming a skydiving instructor examiner, someone who teaches the teachers, before her accident.

"A lot of people go through their entire lives and don't change," I said. "They don't put themselves into hard situations in order to learn what they're capable of."

"How *boring*," she said.

"You're so inspiring," I said, then clamped my mouth shut. I saw a shadow cross her face and quickly changed the subject.

The second time I said the "I" word, she was telling me about her post-accident identity crisis. "I felt so inadequate. I'd meet new people and need to show them photos and videos of who I was before, because that's where my value came from," she said. "I'm trying to work through that and be like, no, I can still do cool shit now. I'm still a person of value."

"I can only say what I've seen having known you via Instagram for like four days," I started, then stopped. Was I really going there? I didn't see any way around it. "Which is that . . . I have been really inspired by the things you've done . . ." *Doh.* "I mean . . . your story is really inspirational." *Double doh.*

She smiled so aggressively and said "thanks" so sweetly that I felt like I'd given her a cavity.

"You're still not afraid?" I asked.

She told me the story of how, exactly two years after her accident, she did it again. Her old crew in California had planned a fundraiser for her, a "boogie," drawing skydivers from across the country to jump in her honor. She told her old boss that she wanted to be in the plane to celebrate Not Dead Day with everyone. He said okay, but let's make sure there's a tandem instructor with you in case anything happens. And she said that if a tandem instructor was going to have to be there anyway, they might as well just jump out together.

One week later, she woke up and thought to herself, *What the hell am I doing?* But her doubts melted as soon as she was lifted into the plane. Her best friends surrounded her on all sides, including her mom, who jumped right after her, and her dad, who sat by the door and sent them on their way. They soared like human confetti. "The stoke level was so high," she said. She was a skydiver again, a woman who had been training to teach the teachers, a woman with seven thousand jumps behind her. "It was all I could do not to nitpick my instructor," she said. There's a feeling you get when you've put in your hours but been away long enough to truly appreciate the competency you earned. I recognize it anytime I'm back in the pool. Becca, back in the air, felt it too. Free fall was just like coming home.

Becca has no plans to skydive regularly again, for similar reasons to why I don't like to dive anymore. After that initial elation has worn off, you stop thinking about what you can do and start focusing on what you've lost. She'd like to do it once a year on Not Dead Day, but that's it. "I really don't want it to lose its wow factor," she said.

I was on the verge of letting that goddamned "I" word escape my lips again when I gave myself a mental smack and redirected to the real question.

"Do you feel comfortable seeing yourself as inspirational to others?" I asked. "I know I've kind of gone fan girl on you but . . . is that a weird position to be in?"

Her eyes went wide with relief.

"I freaking hate being called inspirational," she said, and I had the opposite of that foot-in-mouth feeling. I've never been gladder to have asked a question.

"When a woman comes up to me in Costco who doesn't know me from Adam and says, 'You are just amazing. What an inspiration that you're out and about,' I'm like *bitch*. Just because I'm in a wheelchair and out in public is not enough."

"Sorry!" I said.

"No, let me finish that up," she said. "I don't like it when strangers come up and tell me I'm inspirational. I am honored when people find what I do, or what I've overcome, or what I'm capable of inspirational."

I couldn't quite decide which category I fell into. Maybe somewhere in between.

"You stalked me enough on Instagram. You're allowed to say that," she said with a smile.

While we were on the subject of taboo things to say to someone who's recently been paralyzed from the neck down, I brought up another thing I'd been wondering about. Nearly everything she'd said so far, I found strangely relatable.

Like the pain of watching her body fade. "I used to wear a fifty-five-pound rig and throw 240-pound dudes out of an airplane," she said. "And then I watched my muscles literally melt away." I conjured up the memory of watching my body soften in the months after I stopped training five hours a day.

Like how scary it was to date. "It's so hard to remind myself that if I am rejected, it does not mean that my chair is more important than my personality," she said.

Becca described working with her family to write down all the ways that others could support her, a list with three tiers ranging from "insert a catheter" to "things you ask from the church ladies." I cannot imagine asking a buddy to cath me. But I did relate to how vulnerable it feels to ask for help.

"Do you find it annoying when people say things like, 'Oh, your situation reminds me of this other thing I experienced?'" I asked. "Are you ever like, 'Just stop, it's not the same'?"

Her answer to this one was an emphatic no. "What I actually find annoying is when people don't want to talk about what's hard in their lives because they think my life is harder," she said. "Just because your issues are different or not on scale with what I'm dealing with on a daily basis does not make your struggles any less valid. And it does not make me not want to be there for you."

In Ella Wheeler Wilcox's poem "Solitude," she writes:

> *Laugh, and the world laughs with you;*
> *Weep, and you weep alone;*
> *For the sad old earth must borrow its mirth,*
> *But has trouble enough of its own.*

I thought of it now, and all the social pressures that keep us grinning through clenched teeth. No one likes a Debbie Downer. "There's this misplaced instinct that's like, oh, they've got troubles of their own. Let me not heap anything more on . . ." I said.

Becca cut me off. "That's not how community works. Like, you want me to unload my shit on you, but you're not gonna do the same for me? I'm not paying you to be my therapist. Don't make me feel like I'm the only one with problems."

. . .

Every aspect of Becca's daily life requires help. Her family members insert pills and water straws into her mouth, comb her hair, do her makeup, brush her teeth, and suction the toothpaste out of her mouth with a tube. They slide her onto a vinyl hammock and clip her into a Hoyer lift to move her to a special shower chair, then wash her hair and body. They empty her bladder. They dab tears from her cheeks, scratch her ears when they itch, and remove fuzz from her eyes. They pour coffee into her mouth and feed her small bites of steak dinner. And those are just the mundane things. They also take her fragile life into their hands on the daily. "Trach care" means cleaning every piece of the ventilator, which means someone holds the trach tube up to the hole in her neck while the gauze, cannulae, and industrial-strength Velcro are replaced and a baby washcloth is folded neatly into sixteenths and jammed under the tube to keep it from drooping. All the while, Becca grimaces. This hurts.

Becca's Tinder dates pour her beer into her mouth. Her dearest friends suction her lungs. Her parents will need to spend the rest of their lives caring for her. Becca now has to ask for—and accept—help in every aspect of her life. And she does so with remarkable grace and dignity. But the one thing she wants even more than help is the opportunity to help others.

When I asked her what she missed most about life before her accident, she said, "Hugging people back. Like, being able to squish someone." Later, she cried freely describing the frustration of not being able to give as much as she gets. "It's quite the mindfuck," she told me through tears. "Forgiving myself for being in a situation where my parents have to take care of me, and I can't take care of them." Her disability bars her from contributing in the ways she used to. She can't accompany a terrified skydiver on their first jump anymore, talking them into becoming a better version of themselves. When a friend squeezes her, she can no longer squeeze back.

Most of her goals and accomplishments now center on helping, giving, and supporting. After years of trying, she recently persuaded her parents to go to therapy. A few months ago, she started managing the family calendar, an enormous burden off her dad's plate. She's taking courses in sales in the hopes of someday getting a job and, eventually, being able to pay for her own care.

I had a lot of questions about coping. But I didn't even know how to finish the sentence. *How on earth do you cope with . . .* the end of your life as an elite skydiver and instructor? The grief of losing your independence? The murk that sets in when the future you used to imagine becomes impossible? I kept it general. "How do you cope with . . . the negatives?"

"I feel like I'm really, really lucky with the people that I'm surrounded by," she replied. "I have a group of friends that is getting bigger and bigger every day. And people that are intensely supportive and encouraging and just want to hang out with me because I'm me."

A few months after she got home from the hospital, she started hosting "Tater Tuesdays," a three-hour come-one-come-all potato party at her house every week. Someone throws a bag of potatoes in the oven and sets out all the fixin's, people show up—a different random assortment of new and old friends every time—and everyone sits around talking shit. It takes a lot of logistics for Becca to leave the house, so Tater Tuesdays bring the outside world in. "That's been a lifeline for me," she said, "and a highlight of every single week."

I mentioned the story of Carolyn's forced early retirement to Becca. "An awful lot of people are cut off from their work or their friends and then never seem to fill that gap," I said. "It's actually really heartening to hear that you have been able to build this thriving community."

"It takes conscious effort," she said. "I don't think it's something that just happens. I think you have to really have that as your purpose in order to find it." Becca's got the gift of fast friendship—for example, one of her best friends is the guy who retiled her bathroom after her accident.

But when life has curtailed your activities in the way Becca's has, charm isn't enough. Her greatest piece of advice for transitioners was on that theme: "Don't isolate yourself."

Even before her accident, Becca recognized community as an indispensable lifeline worthy of all the effort and energy she could pour into it. Her story made it so clear to me that asking for help is just as important as giving help to others. We are all social creatures, hardwired not just to give and receive help, but to *enjoy* giving and receiving help. Help isn't just a selfish request—it's a chain reaction that creates community.

Tools for Asking for Help and Finding Community

Transitions often make us feel alone, but connections are always possible. Building relationships takes time, energy, and vulnerability, but it's a good investment.

How to Help Your Friends and Family Support You

Tell Your Story: Write It Down

Your friends and family love you, but they don't always understand your transitions. You are certainly not obligated to explain yourself to others, but it can feel less lonely if you share what you need. Sarah's email started with some quick context about how she was feeling and what not to do ("I imagine it is probably only natural to want to suggest things that feel like they might offer a solution. But there is no solution on Tuesday."), then included a section on what she needed from her parents, a section on what she needed from extended friends and family, and a heartfelt thanks at the end. Becca didn't send out an email, but she did sit down with her family to brainstorm what they could delegate to people, in three tiers based on closeness. Write a letter, email, or just talking points for yourself to help communicate what you need and what you want friends and family to know.

How to Find People Who "Get It"

Know That You're Not Alone

It is almost always possible to find organized support systems for people who "get" what you're dealing with. For job seekers, alumni associations generally have career support programs. For retiring athletes, colleges and national sport governing bodies often have or sponsor "pivot" advisors. *Psychology Today* maintains a list of support groups for coping with transitions like divorce, depression, or death. The Reeve Foundation and United Spinal Association both facilitate support groups for those coping with spinal cord injuries. You get the idea. Do a quick Google search for community or support for your particular transition and see what you find.

How to Turn an Activity into a Community

Don't Just Wait for Connections to Happen

Think of all your communities and potential communities, including family, hobbies, support groups, neighbors, or your Commit for a Bit activities from the previous chapter. Which of these have people you'd like to get to know better? When you're at your activity, don't just go heads down—pay attention to the people around you. Notice haircuts, ask questions, offer support. Invite the community to something outside your standard meeting place, like a pre-work exercise class, a post-game drink, or a Saturday afternoon in the park. Bring baked goods. Actively welcome newbies.

How to Enhance the Warm Fuzzies of Social Interaction

Show Your Gratitude

It feels good to invest in others, whether that's sharing career advice, sending a cat video, or hosting Tater Tuesdays. It feels extra good when we feel like that investment is appreciated and impactful. Write specific, heartfelt thank-you notes. Notice what people are doing (on your behalf or for the good of your group) and share your appreciation. Also, notice the impact they've made, whether it's a successful work project, good community vibes, or just something you feel, and tell them.

Don't Forget

Hang Up Your Hang-Ups

Making new connections and asking for help are scary. But our fears are like evening shadows: taller than they should be. If you're like most people, you underestimate how willing others are to help you. There's no shame in vulnerability, particularly when you're fighting with all your brain, heart, and muscle to wade through the murky tar of transition. It's rare that that help will come to you unbidden. You have to ask for it.

5.

Connect Your Dots

New environments can be unsettling. How do we keep our composure, identify our strengths, and apply our lessons and passions to new challenges? What of our identities do we bring with us?

After my meeting with that first strategic planner, Patty's friend, I sent her a thank-you note. She responded with an offer to forward my resume to other strategists she knew. Several of those people were hiring and set up formal interviews. Within a few weeks of my New York trip, I had two job offers.

I turned them both down.

In addition to being the year I competed at the Olympics, 2012 was also the year of the diving reality TV show. *Dancing with the Stars* was in its fifteenth season of solid ratings and networks were nosing around for the next great celebreality hit. That year they'd nosed their way to the pool. On a lark, I'd applied to be a coach on the upcoming show *Splash*, a diving competition featuring an array of celebrities from Drake Bell to Kareem Abdul-Jabbar. The week I got both strategy job offers was the week I flew out to Los Angeles to audition for the show. Though I was excited about advertising, it seemed unlikely that I'd ever get another opportunity to teach celebrities how to dive on TV, so when they offered me the coaching role, I packed my bags and moved back across the country. Filming was to last four months, from January to April.

To hedge my bets, I also got a ten-hour-a-week remote internship with a New York agency. During downtime at the pool, I tracked cereal content on Twitter and analyzed press releases on new flavored vodka launches. I still wasn't entirely sure what a real strategist did, but I was glad not to let my options go cold.

I was anxious about my role on *Splash*. Despite talking a big game in my audition about all the great coaches I'd learned from, I had never actually done much coaching. The other three trainers on the show were professionals with decades of experience. Plus, I would be learning to coach in front of TV cameras.

"I feel like I'm keeping up some charade," I journaled in week one. "I can't afford to make rookie mistakes." But once I worked up the courage to ask my fellow trainers for pointers, I learned they were happy to give them. I also realized I had a big advantage over the professional coaches. They'd spent decades preparing relatively invincible children to compete. They often grew frustrated with the aging bodies and fearful brains of adults, not to mention the "drama over perfection" mindset of reality television. I, on the other hand, soaked it all in. I learned a lot about how to coach diving. I helped the producers brainstorm storylines to showcase the inner journey of each competitor. I made friends with my athletes. In four months, I helped Chuy Bravo, Chelsea Handler's sidekick on *Chelsea Lately*, learn to swim, then dive headfirst from a three-meter platform. I taught Brandi Chastain, a retired soccer player famous for celebrating a World Cup–winning goal in her sports bra, to do dives from the ten-meter that I, myself, had never done. And I helped Nicole Eggert, a former child star who'd gone from *Baywatch* babe to full-time mom, learn to appreciate her body and take pride in her bravery. And while I wasn't Kareem Abdul-Jabbar's main coach, I like to think I gave him some useful pointers on his back flip.

When I wasn't coaching or scanning the internet for mentions of Smirnoff Sorbet Light Raspberry Pomegranate vodka, I played around on the diving boards. During my time on the show, I didn't come close to getting back into competition precision, but I did start to imagine a world where I might. I wondered more than once if it could always have been like this: no coach raising the heat on every moment, no forcing myself to practice through sideways rain or sprained toes, just this cozy Hotel California version of the sport.

When filming ended, I flew to New York for a few months to finish out my agency internship in person, but I told anyone who asked that I was holding out for a second season. A plan had begun forming in my head: work on *Splash*, start diving again, and try to make another Olympic team. It never materialized. The show never found its place between earnest intensity and slapstick comedy, never earned the ratings that would have made it the next great celebreality sensation, and never got picked up for another season. Meanwhile, my internship boss recommended me for a role as a junior strategic planner at a venerable old ad agency that had created several of the commercials I'd loved as a kid. After a series of interviews, I accepted my first full-time, long-term job.

The demise of *Splash* highlights another important facet of transitions: You can plan and fixate and play every possible scenario out ten steps ahead. But inevitably, life makes the decision for you. Some paths open. Others never do. You go where you can. Also, if you think this all sounds like an extension of the murk from chapter 3, you're correct. The murk isn't a stage you pass through like clockwork. The phases of transition stretch, shrink, overlap, and double back on themselves, coming in any order.

· · ·

I arrived at my new job with the same plucky anticipation as when I had first arrived at Stanford freshman year. I had hyped up college as the place I would find myself, the place that would set the tone for the rest of my life—if, that is, I could hack it. Now, a decade later, I had the same hopes that New York would inspire a new *me*.

On day one of work, I lost my pluck. After an hour of onboarding, my boss came to collect me from HR and introduce me to the team. We found all ten of them crammed into an office, reviewing the first "rough" cut of a new commercial. One by one, like a *Sound of Music* roll call, they shared their names and titles. What were all these titles? One man, who I assumed must be an intern because he looked young and reminded me of a golden retriever puppy, introduced himself as an account executive. An executive? My instincts were totally off. I sensed a deeply structured hierarchy but couldn't intuit who sat where. I was haunted by a feeling, which grew stronger over time, that there were a great many things I should know—but didn't.

In retrospect, the intense strangeness of this transition makes sense. From infancy on, I spent more waking hours on the pool deck than I did at home. By the time I retired from diving, I knew my competitors, their coaches, and where each of them sat in the hierarchy, whether you organized it based on raw talent, standings, or popularity. I knew Stanford's pool so well I could have gotten from the stands to the three-meter blindfolded, while telling you exactly how much splash each diver had made while I was getting there. I knew how long it takes to warm up when the air is 51 degrees versus 53 degrees and the difference between holding onto a pike with one, three, or five days of leg hair. I knew all fourteen ways that Rick knew to try to fix an entry that threw too much splash, plus one or two more. I was used to having a precise understanding of my environment. The newness of this office unmoored me.

When introductions were over, they resumed critiquing the commercial, seemingly trying to one-up each other with small frustrations about how it had turned out. Then one of the executives—this one gave off more of an alpha border collie vibe—said, "Let's ask the new strategist what she thinks," and my stomach dropped. The introductions had made

me keenly aware of all that I didn't know. I prepared to hide my igno-
rance. Someone hit play on the commercial, but I hardly watched, fixated
as I was on the fact that when it ended, I would have to say something
smart about it. Colors danced in front of my face, but it felt like a wall had
gone up in my brain between the part that saw things and the part that
understood what she was looking at. When the thirty seconds were up, I
parroted a version of what I'd heard when we'd first entered the room,
something negative and a little bit sarcastic. Whatever it was, it was the
wrong thing. The executives "heh heh'd" uncomfortably. "Shots fired!"
someone said. "You know that the people in this room made this spot,
right?" said my boss. I was mortified. Day one, and everyone hated me.

That set the tone for my first year of agency life. The boundaries and
rules of sports are sharp and well-defined. But advertising is a lawlessly
creative field, built more on conviction than canon. The trouble was, I
had no idea where that conviction was supposed to come from. Even
words let me down. I had a creative writing degree from Stanford University. I figured I could count on my vocabulary to keep me afloat in
corporate America. But the language of advertising is not the language
of poems and short stories, and I was overwhelmed by the jargon. My
boss corrected my work with changes I didn't understand: Don't call this
an "insight," call it a learning. Don't call this a "learning," call it an observation. Don't call this an "observation," call it an insight. All the
while, I watched as coworkers years younger than me attacked their jobs
with an alacrity that wasn't in my muscle memory. I knew it would be
hard to start over, but I had no idea I would feel so inadequate. When I
described my struggles to my now-roommate Jess, who'd been working in
New York for years, she said, "Just fake it 'til you make it." In retrospect,
it was good advice. But at the time, the concept was so far outside my
worldview I assumed she was joking. There's no faking it in sports.

As a diver, my athletic prowess was currency. I had spent my life earning strong quads, precise aerial awareness, and podium placements.

These things all had value on the pool deck: kids looked up to me, competitors respected me, and the skills and accomplishments I'd banked gave me confidence. Even on *Splash*, as a coach and not an athlete, that currency still mattered. But I didn't know how to exchange my diving earnings for something that had value in the workplace. I was proud to be an Olympian, but it felt like it came with expectations I didn't want. An "Olympian" should be loud and confident. An "Olympian" should have an inner fire that makes her bright and shiny. An "Olympian" should pick things up quickly, deliver flawless work, and always know the right thing to say. But I'm a low-key person, more likely to be taking in what's around me than opening a conversation, more comfortable sharing an observation than a bombastic point of view.

I found that the only way to deal with the dissonance was to hide the part of myself I was most proud of. I remember the first time I told a co-worker that I was an Olympian, months into our working relationship. We were in a fluorescently lit meeting room that smelled like whiteboard cleaner. We were brainstorming intersections between football and detergent, and my sports background felt relevant. "You went to the Olympics?" he asked. "I never would have guessed." The next day, he was still on it: "I can't believe you're an Olympian."

In retrospect, the skills I'd gained in my previous life as a diver *did* have value in my corporate life—I was just so overwhelmed that I forgot what I already knew. I knew how to find creative solutions to challenges. I knew how to fail at something and try again. I knew how to intuit what people needed from me and deliver it. I knew that I had a tendency to feel nervous, to freeze under pressure. But I also knew how to overcome these obstacles.

· · ·

At my first international meet in Zhuhai, China, in 2004, I had a panic attack. My legs spasmed, I lurched to the side of the board, and the dive, which was supposed to be three and a half somersaults, crashed in at three-and-a-quarter. I emerged to thousands of people laughing at me. I was nineteen.

I've always been a jumpy person. I startle at sudden noises and hide behind pillows during scary movies. When I began competing at a higher level, the pressure to execute dives perfectly exacerbated my natural jumpiness, and I found myself dealing with unexpected muscle twitches and brain fog.

Sports are about seeing your natural limitations and working through them, day by day, rep by rep. I did dead lifts to help me jump higher off the board. I practiced my entries thousands of times to make them cleaner. And I put in the mental work to perform consistently under pressure.

I worked with three different sports psychologists over the course of my career, plus Rick, who happened to have a PhD in the subject and taught a Stanford course on it. They taught me that deep, controlled breathing can reduce stress. Smiling—even forced smiling—can elevate your mood. Music has been proven to reduce anxiety and blood pressure. I learned by trial and error. At one US Nationals competition, I discovered that an overly upbeat playlist led to overstimulation—when my turn came I lost my balance and vaulted off the side of the diving board. Music that made me feel calm and unemotional led to better results. I learned that my mind was more likely to spiral when I retreated too far into myself, so I tried to make small talk with my fellow competitors while I was waiting for my turn. Mental practice helped me feel more prepared, so each night before I went to bed I visualized my dives two times, once in the third person like I was watching myself on TV and once in the first person, feeling the moves in my muscles. I created a "greatest hits" video of my best work, a reminder of how much I was capable of.

Rick helped by putting as much care into shaping my attitude as he did into shaping my dives, raising and lowering my anxiety level like a thermostat. If I needed to learn a new skill or technique, he'd lounge and make jokes from his chair to decrease the tension. If he wanted to simulate competition nerves, he'd stand and bark orders. If I stepped onto the pool deck too stressed, too proud, or too distracted to be at my best, Rick nudged, cajoled, or shook me from my funk. "Are you even here today?" he'd ask in a warning tone after one or two bad hurdles. If I made a third mistake in a row, he'd be on his feet yelling, "If you don't want to practice, maybe I should just go home," and I'd get a jolt of adrenaline and the next dive would be impeccable.

All those strategies—the positive self-talk, the visualization, the greatest hits reel, and Rick's psychological artistry—were designed to "make the butterflies fly in formation," as one of my sports psychs often said. And each of them helped. By 2012, I had won ten US National titles and two NCAA championships. I was the American front-runner in my event. But on that one dive—the front three-and-one-half pike (the one I'd messed up in Zhuhai)—I continued to get that buzzy feeling and make strange mistakes.

The final piece of my mental puzzle didn't click in until a few months before the 2012 Olympic Trials. On a recommendation from a friend, I drove to a brick and beige building of medical suites and investment advisors in San Francisco to meet a therapist with a long, Romanian-sounding last name. She explained that we would use the memory from Zhuhai as a way to neutralize and reframe the negative emotions I carried with me. It felt a little woo-woo, but I was willing to give it a try.

"Let's start at the bottom of the ladder," she said. "What do you see?"

I described it as I remembered: the chill in the air, the haze of smoke near the roof, the shaking of my legs. The cold metal ladder with drops dripping down it. My chest trembling at the top of every breath. I remembered things I'd forgotten—the tiles under my feet, slick enough that I had to walk cautiously. The smell of dust, chlorine, and cigarettes.

I was sitting in a comfortable, if dated, chair in a small beige office, but my body thought it was at the pool. I shivered. My lungs tightened; my muscles tensed.

"What do you feel?"

"I'm trying to feel normal but I don't feel normal at all. I'm jittery, like I don't have control of all my limbs," I said.

"How could you reinterpret that feeling in a positive way?"

"Nerves can be good, I guess," I said. "They can make you stronger, sometimes."

"That's good," she said. "The nerves are a gift. They're here to make you stronger."

To my surprise, I felt myself actually calming down. My time-traveling body eased its fight-flee-or-freeze preparations.

We walked through every moment of that memory. At the bottom of the ladder, I wasn't nervous, but excited. At the top of the ladder, that extra wave of butterflies that hit me wasn't menacing, but helpful. When I started my hurdle, my legs weren't shaky, they were powerful. After the dive ended, instead of emerging mortified, I emerged grateful. What a gift, to be able to travel all the way back in time and redo the past. At the end of our fifty minutes, I felt calm, and strangely proud.

A month after my work with the Romanian therapist, I went to Federal Way, Washington, for the 2012 US Olympic Trials.

The nerves didn't wholly disappear. The night before the contest, I prayed I could fall asleep before I threw up. But at Olympic Trials, the nerves stopped when the job started. Normally it was a struggle to keep the bad possibilities at bay. What if I start walking with the wrong foot? Fall off the board? Crack my head open? That day, my brain recognized them as irrelevant wisps of thought and gave them no space.

I won the competition by so much I could have skipped my last dive and still made the 2012 Olympic team.

At the Olympics themselves, two months later, my confidence held.

Between every dive I listened to music that helped me stay neutral, focusing on my breath and clearing my mind of stray worries. Before my front three-and-one-half pike, I went to Rick and he gave me a few words and a hand gesture. "Have a blast, buddy," he said. It was all I needed. I climbed the ladder and smiled out at the crowd, which was packed into stands that went up a hundred rows higher than in Zhuhai. This wasn't a fake smile, but one with real gratitude behind it, to be this alive, every cell singing in harmony. I keep the high of that moment tucked in a precious space in my brain. Yes, I messed up my last dive. But the shine has lasted all these years without fading.

· · ·

Rick taught me that anxiety has the same effect on the body, no matter its cause. By his logic, if I could learn to dive through a windstorm, then I could learn to dive in the highest-pressure competition. If I could learn to keep my cool when my coach was yelling at a Stanford practice, then I could learn to keep my cool while my name was being announced across the packed Olympic Trials stands. Eventually I realized if I could make my butterflies fly in formation at a diving meet, then I could do the same in a business meeting.

Gaining confidence at work wasn't a light switch. Unlike my quick adaptation to coaching on *Splash*, it took years to find my footing in advertising. The biggest thing my transition took from me was familiarity, which is impossible to build overnight. But eventually, simple exposure to the rhythm of ad biz interactions—from high-stakes meetings to impromptu huddles—dulled my nerves. The lessons I'd learned as a diver came back to me in a series of small epiphanies. If I had an important conversation coming up, I prepared the night before. If I was feeling scattered, I took deep breaths and smiled. If I was scared, I dwelled on the upside of that fear and carried it with me like a candle. I lost my white-knuckled sense of panic. In big meetings, I discovered I had a knack for presenting with authority. I began to take a modicum of pride in my work. After two years at the ad agency, I left for a different type of firm, where instead of making TV commercials, we developed and sold new brands and products. From there I gained more respect, took on more responsibility, and earned a higher paycheck.

. . .

Sometimes I still wonder: How was I able to perform at my peak on the largest stage in the world, but couldn't manage a standard Tuesday morning in the office? Why did participating in a class discussion back at Stanford feel so natural, while participating in a conversation at the agency felt so forced? Why was I able to overcome my fear of messing up as a celebrity diving coach more quickly than my fear of messing up at work?

This chapter is about connecting the dots between your past and your present. How do you apply what you've learned to a new problem? How do you use the passions and interests you've developed to build a new life? How do you bring the best version of yourself to a new world? And how do you give yourself the grace and time to figure it all out?

I've learned that "the best version of yourself" is a complicated concept. In his book *Me, Myself, and Us*, personality scholar Brian R. Little describes three layers of personality: traits (blanket descriptors, like "I'm an introvert"), personal projects (goals that might require us to step outside our traits, like "To get people fired up about my idea, I'll be more extroverted"), and narratives (circumstances that lead us to behave as we do, like "I felt in over my head at work, so I retreated inward"). "Your personal constructs serve as both frames and cages," he writes.[1]

Unfortunately for me, the moment I got to the office, a layer of self-doubt clicked into place. One might also call this a gnarly case of impostor phenomenon. Back in the 1970s, psychologists Pauline Rose Clance and Suzanne Imes coined the term to describe people who tend to question their abilities, doubt their value, and underestimate objective signs of aptitude like test results, IQ scores, and competitive success. Experts estimate that around 70 percent of individuals will experience impostor phenomenon at some point in their lives.[2] It's a lot harder to bring your best self to work when you don't believe you're capable of doing the job.

For me, the key to connecting my dots at work was realizing I could apply what I already knew to a new environment. But is bringing your best self forward just about translating skills? What about the other things that major transitions so often take from us: our passions, our dreams, our ways of making meaning in the world? How do we connect the dots to those things?

• • •

When William was ten, a woman walked into his younger brother's second-grade classroom and started shooting. His brother was okay, but several of his brother's classmates were hurt. That night watching the news, his mother told them both to focus on the helpers: the first responders who rushed to the scene. It was a lesson that stuck with him.

William's dad was a Green Beret. Both of his grandfathers fought in World War II, one as a fighter pilot in the Marines and the other as a naval beachmaster. To William, "helper" meant serving his country. His childhood dream was to work for the CIA and join the Marines. He eyed that future as resolutely as any Olympic athlete; it was part of his identity long before he went through basic training.

After college, William joined the Marine Corps Reserve, balancing a series of civilian intelligence agency jobs in Washington with monthly drills. During his first deployment to Iraq, a POW was captured in Abu Ghraib, not far from his forward operating base. His team worked to locate the man, but his tour ended before he could see it through and the investigation floundered. Back home, William grew increasingly frustrated by the lack of progress. He wrote an email to the Secrètary of Defense POW/MIA office that criticized the search and offered up a solution. He believed he was doing the right thing, but criticizing military leadership from a personal email address prompted the ire of the intelligence community. Despite filing for federal whistleblower protection, he was questioned on a polygraph machine and accused of unconscionable things, from mishandling of classified information to spying for foreign intelligence services. For a time, he lost the security clearance on which his entire civilian career relied. Eventually, William got his name cleared and security access reinstated, but his dream never recovered. He had spoken out for what he thought was right, only to be severely punished. "I was like, fuck this. I don't want to do this," he said. "But in that moment, it was my life."

William was also starting to doubt that his service was really *helping* anyone. He was frustrated with US foreign policy. His second tour in Iraq, from August of 2008 through May of 2009, reinforced his disillusionment. "I was doing this because I wanted to feel like part of a solution, but there was no identifiable progress," he said. William experienced his own transition as one of losing faith in the dream that had guided his life.

When he returned home, he knew only two things about his future: He didn't want to go back to Iraq, and he didn't want to go back to Washington. "I'm very proud to have served in the military, but when I was done, I was done," he said. At first, the freedom of day-to-day life was a rush. "You don't have to shave anymore. You don't have to report at 6 a.m. You don't have to do bullshit tasks like cleaning the squad bay," he said. "But then it strikes you. What do I do now?"

Even though William could no longer stomach his old military dreams, he still missed the service like hell. "There are three things that you lose, and it hits you maybe several weeks, or maybe two months after you take off the military uniform," he said. "You lose a sense of purpose or a mission, you lose a community, and you lose a sense of identity." He paused. "And that's when despair sets in."

On January 12, 2010, six months after he returned from Iraq, William was sitting at home, depressed and unsure of his future, when a magnitude 7.0 earthquake hit Haiti. Immediately, the news was full of images that rivaled any war zone William had seen, and his social circles started buzzing. William's family doctor reached out and asked if he wanted to fly down to help. Another marine he'd only met on Facebook shared a post: "I'm going to Haiti. Who's in?" Five days later, he and a makeshift team of eight, including five who happened to be veterans, crossed from the Dominican Republic into Haiti, heading toward Port-au-Prince to prepare for a convoy of medical supplies and volunteers. When they got to Port-au-Prince General Hospital, there were no doctors left—they were all tending to their own injured friends and family.

Meanwhile, the international relief response was succumbing to chaos. At the airport, William saw crates of supplies piling on top of one another. With one functioning landing strip in Port-au-Prince, one rocky, debris-covered road from the Dominican Republic, and a port in ruins, response teams struggled to get in and start working. Large relief organizations, scared by CNN reports of "a frenzy of looting," were waiting for government peacekeepers to secure Port-au-Prince before they could safely operate.[3] William and his team of veterans and doctors, by contrast, were able to mobilize more quickly. William connected with a Jesuit missionary in Haiti, which provided local guides, interpreters, and credibility so the team could operate safely. They reestablished the emergency room at Port-au-Prince General Hospital and ran it for several days before larger relief groups could take over.

He realized there must be others like him: trained under pressure, hungry to serve, but unsure how, and cofounded Team Rubicon, a global group of veterans who provide aid in crisis. Today, Team Rubicon has helped over one hundred thousand veterans bring their skills and values to disaster relief. It provides veterans with those three critical things that are lost when one leaves the military: purpose, community, and identity. "When you're serving together in a disaster, like mucking and gutting a village because it's been struck by a flood, the work that you're doing is immediately tangible," he said.

William reminded me that the act of translating your skills doesn't just enable you to fit into a new role—it makes you innovate. By bringing battle-trained volunteers to disasters, Team Rubicon was able to provide better relief. It's another way to kick your impostor to the curb: No, you don't know all the rules and norms of this new world, but that means you aren't constrained by them.

William leapt from military man to his next evolution. That's one good way to connect the dots on your dreams: simply doing the things that call to you, whether or not you've exhaustively thought them through.

But what if your gut doesn't call to you as clearly as William's did? What if you have responsibilities that limit your ability to leap blindly into the unknown? In those cases, there are more deliberate, incremental ways to carry your best self forward.

"We really tune into feelings in the work that I do," said my former Stanford Alumni Association colleague Meredith, who's now a clarity coach. Her work is similar to that of a life coach, with a focus on trusting and channeling intuition to make life-changing choices. She told me about a client who feels lackluster in her day-to-day home and work life but loves the version of herself that comes out when she travels. "I asked what it was about travel that she loved, and she said, 'It makes me feel alive,'" said Meredith. "And I was like, cool, that's your feeling." She then worked with her client to incorporate that feeling more deeply into her life. "What does your business look like with that feeling of alive? What would alive do? What decisions would alive make?" she asked.

Meredith went through a similar process in her own transition from overworked marketing exec to clarity coach. "I wanted to feel nourished," she said. "So I did everything I could to feel nourished. And it eventually led me to become a coach."

I spoke with another coach, Jason (who you'll meet in more detail in chapter 8), who starts his work with his clients by asking them to share "examples of authentic pride." He then works with them to incorporate more of that into their lives. This may feel drastically different from William's drop-everything-and-run-to-the-disaster approach, but the principle is the same: It's about learning what really lights you up and doing more of it.

Sometimes taking the time to identify and say out loud how we are feeling when we are feeling our best can open new possibilities for the future.

. . .

The Team Rubicon website is packed with feel-good quotes about veterans' experiences: "We do hard work and heart work," wrote one volunteer. But there are people who take it too far. William told me about a friend of his who dropped out of school so he could go on more missions. "That's when it starts to become a problem," he said. "We're not paying them. So when it starts detracting from their ability to live, it's almost like a drug problem." It illustrated a risk of passion: When you live your passion in a way that's so all-consuming it detracts from creating a sustainable life for yourself—that's not good.

What can we salvage from the rubble of our former dreams? It's a question that came up a lot in my conversations with other retired Olympians. For many of us, our sports were passions we left behind because they didn't fit us anymore. But that loss left a vacuum. A conversation with my old friend David illustrates how to carry forward a former passion and the surprising ways that it can help heal old wounds.

. . .

Back when I was in college, my fellow divers and I would arrive at Stanford's Ford Center to train before dawn. The campus was dewy and sleeping—except for the rowers, who were already dripping with sweat. All morning, while the divers somersaulted and the sun rose, the rowers rowed on machines outside the great glass windows. I'd often wave hi to David, my friend's brother, when we walked in. He was tall, broad, muscled, and agile. His rowing was precise, each roll and pop of his body a mirror of the previous roll and pop. His face grimaced and calmed in time. He didn't always see me, but when he did he'd interrupt his rhythm with a nod and half a smile. Usually, he was there when I got there. Usually, he was still there when I left.

Seventeen years later, I called David over Zoom at 6 a.m. West Coast time. He was already at the office. His hair was buzzed short, as it was in his rowing days, and he didn't seem to have lost an ounce of muscle since those mornings, decades ago, on the erg machine. Behind him were white walls, fluorescent lights, and a bright orange vest hanging on a hook. The space fit what I knew of him, ascetic and efficient, no embellishments necessary. He's now a project manager for a construction company, an industry with hours almost as early as he used to keep as a rower. Just across from his office was his latest ambition—a housing, practice, and performance space for the San Francisco Conservatory of Music—rising slowly from the ground.

An eight-hundred-meter runner in high school, David planned to run track in college until a men's rowing recruit got to him first. He had no idea what crew was, but the promise of free dinner lured him to a meeting to find out. A dearth of scholarships for Stanford's varsity team meant that totally green rowers were often wooed from freshman dorms with promises of free meals, not unlike an Orlando time-share marketing scheme. A lot of my dorm friends heeded the call at first, seduced by a snazzy pitch, then dropped like flies through October and November. Not David. When he first started rowing in 2001, he was six feet three and 165 pounds, and his Stanford coach, Craig Amerkhanian, recalled him as "one of the skinniest, smallest guys." By his senior year, he was a 190-pound member of the All-Conference team.

I asked David about the transition from running to rowing. Having spent ten minutes on an erg machine, I couldn't imagine how an hour on it must have felt, much less all the hours he put in every day back at Stanford. And the monotony of that exertion!

"Erging seems like pure pain," I said. "Like, just awful."

He smiled and shook his head. "There were some rough times. Not painful exactly. . . . But yeah, it was torture." While I was trying to figure out the difference between pain and torture and whether it had anything to do with pain and suffering, he continued. "I remember looking at the monitor on the erg machine and literally feeling every second and realizing . . . somehow I've got to go for twenty minutes. And then you realize it's only January. How am I going to make it to June? How am I going to make it through the next four years of this?"

Over time he learned rowing 101: how to manage torture by managing time. Each day's workout became a series of smaller games: how hard could he go for five minutes, then ten, then twenty. "Finally, I got to the point where I could look back and see how far I'd come in six months," he said. "Then it was like . . . where can I be in another year?"

Despite David's progress through his college career, he remained an underdog: tough, tireless, and never quite at the top. He missed making the national team in 2005 and returned to Stanford for one more year of school. After earning his master's in 2006, he tried out for the national team again and failed. Still, he stuck around Princeton, USRowing's headquarters, that year, erging on his own through the dark New Jersey winter while the team traveled to a seasonal training camp in Southern California. All in all, David failed to make the US National Team three years in a row.

Again, I had to ask. "What kept you going?"

"I could still see myself getting better," he said. "And so it was just one day at a time." But after the simple answer, he started to explain something more complex, and I saw there were two sides to David's discipline: the focus to keep grinding through the seconds, and a deeper mission that drove him through the years.

"My dad's African American, my mom's Jewish, and I know how many people with my background, no matter how talented they were, would never have had these opportunities," he said. "I was so fortunate that all these people had laid the groundwork for me. It became . . . almost a mission. To keep moving. To keep riding it out." As of the 2024 Paris Games, the United States has sent only five Black rowers to the Olympics, and David is one of them. At first, he kept rowing to represent those who'd come before him. But then, his mission evolved to sharing his sport with those who would come after. "That was a big way I justified training after I graduated," he said. "The better I could be, the better position I would be in to help change the sport."

It wasn't until 2008—the year of the Olympics—that all those lonely Princeton winters started resulting in tangible success. The first time David represented the US internationally was at a regatta in Lucerne, Switzerland, in May of 2008, where he went from being an unknown to beating world champions. Two months after that, he left for Beijing to represent the United States at the 2008 Olympics.

In Beijing, David and his team took ninth. He summed up his performance with a shrug: "I wish we would have done better," he said. "But it was the biggest rush in my life, and I just knew I needed that again." Some athletes are celebrators. They see every win as an opportunity to spray the champagne and feel their thunder. Others are braggers. They celebrate the wins even before they happen, à la Muhammad Ali, "I am the greatest." David and I were both grinders, perpetual underdogs. It was pounded into us that pride cometh before the fall and laziness cometh after the peak; tamp down on the highs, we thought, and you can also avoid the lows. "I trained myself to not get too excited or too upset, knowing there was still another race or practice the next day," David said. Most athletes take at least a few months off after the Olympics to recharge, but David was too hungry for that. He was back on the erg machine in weeks.

By the time London 2012 rolled around, there was only one possible outcome: a medal. If all went well, it would be a chance to celebrate, finally, after a lifetime of even-keeled work. Beyond that, he saw London as his chance to become the next barrier-obliterating phenom to revolutionize a white, waspy sport. "I put pressure on myself to be the Serena Williams or Tiger Woods of the sport," he said.

At the 2012 Olympics, David rowed as part of the men's eight. An eight-man boat is a machine made of bodies. So smooth it must be organic, so rhythmic it must be mechanical; watch boat races for too long on YouTube and the eight starts to look like a mix between a locomotive, a centipede, and a giant toothpick. Eight men move as one, down to the muscle: glutes and hammies, abs and lats, bis and tris, repeat, repeat, repeat, until the parts blur into arcs and angles. They face the starting line. It's not for them to know where they're going—only to know and replicate the exact pattern of the man in front of them. The front of the boat, the bow seat, is all about precision. It can get rocky up there in the narrow toothpick taper. The bowman's balance is sure, his technique, impeccable. Not the loudest, not the strongest. The steady stoic, never letting a whisper of the waves he's broken reach his teammates. David, of course, rowed bow.

Five days after my own Olympic final, David raced in the final of the men's eight. The announcer named each boat, and for a few seconds the silence thickened and even the water seemed to hush. Then the buzzer sounded and the air reverberated with the groans of men and oars overcoming inertia.

Their start was abysmal. A minute in, the US was nearly a full boat length behind. They spent the majority of the race in last place. It wasn't until the final stretch that they seemed to find their fire. With a hundred meters left, as the bike track alongside the reservoir gave way to screaming grandstands, the US pulled ahead of Australia, then edged past the Netherlands. They seemed to just reach the flagging Brits and then, about an inch too soon, it was all over. The difference between Great Britain, who earned the bronze medal, and the United States, who placed fourth, was three-tenths of a second.

"Some people win, some people lose, but it's not like they're better people," he said, because that's what he's supposed to say. That's what he's told himself, time and again, for a decade. But underlying those things we tell ourselves, are the things that every TV show, every movie, every sportscaster, and every sports fan tell us: "I guess in this country, you always hear about the medalists," David said. "You hear about 'the hearts of champions' and all that. And it kind of still nags at you." After eleven years of dedication, tens of thousands of hours on erg machines, an unquantifiable number of choices made, priorities ranked, and opportunities sacrificed, the difference between the podium and the floor—eight men with hearts of champions and eight men whose hearts didn't quite pass muster—was three-tenths of a second. That's less than half a push on the erg machine.

David kept at rowing for a few years after 2012, but it wasn't the same.

He just didn't have the same drive. "All these young guys came in gung ho," he said. "And here I was just that old guy who was bitter and jaded." After a few seasons with one foot in rowing and the other in a budding construction career, he retired in 2014.

The lessons he learned have carried him well beyond rowing. It's not just the punctuality and buzz cut that make him still seem like an athlete today—it's that he applies the same stroke-by-stroke discipline to his job. "They're really kind of similar," he said. "You just do the little things, look for the little wins."

For the past four years, his twelve-story building has been rising slowly, painfully, from the ground, inching upward toward its neighbors, the opera house, the symphony hall, and City Hall. A recent construction update introduced the project as "on the drafting board for years, delayed by the COVID-19 pandemic, but prevailing over all challenges." It's eerie how closely it parallels his athletic career.

To this day, he has a hard time watching sports on TV—not just rowing, but sports in general. "It's tough to see that victory moment for others," he said. "Not that I don't want that for them. But it's still difficult."

"Do you think your life would have changed if you'd gotten a medal?" I asked. David would start to speak, but then stop before he could get an idea out. The next day, he followed up with me in an email: "[I wanted] a moment in time that could never be taken, where it was just a sense of joy. . . . We crossed that line and it flashed fourth and it was ripped away. And there was no moment like that."

For years after his retirement, David steered clear of rowing. There was too much pain. But the racial reckoning of 2020 brought him back. The Black Lives Matter movement shined a light on rowing's unexplored barriers. David was inspired by a growing community who refused to accept the status quo. "It reminded me that my place in the sport—one of five Black Olympians—*is* important," he said.

Since 2020, he has started coaching part time, mentoring coaches and athletes, and serving on USRowing's DEI committee and on the board of his local club, the Oakland Strokes. The club sits amid a low-to-middle-income Black and brown community, but most of its patrons are white high schoolers from the suburbs. So now, on Sundays, David brings a bunch of erg machines to a park in Oakland and runs circuits to introduce the sport to the neighborhood kids.

"For me it's about trying to find ways to make the sport more relevant," said David. "How can rowing become something that people know so it becomes part of the community?"

David does this work because he wants to make a difference for the kids and to help the sport grow. But there's another benefit, one on his own psyche. "I think the sense of mission has helped me to make some peace with the sport," he said. "In my mind, I still think about that fourth place, but it's not the most important thing in the world." David's return to rowing has helped him see those three-tenths as one small part of his larger story. "I used to think the only way I could help was to be Lebron," he said on a podcast called *Rowing in Color*.[4] "But I've learned there are other ways to be impactful than just on the water." He's not just an athlete who fell short of a medal. He's a coach to future generations. A role model for kids who look like him. A mentor whose impact doesn't solely depend on his athletic prowess.

David's rowing story could have ended when he retired: a passion that sparked, grew, and flamed out, leaving charred spots too dangerous to revisit. But it didn't. It's one thing to evolve old skills to meet the challenges of a new world. But what really awes me about David is how he's evolved his passion for rowing to a mission that lends purpose to his present and future.

The other thing I noticed is that this evolution took time. It took time away from rowing before he was able to come back with a different mindset that didn't hurt so much, just like it took time for me to adapt to the workplace. When I look back on my early career, it's hard not to be impatient with young Cassidy. But I've realized, we're not all Williams. We don't all connect our dots quickly enough to go from sitting on our couches to running a disaster-stricken hospital in days. It takes time to understand new dynamics and figure out your skills and needs in new situations. And it takes time for pain to subside enough to bring an old passion into a new life.

A transition is a great opportunity to be intentional about what you bring forward. How can old dreams point you toward the future? How are past skills relevant to your present? How can your unique perspective point to a better way to do things?

Tools for Connecting Your Dots

Your past experiences, skills, and passions have prepared you for what comes next—but they require some translation.

How to Bring Your Best Self Forward

Tell Your Story

Celebrate your greatest hits. Our greatest accomplishments aren't really medals and promotions—they are the skills we developed, lessons we learned, and passions we nurtured. And because they aren't as obvious as trophies and bank statements, it takes extra work to celebrate them. If you're feeling unworthy, take a minute to remind yourself of what you've actually accomplished. Choose the positive interpretation. Pride decays in storage. Don't be stingy with it.

Think of your life before your latest, greatest transition:

- What lessons did that life teach you?

- What skills were you most proud of?

- Celebrate those wins—even if it feels like they no longer apply to your life today.

Now think of your life today:

- What new lessons have you learned?

- What have you done that you didn't think you could do?

- Reflect on these accomplishments. You are capable. You are growing. You are worthy.

Now think of a big transition you're coping with or anticipating:

- How do your past lessons, skills, passions, and accomplishments help you now? Give yourself the benefit of
  the doubt here, but also think critically. Not all past
  skills have a place in your future. More on that in the
  next chapter.

How to Reset Your Framework

Borrow Someone Else's POV

As with most relationships, your relationship with yourself can
get into a rut. Maybe you've allowed that damned impostor to
become part of your personality. If you can't figure out how to
ditch the self-criticism, pretend you're talking to a friend who
seems to underestimate their own capabilities in the same way
that you are. What would you tell them?

How to Get into Your Zone

Expand Your Happy Place

Spend two weeks keeping a heat journal—a notebook or phone
note in which you jot down the moments that you feel most alive,
the most on, and the most in your zone. What's happening in
that moment? Can you describe what your mind and body feel
like? What do you think caused that feeling? After two weeks,
review. What are some small ways that you can change your life
to provide more of these moments? What are some medium
ways? What are some large ways? Reflect on these lists—what
level of shake-up is right for your life right now?

Don't Forget

Set Boundaries with Your Exes

When bringing the best of your past into the present, don't forget to set clear intentions for how you want to move forward. What do you want to accomplish that you haven't already? What were the downsides of your past passions and experiences? What do you need in order to build a sustainable life for yourself in the present? A past passion can consume us. Set boundaries on the ways in which you bring it back into your life.

6.

Leave Your Baggage

Transitions are opportunities for reinvention. How do we identify the habits and mindsets holding us back, unlearn the lessons that no longer apply, and adapt to a new world?

It was another late night at the office. A "dumpling night," my co-worker Flora and I called them. Seven years had passed since I'd boxed up my swimsuits and become a brand strategist. Outside the sky was a cold black lit with NoHo's red and yellow streetlights. Most of the shades in the hotel across the street had been drawn, but here and there were vignettes of disparate lives: a woman putting on her going-out boots, a man watching TV, a naked couple looking out over the city, bold and anonymous. It felt like it had been days since the sun had gone down. We'd passed 8 p.m., which meant dinner was on the company, and empty aluminum dumpling trays and half-full containers of soy sauce languished on our desks. I'd long since texted my trapeze coach, Josh, that I wouldn't be able to make it to practice that evening.

Not long after moving to New York and starting my first agency job, I tried trapeze for the first time at a circus school in Queens. There were familiar echoes to diving: I climbed a ladder; stood, shaking, on a platform; and made a leap. But now, instead of descending into water, I grabbed onto a tape-wrapped metal bar that took me in a long arc through the air. My body recognized the push and pull of gravity like an old friend. Even the fear was comforting: the sharp urgency of a new dive, rather than the blanket of anxiety that weighed me down at work.

Trapeze was foreign enough to give me something to learn, yet familiar enough that I learned very quickly. It was everything I had loved about diving: the thrill of flight; the ability to develop new skills; the chance to impress. And more. In diving, I had spent years pressed against the ceiling of my own potential. But trapeze was a wide-open frontier. I hadn't felt that much forward momentum since my first days diving with Rick at Stanford. In trapeze, I, like Emma from chapter 3, found my people: a community of weirdos who took this strange not-sport seriously. Here were grown adults, with jobs and classes and adult responsibilities, spending massive amounts of time and energy at a chalky warehouse because they liked how trapeze felt in their souls. They welcomed me. At the circus school, all the currency I'd earned as a diver was valuable again. But I did what I could to keep the passion at bay. Trapeze felt too close to the world of diving I'd left behind. I needed work to be my next great pursuit.

This particular dumpling night wasn't the first time I'd canceled trapeze last minute, or the tenth. Though it brought me joy, it was always the lowest priority, easily sacrificed for a sixtieth hour in the office.

Flora was creating a set of design directions for a coffee company. I was working on an internal mission statement for a hotel chain. We were the last ones left. The long desks and corkboard walls were full of the odd miscellany that creative consultancies tend to acquire: a collection of crispy non-potato-chip snacks with "natural" semiotics covered one table, several boxes of feminine hygiene products were stacked next to them, and a giant printed-out poster of a cat kept watch over the room.

The document in front of me was full of short sentence fragments, sets of four or five words attempting to capture the hotel chain's essence: an essence that must (a) differentiate this brand from all the other chains in the world, (b) make guests feel loved, and (c) warm the graveyard shift manager's heart.

I typically loved this part of my job. I loved searching the world around me for a new metaphor to bring out the idea in my head. I loved nerding out with my coworkers about the nuances of synonyms and the hardness and softness of sounds. I loved condensing a universe of possibility into one idea, then expanding that idea back out again into tangible actions a company might take: products they might offer or services they might invest in to fully embody their own essence.

But on nights like these, I lost faith in the power of words. Semantic satiation happens when a word is repeated so many times that it loses meaning. I'd passed the threshold. I rubbed my eyes, which were sore and watery. I felt like I hadn't blinked in hours. It was just after ten. Certainly not the latest I'd ever been in the office—the industry runs on procrastination, and midnight rushes weren't unusual. But there was no big meeting tomorrow, just an endless push to get ahead of the next milestone. Night after night, we worked until our creativity ran dry.

· · ·

In addition to falling in love with a hobby, I'd also fallen in love with a human, Nicholas, an old friend from my Stanford days. We had both moved from California to New York separately and had become close-the-bar-down-one-night-a-year friends, meeting up for happy hour and not leaving until it became abundantly clear we could no longer stay. At the end of those nights we'd say, "See you soon!" and then another year would pass. Until one night, after the moon had set, we made out.

When I first met Nicholas, all I knew was that I liked his energy. We'd banter bad ideas back and forth until they sounded good. Most people are good brainstormers or good executors, but he was both, recognizing possibilities and immediately taking them seriously. As we started spending more time together, his mix of ambition and stop and smell the flowers boggled my mind. He was a professor working at the intersection of medicine and big data. In his job he had a major impact, not just on his grad students' lives, but on the hospital where he based his research. He took that impact seriously, but somehow his work always seemed to fit easily with the rest of him. He'd grown up on a farm in Ohio and organized his schedule so he could take a few mornings a week to go ride horses an hour and a half north of the city. He nearly always got out of work with time to cook dinner. A couple times a year, a work project would get lodged in his brain and he'd code all weekend.

Over time, he came to terms with the fact that I'd always be making him wait in the lobby while I sent one last email, would always be getting home after dinner had cooled, would always be buried in Slack while he watched TV next to me.

. . .

Eventually, Flora threw in the towel. "I'm heading out for the night," she said. "You should too."

"Yeah, I'll be on my way soon," I said.

Half an hour later, I was spent. I sent the output of today's morning, afternoon, and evening—a bunch of lines in a Google Doc—to my boss, wondering what she'd say in the morning. I didn't think I'd nailed it but couldn't be sure. There was a lot I wasn't sure about.

Confidence, or even a ghost of confidence, was my moth light. Just tell me what to do, so I know how to get a ten. I was a strange kind of perfectionist, working all day and night to try to get something right, but without an internal compass to know what "right" was. I relied on everyone—bosses, junior team members, and people who were simply nearby, like Flora—to give me a sense of direction. In situations where it felt unseemly to ask for help, I waffled away the hours. I would stew over an email forever, softening recommendations then hardening them, removing exclamation points and then adding them back in, making caveats and then erasing them, then finally hitting send, dissatisfied. Every once in a while, someone would bcc me a "nice response!"—a crumb of positive feedback—which I'd reread and glow. But in reality, perfection wasn't just impossible to reach—it was impossible to even define. I once asked a mentor how to become the best strategist in the world and she started laughing. "No one thinks like that!" she said. But I didn't know how else to set goals.

In retrospect, it was fairly obvious what I needed to do to become a better strategist. My 360 performance reviews from that time were mostly positive. According to my colleagues, I was good at leading consumer research, scanning the wider world for inspiration, breaking down complex ideas, communicating clearly, thinking outside the box, and building trust with clients and coworkers. But they also recognized my Achilles' heel: to sum it up, *Cassidy tends to overthink things which has created unnecessary stress and work.*

But I couldn't stop. Every night I watched the sun set from the office windows. On the rare occasions I did make it to trapeze, I usually had my phone on and my laptop at the ready, typing frantic Slack responses with my grips (strips of leather that protected my hands from the bar) folded against my wrists. But mostly I skipped it. I canceled dinners with friends at the last minute. I stopped reading and writing entirely. I'd been raised to believe that the more energy you invest in something, the more it will matter to you. But every time I doubled down on work I felt like there was less of me.

· · ·

Years later, I had a chance meeting with another retired Olympian, a former hockey goalie named Molly. It was one of those conversations you keep thinking about. Our words piled on top of each other, with "Yes!" and "That reminds me of" and "I felt that too!" Molly's story helped me see my own life from a new angle.

Molly was four years out of Olympic training and into a career in community development with the Anaheim Ducks, fighting an uphill battle to grow the sport of hockey in sunny Southern California. We started talking about the transition from sports to work and she lamented how hard it was to understand clearly what her goals were. "I can go a million directions at a million miles an hour trying to fill that space of uncertainty," she said.

"*Yes*," I said.

We spent a few minutes admitting our perfectionist tendencies. I told her about my email waffling and word stringing and desire to be the "best strategist in the world." She described getting frustrated with people who messed up the colors on Excel spreadsheets and her quest to get to inbox zero every day and the period when she basically didn't sleep for seven months because she was generating support for a USA-Canada women's game (it ended up being the most well-attended women's hockey game in US history). Though we had landed in different fields, our shared Olympic drive produced similar consequences at work. "It controlled me, to be honest," she said. "It worked. But it wasn't healthy."

"My boss told me once, 'Don't make work your Olympics. Go have a life, have a family,'" she said, and a little explosion went off in my brain. *Making work my Olympics*. Of course that's what I'd been doing. Work had moved to the center of my universe, the same spot diving had previously occupied. But I'd never paused to consider that that might be a bad thing. I'd assumed that's how people were supposed to live: one big thing, with others orbiting it like satellites.

But in diving, the amount of time I could physically devote to my sport was finite. My body could only do high-quality repetitions for so long without giving out, and Rick was always monitoring me for signs that I'd reached the level of fatigue where my technique slipped. Without a moderating force, work swallowed up both trapeze and my social life.

"My boss tells me all the time, 'Perfect is the enemy of done,'" Molly continued. When I was diving, one of Rick's favorite phrases had been "Good is the enemy of great." The sheer truth of that contradiction caused me to let out an involuntary snort.

Under Rick's watchful eye, I spent entire years as a diver fixating on whether my arms were swinging in a perfect circle in my hurdle, whether I was initiating the somersault at exactly the right moment for maximum lift and speed, whether my biceps were hugging my ears at a ninety-degree angle as I entered the water, whether my hands were moving fast enough on entry to prevent the slightest splash. This kind of pursuit of perfection is necessary in sports. But having, or even attempting, this level of perfection on any single work project was insanity. No one has time for that. Besides, in a creative, subjective world like brand strategy, there is no perfect ten.

. . .

Being successful—and sane—at work required me to *unlearn* the ideals I'd internalized as a diver. Self-help books tout the life lessons of sports, and they're not wrong. Try diving through a panic attack and those Big Word motivational posters—Perseverance, Courage, Dedication—get real. But it's not a seamless fit. There's this myth that everything we learn is additive. In truth, we optimize ourselves for one season, then realign for our next. Every new learning involves an element of unlearning.

It wasn't just diving that gave me the impression that life's greatest goal was to meet some arbiter's definition of perfection. On my last trip home to Pittsburgh before my parents sold their house and moved into a condo, I sat on the bubblegum-colored carpet, going through boxes of old drawings and A+ tests, a disintegrating cardboard box for each year of school. As the years went on, stickers and fast-penned happy faces on multiple-choice tests gave way to whole sentences scrawled in the margins of essays, praising my use of *juxtaposition, imagery,* and *foreshadowing.* I remembered the effort I'd put into these papers, and the pride with which I'd placed them in my box of accomplishments.

Psychologist Lisa Damour notes that girls study longer and more intently than boys, earning higher grades and graduation rates. But at work, they fall behind in pay and leadership positions. According to a 2023 analysis of S&P 100 companies, women make up nearly half of their workforce but only 28 percent of the C-suite positions.[1] Damour surmises that perfectionism and discipline may stunt confidence, which ultimately limits career advancement. "Our daughters may miss the chance to gain confidence in their abilities if they always count on intellectual elbow grease alone," she writes.[2] It bears saying that this gender gap in confidence isn't the only explanation for the gender gap in leadership, and also that many boys also stress about school, get good grades, graduate with fancy degrees, and then founder away in middle management. But her insight resonated with me. It's a lesson I learned twice, first as a people-pleasing straight-A student, then as a coach-pleasing Olympic diver: Don't rest until you're perfect. But in the real world, confidence and conviction matter much more than exhaustive work.

In order to bring forward the best, most confident version of myself, the one who deserved her promotions and pay raises and who was capable of making good choices without crystal clear foresight, I had to shed something: my all-encompassing reliance on elbow grease and A+ work. Not holistically, as doing the bare minimum on everything would have felt empty. But surgically. I needed to figure out what was worth my time and perfectionism, and what wasn't.

. . .

Once I stumbled upon the concept of unlearning, I noticed a lot of old baggage that was no longer serving a purpose. As a diver, I had made a calculated choice to share control of my athletic career with Rick. We shared a dream. He helped make me an Olympian. But to succeed at the office, I had to unlearn some of the behaviors that made my partnership with Rick successful. During my nine years with him, I learned how to react to negative feedback with aplomb, but not how to shift my own moods. I learned how to execute spoken and unspoken demands, but not how to judge my own success. I learned how to see things from another person's perspective, but not how to commit to my own.

Every transition story I've told so far has required its subject to unlearn something, usually something significant. Nora's ongoing post-cancer symptoms have made it hard to predict what her body and mind will be capable of each day, forcing her to unlearn the notion that great ambition makes life meaningful. Emma's recovery from depression has meant unlearning the coping technique that she used to turn to every time she felt anxious about the future: "If it doesn't work out, it's fine, because I'm not planning to be here anyway." To get through her divorce, Sarah had to unlearn the belief that true friends should automatically know exactly what to say or do to help you.

· · ·

Connecting our dots and leaving our baggage are two sides of the same coin: adaptation, the process of change we undergo to be better suited to our environment. In the natural world, a species' ability to adapt determines how likely it is to survive. It's just as essential to our humanity. Transitions cause a lot of suffering if we can't adapt to our new environments.

In a 2021 study of eighteen thousand individuals in fifteen countries, management consultancy McKinsey found that "adaptability" was the skill most closely correlated with employment, even more than achievement orientation, optimism, or digital collaboration.[3] A lot of the buzz about career adaptability these days surrounds AI and its effect on the job market. And yes, if you're a graphic designer and haven't explored how AI design tools can help your creative process, you risk losing a job to someone who has. But career adaptation isn't new, and it isn't always about technology. A few years ago, I caught up with Rick over a Tanqueray and tonic. "I'm a different coach now, buddy," he said. College kids had changed in the forty years he'd been coaching, and even in the twenty years since I'd first started with him. Rick speculated that parents were less likely to yell or ground their kids, which meant the kids, when they got to Rick's college team, were more likely to take negative reinforcement personally, making it a less productive coaching technique. He'd had to find a different style. When I saw him coaching on the pool deck he was like a Santa Claus version of himself. It wasn't easy to change, and he did a fair share of grumbling about kids these days, but to be fair, so do I. To be a successful coach, Rick had to adapt.

. . .

Adaptability is hard. And unfortunately, it's hardest in times when we're stressed and under pressure. A team of researchers from McKinsey call this the "adaptability paradox": "When we most need to learn, change, and adapt, we are most likely to react with old approaches that aren't suited to our new situation, leading to poorer decisions and ineffective solutions," they write.[4] In other words, the moments that most require fresh, new approaches are the moments we're most likely to turn to familiar, old ones.

Adaptability is not just a business buzzword, and psychologists are trained to help us cultivate it. In acceptance and commitment therapy (ACT), people cope with fear and trauma by accepting what is out of their control and committing instead to actions that enrich their lives. The gist is that it's more effective to acknowledge your emotions than to try to prevent or ignore them. (This differentiates ACT from most of the cognitive behavioral therapy techniques I used as a diver, which were more about changing or controlling my feelings.) This doesn't mean it's *okay* that a terrible thing happened. But it does mean that you accept that it happened and learn to adapt to that reality. An ACT therapist might wear a T-shirt that says "feel it to heal it." (These are, in fact, readily available on Etsy.) ACT is a robust process that takes years of schooling to facilitate well. But it boils down to a simple heuristic: accept, choose, and take action.

Imagine a man is mugged as he's walking home from the school where he teaches. His assailants knock him down, steal his wallet and phone, and leave him on the ground with a broken nose. Long after his physical injuries have healed, the mental ones remain, including an overwhelming fear of walking outside alone and a livid fixation on the anonymous strangers who did this. After his mugging, the man, who had been an avid runner, stops leaving his house unless he's in a car.

An ACT therapist might start with helping him *accept* his fear and anger, teaching him breathing techniques and positive thoughts to help him cope with strong emotions, e.g., *I am angry and afraid, and it's okay that I feel this way.*

That therapist might also help him *choose* his values and the actions that represent them. He values being an active person, but his terror of going outside alone keeps him on the couch. He and his therapist identify activities that are important to his sense of self but that he's avoiding due to fear.

His therapist might then help him to *take action* according to his values, cueing him to practice his acceptance techniques while jogging around the block. Slowly, he gains confidence in his ability to feel fear without allowing it to control him.

When a new environment or challenge calls for adaptation, the principles of ACT help you keep your baggage—your emotional triggers, angers, insecurities, and biases—from determining your reaction. Instead, you can react purposefully, based on the values you've chosen and the version of yourself you want to bring forward.

. . .

I was curious to talk with a trained therapist about how she's left her own baggage behind, so I reached out to my friend Shelby. Professionally, she's a relationship therapist for queer and nonmonogamous people. Personally, she's devoted a lot of thought and energy to unlearning various facets of the culture she was born in.

Shelby grew up in the Church of Jesus Christ of Latter-day Saints. She was raised to believe that sex was for procreation, not pleasure, and that her greatest earthly goal as a woman was to attract a worthy man, marry him, and dedicate herself to him for eternity. Today, she has left the church and identifies as queer and nonmonogamous.

I wondered, how do you leave behind a religion? How do you build a new life, acting on the values you choose?

"How did you become the fun, fabulous Shelby we know today?" I asked.

Shelby started questioning her culture's treatment of women and their bodies back in middle school. It just didn't seem plausible that she'd go to hell for wearing a spaghetti strap tank top to school. She was a dancer, and her closest friends were other dance kids pushing against various boundaries: queerness, body autonomy, sexuality. By the time she got to college, she'd long since made her choice. "I knew for a long time the religion did not resonate with me," she told me. "But I was performative for my family. So when I left it didn't feel like a big thing." I had thought that the hardest part of leaving behind a faith was finding the courage to do so, but that part seemed relatively easy for her.

The bigger challenge has been expanding beyond the moralisms and mandates she internalized as a kid. For example, she started having sex when she was still a teenager in Salt Lake City but felt so much shame around masturbation that she couldn't bring herself to do it until she had been living on her own in New York for years. "It's wild, how we're taught something, how it's internalized, and how it reflects in our behavior," she told the host of a podcast called *Open Late*, which explores alternative relationships.[5]

Even now, as a professional psychotherapist with years of schooling, she continues to peel back the layers of childhood baggage. When we first spoke, she was happily dating a man in Texas and a woman in New York, but a few months later, she woke up in the middle of the night with the realization that, although she was falling deeply in love with her female partner, she didn't value the relationship as much as she should. "I was like, 'Oh my God. There's this story that I'm telling myself that if it's two women, it doesn't matter,'" she said. "I thought I was a proud queer person. But I was coming up against internalized homophobia from this deeply religious place." It underscored the messy process of unlearning. Culling your old root systems isn't linear, and no amount of intention in any one moment of your life is enough to fully excise them. "The more life experience I had, the deeper the roots that were exposed," said Shelby.

Her epiphany spawned weeks of heart-wrenching conversations with her therapist and both partners, culminating in the awareness that to fully step into herself, she couldn't be dating a man. So she broke up with her boyfriend.

She paraphrased the advice of one of her role models, Oprah's life coach Martha Beck, who described setting a timer every thirty minutes to ask herself, *Am I doing what I want, when I want, where I want, with who I want?* Shelby doesn't go to that extreme, but she often recommends that her patients try it a few times a week. "It forces you to ask yourself, *Am I moving and behaving and navigating the world in a way that is truly in alignment with my authentic self, my wants, my needs, my desires, and where I want to go?*" she said.

Sure, life is renovation, but Shelby puts this principle into practice like few people I've met. Think of the psyche as a house. Some spend years doing the bare maintenance to keep it standing. Some update the kitchen every decade. Shelby is always remodeling, knocking down walls, building doors, retiling the bathroom. There's an ease in taking things for granted, one that she has given up.

The upside of this work is that her identity fits her like a glove. She doesn't get stuck with paint colors that don't feel as fresh as they did five years ago. She doesn't experience the malaise of spending too long living in a kitchen where the cabinets aren't where she wants them. She doesn't get attached to the parts of herself that aren't serving her. She lets them go and builds a better self.

. . .

"Transitions are tricky enough when they involve one person," I said. "How on earth do you navigate the process of adaptation within a relationship?" I could think of many complex scenarios in Shelby's line of work. Opening up a monogamous partnership. Coming out as nonbinary to a partner who's only ever known you as a man or woman. Sharing that you changed your mind and don't actually want kids. It would seem like you have to be so surgical in your process. How do you move on from one thing while protecting and bolstering the things you don't want to lose?

For couples who are diverging from the beaten path, Shelby recommends they work to ground themselves in whatever makes them feel strong together. "What can you do to double down on your intimacy in order to expand in other places?" she said. "Is it being in community with others? Is it date nights every week? Is it watching a movie? How do you touch the part of yourselves where you are completely safe?" I appreciated that these suggestions weren't just conversation prompts. We don't just talk ourselves into trust and stability. These emotions come from the environments we create, the activities we do, and the things we feel together—not just words.

"It comes back to how comfortable people are with ambiguity and the unknown," she said. "I ask my patients, 'How can you be curious?' People often talk about creating safe spaces, but I think more about creating brave and courageous spaces."

I saw her point—when exploring new territory, either alone or with others, it's unlikely that we'll feel totally safe. Instead, we can set an intention to be curious and brave, not judgmental or defensive. I loved this reframing of fear as curiosity. It felt empowering to have a choice over where you want your butterflies to fly.

Author Paulo Coelho wrote, "Maybe the journey isn't so much about becoming anything. Maybe it's about un-becoming everything that isn't really you, so you can be who you were meant to be in the first place." Molly, Shelby, and I all found power in unlearning specific lessons from our pasts. We all navigated the two sides of the adaptation coin, bringing some parts of ourselves forward and leaving others behind. But what happens when your transition requires more radical unlearning?

· · ·

Growing up, I saw my cousin Jacob about once a year at our family reunion. He was twelve years younger than me, one of a gaggle of tow-headed children building driftwood forts on the beach and piling on the rumpus room couch to play Mario Kart. Over the years, I was vaguely aware of him becoming tall, going to high school, and turning into a quiet, sort of angsty music kid. Shortly after his college graduation, I heard through the grapevine that he was heading to Myanmar for a three-week silent retreat. I remember feeling puzzled—he must be really into this Buddhism thing. The next I heard, he was wearing white robes, changing his name to Tyberius, and moving to a monastery up in Mendocino, a few hours north of San Francisco. A year later, his dad sent around photos of him at his ordination, his face and head hairless, smiling serenely in the orange robes that signified full monkhood. His name was now Obhāsī.

Everything I knew about Buddhism I'd learned from a handful of Thich Nhat Hanh books and a documentary I watched on the Dalai Lama in high school. I didn't understand. What experiences could lead my cousin to want to leave behind so much of the world he grew up in? I was also curious. Obhāsī was in the middle of relearning everything— how to live, how to find joy—not just his identity but the very concept of identity. I wanted to learn from him.

To get to the monastery in Mendocino, I drove past small vineyards, ranch houses with tchotchkes and goats in the front yard, and clusters of mailboxes beside unpaved lanes. As I got closer, the road narrowed and the fields of grass and grapes turned into patches of redwood forest. The monastery covers 280 acres spanning across three biomes. The grounds are steep, with epic views of tree-covered valleys that make fully fledged humans feel like insignificant specks. When I arrived, the monks were busy finishing their morning work assignments and a friendly band of laypeople were in the industrial kitchen, making a meal.

In addition to the sixteen monks and novices who make this place their home, there's a revolving set of residents who stay for days, weeks, or months at a time. Everyone, ordained or lay, seemed cheerfully, mind-blowingly committed.

The monks are on a tight schedule: They wake at three or four in the morning, pray at 5 a.m., and work for a few hours on daily assignments that range from clearing underbrush in the forest to managing book orders for the reading room. At 10:45 a.m. the monks change out of their work robes and everyone enters the prayer room, the monks through one door and the laity through another. It's a simple rectangular building with wood floors and walls, but the atmosphere is hushed and holy. The monks kneel and chant in two neat rows on one side of the room, and the laity kneel on the other. Sometimes they face each other, sometimes everyone turns and genuflects toward the Buddha perched in a lit alcove behind the monks. Then the monks walk out of the room single file with smooth, deliberate heel-to-toe steps.

"The meal" is a big deal. No one eats after noon on monastery grounds, and, to ensure that they are dependent upon the community, the monks are not allowed to grow, acquire, prepare, serve, or store food. After the prayer they bring their wooden bowls through the meal line, followed by the other residents who haven't eaten since noon yesterday, followed by day-trippers like me who grabbed a buttered bagel on the drive up. I ate with a kid finishing his last semester of college and a middle-aged woman who'd grown up Buddhist in Sri Lanka. Both were contemplating ordination. Both were feeling family pressure not to go through with it; the boy to do something lucrative with his college degree, the woman to practice Buddhism alongside a secular life, like her parents. Both wanted to know how my family had taken the news about my cousin. "No judgment, but a lot of curiosity," I said.

After the meal, Obhāsī and I sat down to catch up. I hadn't seen him since he was in college, a few years before his ordination. Years of single-meal days and hard labor in the forests had made him just this side of gaunt, with pronounced shadows under his eyes and sharp cheekbones that might have been camouflaged if he still had hair or eyebrows. There was a perpetual closemouthed upturn to his lips, like someone who knows a secret, or someone who is in the process of achieving joy through enlightenment, or someone who is playing a monk on TV. He spoke like he smiled, the tenor of his voice peaceful and affectless.

I asked my first question. "How did you end up . . . here?"

At ten or eleven, Obhāsī had begun asking questions that no one around him seemed inclined to answer: "Why am I going to class? Why are people going to their jobs? What's the grand purpose behind all of this? Why does nobody seem to know what's going on? Why is nobody satisfied? Why does nobody want to talk about this whole life thing?" His intonation was as steady as a Theravada chant. For some kids, existential wondering is a phase, but for my cousin it was a constant undercurrent. By college the questions had taken on an air of desperation. "I'd be like, 'We all die, and what's up with that?' And everyone was like, 'Don't be such a downer, man, come to this party with us,'" he said.

He went to a Buddhist meetup group in college but wasn't yet ready to heed the call. The chanting seemed scientifically dubious and made him uncomfortable. "It was like they took everything that I thought and believed and put it into a religion," he said. "But I didn't really believe in religion." Instead, he decided to major in neuroscience. "My aspiration was to try to figure out some way of viewing this human life that made any sense through the realm of the brain, the consciousness," he said. But the deeper he got, the more overwhelmed he was. Near the end of his degree, he attended the Society for Neuroscience's yearly conference, where he examined a sea of PhD poster boards, each one explaining a very specific enzyme mechanism influencing a very specific part of the brain. Obhāsī smiled ruefully. "I was like, there's just no way it's all gonna come together to make an answer," he said.

It was around then that he started meditating. It began as a secular, scientific pursuit. Peer-reviewed studies have found that meditation improves attention span, memory, creative problem-solving, interpersonal skills, contentment, and empathy and reduces blood pressure, the stress hormone cortisol, and inflammatory chemicals called cytokines. But while science was the doorway, the path was intuition. "The one thing that I knew immediately was that I needed to meditate more," he said. Buddhism entered the fray as a lifestyle that could support his jones to meditate. After graduation he went on that three-week retreat in

Myanmar. By the end he was asking the monks there what it was like to ordain.

Between every one of my dives at the Olympic Trials and the Olympics, I wrapped my body in a soggy towel, tucked myself into a parka, and lay on my back with my eyes closed, breathing in four counts and out four counts to the metronomic beats of "Sail" by AWOLNATION. It helped me stay even in a way that I'd never been able to before—not too nervous, not too excited, not too negative, not too positive, not fixating on what might go wrong or daydreaming about what might go right. Just calm and ready. For me it was a life-changing tactic, not a lifestyle. But Obhāsī was looking for answers in a way I wasn't. Growing up, he had no escape from the barrage of existential questions, not classes or Mario Kart or frat parties or neuroscience. On a day-to-day level, meditation was an oasis. On an existential level, it was an answer. Buddhism provided an explicit response to the question no one else seemed willing to ask: How should I live?

Obhāsī follows a staggering number of precepts—227 to be exact—including bans on any sort of ownership, money handling, or wearing clothing other than hand-dyed orange robes. Even the laypeople who visit the monastery must follow eight, which still manage to cover a good span of potential behaviors. They start with the universal biggie—no taking the life of any living creature. And then they progress from other basic rights and wrongs—no false and harmful speech—to the unique precepts that make this particular life path worthwhile (to believers) and unfathomable (to outside observers)—no eating at inappropriate times, no entertainment, beautification, and adornment, and no lying on a high or luxurious sleeping place.

"What's the relationship between the restrictions and the happiness?" I asked.

"Hopefully, over time, you're cultivating a sense of peace or well-being that can fill the void that used to be taken up by coarser pleasure," he said. "It's giving up the video games or cake or movies in exchange for a sense of ease and contentment in the moment." As he said this, I noticed a tiny spider dancing along his protruding cheek bone. *This*, I thought, *is probably the sign of an adept meditator.*

"Don't get me wrong, it's not an easy lifestyle," he said. "But here I feel I know what's happening. I'd much rather abide in that kind of clarity and purpose than the kind of confusion I felt in the world."

His explanation made me think of Shelby. They both seemed so committed to understanding the innermost sanctums of their brains, and in shaping their outer worlds to match. When Shelby realized that her relationship with a man was keeping her from fully appreciating her relationship with a woman, she put a restriction on herself, breaking up with her male partner. I was not expecting to find common ground between a sex therapist and a Buddhist monk, but there it was: both made radical choices to live by their values. Both limited their options in order to focus on their priorities.

I wanted to learn more about the *unlearning* that it takes to become a Buddhist monk. After my diving career ended, I had to leave behind some baggage. But Obhāsī had to unlearn the entire capitalist Western worldview, starting with his attachment to "coarser" pleasures—the food, the entertainment, the hopes for a family—and progressing to unwholesome thoughts, desires, and ultimately, his identity as an individual.

I asked what Obhāsī thought about unlearning. Did that word feel accurate for what he's experienced? What has been challenging about all that unlearning?

The first part, giving up sex and the restrictions around food, that was easy. He believed in the purpose behind the precepts and was dedicated to the training. But the cessation of unwholesome thought processes, that's been trickier. "It's a reflection we chant again and again," he said. "As one who has gone forth I am no longer living according to worldly aims and values." He closed his eyes and went inward for ten or twenty seconds, then opened them and said, "It might sound banal as a statement, but actually applied to a lifestyle, there are so many ways of thinking, one of them being orienting toward accomplishment and achievement, that are really good to reflect upon." It required my full brain to make meaning out of his words, which I think amounted to, *I'm trying not to put too much stock in accomplishments, but it's hard.*

At least half of the questions I asked Obhāsī were attempts to get him to put something unspeakable into words. "What does it feel like to meditate?" "What do you know now that you didn't know before you became Buddhist?" "What was your three-month silent retreat like?" The answers he gave made words feel like inadequate vessels. Beyond the fact that philosophy can be tricky to ground, this particular philosophy seemed to repel straightforward answers. Since our emotions are not part of ourselves, you can't just say "I was proud." Instead, you say "I was orienting toward accomplishment and achievement." Since judgment is frowned upon, you can't just say "accomplishment and achievement are bad." Instead, you say they are "really good to reflect upon." I felt like I was constantly grasping to make the intangible tangible. You know that thing about how describing a joke kills it? Maybe describing worldview kills it too, but I couldn't understand it any other way. What did this mean to him? What were his dreams? It was hard to say.

The goal of this unlearning is to notice all—pleasure and pain, gain and loss, praise and blame, fame and disrepute—and not be affected by them. "I have this very conscious motivation to look at how I am being habitually swayed by these things and come to a place of clarity where I can see them and not be moved," he said. It could have come straight out of a textbook on ACT or a McKinsey report on cultivating adaptability.

Obhāsī used a wind metaphor that I found helpful: Imagine yourself as a boulder and all your emotions and instinctive reactions as wind. Don't let them move you.

. . .

I didn't leave the monastery with as many answers as I had hoped. But if it was possible to learn the meaning of life from one visit to a monastery, then there wouldn't be many monks. I still can't fully fathom why my cousin chose to leave the world behind in such an extreme way. When pruning a tree, they say never to remove more than 30 percent, and I have to admit, the pruning process Obhāsī is undertaking would terrify me. But I do believe he's found a level of contentment that eluded him before. And that his story reveals a set of principles for leaving behind baggage, even for those who are not planning to shed their possessions, dismantle their identities, and spend most of each day meditating in a hut on the side of a mountain.

Old habits, lessons, and thought processes die hard. First, because they're hard to identify. Second, because their roots have worked their way so fully through us. Meditation can help us see and detach ourselves from lessons that don't apply to our current situation. Rules can help us stay true to our priorities and values. Simply being mindful can help us recognize our pains, urges, and gut reactions and choose how we want to live.

Tools for Leaving Your Baggage

To adapt, we have to leave some habits, assumptions, and ways of thinking behind us—which ain't easy. Train your mind to let go of its baggage through mindfulness and meditation.

How to Prioritize Growth

Tell Your Story: Simplify to Expand

Unlearning is hard. Guardrails help you live according to your values and prioritize what you choose to prioritize. It doesn't have to be as extreme as Obhāsī's precept not to eat after noon to prioritize "finer pleasures," or Shelby's decision to break up with a beloved boyfriend to prioritize her relationship with a woman.

- Take a few minutes and brainstorm old habits or thought patterns that have been getting in the way of your best you—whether that's one too many episodes of trash TV keeping you from getting through a book, or compulsive email checking keeping you from being fully present with your partner.

- Now choose one! Just one. Write it down in big letters. Cut that baggage out, first for a day, then for a week.

- Reflect on how that felt. Are you ready to simplify further?

How to Learn What Baggage to Leave

Expand Your Inputs and Dig Deep

One of the best ways to unlearn is to learn. A lot of our baggage is so deeply ingrained, it's not conscious. Think generally about what you'd like to leave behind. Is it a perfectionist mindset? A religion? The patriarchy? Chances are, someone smart has already been thinking through this. Ask your librarian for books and essays that expand on the frameworks you're shifting and the challenges you might face.

How to Train Your Mind

Meditate

Old habits die hard. Recognizing what to unlearn is step one of a million. You will need tools to help you effectively unlearn, and meditation is a good one. There are two types, both useful:

- Mindfulness meditation, which involves being open and aware of your thoughts and senses without reacting to or judging them.

- Concentrative meditation, which involves focusing on a specific phrase or intention.

Apps like Calm, Headspace, or Waking Up, or YouTube channels like Great Meditation offer guided meditations for a variety of purposes, from gearing up for a stressful day to getting to sleep at night. The voice prompting you can be helpful, but if you want to go it alone, try the following steps for a five-minute mindfulness meditation:

- Find a comfortable space where you won't be inter-rupted. Sit down, set a timer with a quiet, gentle alarm, for five minutes, and close your eyes. Breathe at counts of five: five counts in, hold for five counts, five counts out. Starting at your toes and working your way up your body to the top of your head, tense each part of your body, then allow it to relax as completely as possible.

- Continue to focus on feelings of relaxation in your body and your five-count breaths. When stray thoughts arise, imagine them as bubbles floating on a pond, or breezes drifting around you, and allow them to pass.

- When the timer goes off, slowly open your eyes, and spend a few seconds appreciating and feeling grateful for the world around you. Even if it's a cubicle wall, it's still wonderful.

How to Beat the Adaptability Paradox

Accept, Choose, and Take Action

Our baggage is most likely to get in the way when we're stressed or triggered. For intense feelings and trauma, it's best to try ACT with a trained therapist. But the principles of ACT can help you to react the way you want to, not the way you always have, in a wide range of milder situations.

For example, imagine you and your partner are constantly arguing about work-life balance. Every time you work late or the subject comes up, you start feeling anger, defensiveness, and anx-iety in your body. Then you feel guilty for reacting so strongly toward someone you love.

- **A**ccept your thoughts and emotions:

  The moment you feel your body preparing for a fight, take a deep breath, notice your mental and physical feelings, and say to yourself, "My shoulders are tense, I'm anxious about this conversation, and that's okay." Consider sharing that with your partner and open the door for them to share their own state of mind.

- **C**hoose a valued direction:

  Work with your partner to ground yourself in your shared values. What matters to you both individually, and as a couple? What do you love about each other? How are your conversations embodying those values, and how are they taking you both away from the version of yourselves that you want to be?

- **T**ake action:

  Identify ways to disagree better. Maybe you'll take a minute to say "I love you" and ask each other about your days before launching into the topic at hand. Maybe you'll agree on a safe word that either of you can use when you need to pause and reflect. Maybe you'll both go through the previous meditation exercise before having the conversation. These principles won't solve your disagreement, but they'll put you both in the best state to work together to solve it.

Don't Forget

Vulnerability Is Cool

Share your questions, doubts, and uncertainties with people you trust. They can help you see challenges from outside yourself, call out mistaken assumptions you're holding, help you recognize when you're stuck, and help you stick with your unlearnings.

Adaptation Isn't Instant, Nor Is Progress a Straight Line

Choose simple interventions (e.g., limiting yourself to one TV show a night) and do them daily. Keep doing them, even if they don't seem to be having a large or immediate impact. Evolution takes time.

7.

Know When to Fold 'Em

Quitting is hard. What's the right time to let something go? How do we find the courage to follow through with it? How can we minimize the risks of leaving a secure thing behind?

I was thirty-two when the 2018 Pyeongchang Winter Olympics rolled around. Since my retirement from diving in 2012, I'd been keeping a close eye on other athletes my age, the ones who had stayed on the path I did not take. Those that were left were now past thirty, which, in the Olympic world, was an age bordering on geriatric. I watched them with a set of emotions I couldn't quite parse. A bit of jealousy. A bit of curiosity. And a bit of . . . fandom?

Ironically, I'd never been much of a sports fan. I'd always been more interested in the doing than the watching. But with this small cohort of athletes my age, I cheered hard from the couch. I got into the zone with them and felt my athlete ghost perform alongside them.

One of the biggest names at the 2018 Olympics was skier Lindsey Vonn, who was a year older than me. Two things were foretold before Lindsey got to Pyeongchang: One, this would be her last Olympics—she planned to retire at the end of the season—and two, she would cap her swan song by winning everything. Only one of those prophecies came true. Lindsey took third place in the downhill, sixth in the slalom, and zoomed off the course in the combined event, failing to finish. She was pilloried by the press and public. "Another look at Vonn, not able to handle the run," deadpanned a commentator as she thumped awkwardly over the red pole then zagged to a stop, head down, eerily still, snow falling softly around her. I wondered, as I watched: What will Lindsey Vonn do *now*? Where would she go from here?

An idea started taking root. The US mints five hundred or so fresh Olympians every four years, and sooner or later, every one of us retires. At work that week, as I wrote and rewrote keynote slides over takeout dinners of lukewarm food, I wondered about how others had managed this transition. When you crack open the elite athlete shell, who's inside? Years later, did they feel the same sense of loss that I did? Were there Olympians out there who were thriving in their new lives?

All those years ago, when I'd gone home to Pittsburgh to sit around and try to be a writer, I'd failed because I didn't know what to write. But now I had an *idea*. The weekend after the 2018 Olympics ended, I spent three hours on a Saturday listing out the Olympians I knew. I shared my idea with my friends and they loved it. I daydreamed about the questions I'd ask other Olympians and how the conversations would go.

Then I called no one, asked nothing, and wrote no words for the next two years.

Something always got in the way—maybe an urgent client request, maybe just an urgent need to play Candy Crush. I procrastinated by reading Medium articles about how working professionals made time for creative pursuits: a marketing manager who woke up two hours early every morning to write and produce a one-act play. A design director who always followed up on his "what if" ideas, but only slept five hours a night. I did neither. I could not bring myself to optimize away the parts of my life that brought me easy joy—precious time for sleep, Nicholas, and trapeze—for something that would require creative energy I wasn't sure I had.

I contemplated quitting my job. But where was I actually leaping to?

Was this book a real dream, or just an escape hatch? I hadn't written when I was at home in Pittsburgh, despite having all the time in the world. I hadn't written in New York, despite having an idea I believed in. With my track record—was the idea really worth giving up my salary and health insurance?

Perhaps what scared me most was the idea that quitting my job would make me a quitter.

. . .

In mid-2019, more than a year after I'd started dreaming about writing a book, I was given the kind of assignment that people in my line of work dream of. It was a small organic food brand. Instead of being the middle child on a big account, I was the leader of a smart, scrappy team. Instead of working with middle managers at a corporate empire, I was working directly with a CEO who had a deep personal vision for his company. We kicked off the project with a cross-country research trip, visiting people in their homes to understand the relationship between healthy food and happiness. Flora and I were together on this one, and we drove around in a beat-up rental, navigating Atlanta's beltway traffic and parallel parking in the Los Angeles hills. It was a voyeuristic thrill to sit in strangers' kitchens, with their pets and their clutter and their preferred Glade PlugIns, and ask them deep questions about what they fed their families and why it mattered. Over the next few months, we used the insights we'd gathered on this trip to create several new organic snacks for the brand. My clients and coworkers were inspiring, and it was exciting to imagine my products out there, in my grocery store.

I was moving up. I was working with good people. But it wasn't enough.

During this time—aka my best project ever, the peak of my advertising career—I started grinding my teeth in my sleep and hitting snooze as many times as possible in the morning. My work had begun to feel increasingly meaningless. Did it really matter what specific word we used on a branding campaign? What was the actual value of what I was doing?

I once had looked to work milestones to motivate me: associate strategist to strategist to senior strategist. The corresponding bumps in pay made a tangible impact on my day-to-day existence. But then I passed the point where a bump in salary equated to greater peace of mind or quality of life. I had visions of my boss, alone and working late in a dark office. Did I want her job?

. . .

My breakdown came over winter break. After two weeks off, I couldn't bring myself to go back. When I was in high school, I looked forward to college. When I was in college, I looked forward life post-college, when I could focus my energy entirely on diving. When I was training for the 2012 Olympics, I looked forward to my retirement from diving, when I could explore the working world and find my next passion. Now, all I saw was an endless plateau.

One time, long ago, I'd driven from Stanford to Houston, spending days on a straight two-lane highway, flatness and dust and tumbleweeds stretching out on all sides toward a razor-sharp horizon. That's what my future felt like.

My first day back in the office, I asked the head of strategy for a sabbatical. It was a move of desperation; I knew I couldn't go on like this. The day was cold but sunny, and we walked in slow circles around the block with our coffees. I told her about my book idea, my desire to apply everything I'd learned about strategy to this question of meaning and fulfillment in one's "second life." Then I asked for some time off.

"I was thinking maybe a month," I said, nervously. Sabbaticals are not a common thing in our industry. Why should I deserve special treatment? Her response shocked me. It's astonishing how willing people are to help you, if you have a clear vision of what you want and why.

"Are you sure one month is enough?" she asked. I thought about how many answers I needed, how many people I wanted to meet. I also thought about my dread of coming into the office every day, exactly like this, forever, and whether it was possible that with enough time, I could return to work refreshed and excited.

"Two months then?"

She agreed.

• • •

When do you hold 'em and when do you fold 'em? It's the hardest question that comes up most often in my life, for me and nearly everyone I know. My mom's feeling uninspired by her "retirement job," coaching at the local diving club. Should she stick with it or ask them to find a replacement? My teammate's dog keeps growling at her next-door neighbor, who keeps calling animal services. Should she stay or move? My friend's partner sustained a head injury and started behaving in ways that made her feel unsafe. Should she leave him or take care of him?

My bias is often toward holding 'em. It's a cultural bias—as Americans, we're addicted to narratives of people persevering in the face of insurmountable odds. Think of all your favorite action movies: the essential plot point that runs across the genre is that the main character *doesn't give up*. As my friend Danny wrote in a column for *Seattle* magazine about getting sober, quitting "is seen as the exit ramp chosen by people who don't have the courage and grit necessary to stick with it. Perseverance, on the other hand, is burned into our collective hard drive as not just a virtue, but a trait that is necessary for success."[1]

Danny, in fact, is the person who recommended to me a book called *Quit* by Annie Duke, one of the all-time best female professional poker players.[2] Annie's thesis—which is backed by a quantifiable superpower of high-stakes decision-making, a master's degree in cognitive linguistics, and a PhD in psychology—is that we tend to hold 'em way more often than we should.

"By definition, anybody who has succeeded at something has stuck with it. That's a statement of fact, always true in hindsight," she writes. "But that doesn't mean that the inverse is true, that if you stick to something, you will succeed at it." For every cherry-picked success story, there are a thousand people gritting their way through misery, with no real chance of success, because it's been ingrained in them that quitting is for losers.

We usually don't tell *those* stories, giving us a massive imbalance in the value of grit over quit. But, as Annie writes: "Success does not lie in sticking to things. It lies in picking the right things to stick to and quitting the rest."

· · ·

Our worship of perseverance can lead us to make choices that are at odds with our goals. Danny waffled on getting sober for years after he knew his drinking was a problem, attempting and failing to limit his habit without giving it up entirely. "I somehow thought if I were just more disciplined, a little bit smarter, I'd learn to manage my alcohol consumption," he wrote. The same way I thought that if I was just more disciplined, a little bit smarter, I could work more than full time and pursue my creative dreams. The same way that an aging athlete thinks if he's more disciplined, a little bit smarter, he can get back to his peak. Ironically, the thing that most limits us is the belief that we can overcome all limitations.

One morning, after years of half-hearted attempts to curtail his drinking, Danny woke up on the couch with a hazy memory of his wife finding him in the parking garage of their condo the night before, smoking a cigarette and unable to complete a sentence. That evening he went to an AA meeting. That was the day he quit for real, and he's been sober for seven years since. "The experience of becoming sober and accepting that and talking about it has completely changed how I see myself and what I'm capable of," he said. It was only in losing the battle to moderate his drinking that he was able to win the war, gaining control over his life and confidence in his ability to change. As long as Danny assumed that the only way to succeed was to force a reasonable relationship with alcohol, his drinking continued to do him harm. But when he redefined success around the bigger picture—making *sure* that he never reached that state again—he made the only choice that made sense. He quit.

The pressure to persevere is strong, especially for our major life commitments: jobs, marriages, friendships, religions. But we hold on to the little things just as tightly, and for many of the same reasons. We feel pressure to uphold what people expect of us. Pressure to show that everything's okay. Pressure to keep up the veil of confidence and competency. Pressure to keep faking it until we make it, even long after we've made it. It feels much easier to believe and project that everything's fine than it does to make big, necessary changes.

· · ·

Toya grew up in the eighties and nineties in Irvington, New Jersey. During her childhood and adolescence, Irvington shifted from a working-class haven to an epicenter of the crack epidemic. By the early 2000s, it had the highest violent crime rate in New Jersey. As she came of age, she witnessed the swift decline of her neighborhood. Her older sister had learned to swim in the pool at the apartment building across the street, but before Toya was old enough to take lessons, they drained it. "The message was, 'Nobody's outside. Go inside,'" she said. The stories she learned in church reinforced the idea that the world was a dangerous place and life was a hair away from descending into chaos. "Paradise to hell, that's kind of what was mirroring in my neighborhood," she said. "I really believed the world was gonna end."

That worldview came out in strange ways. As a five-year-old, she was deathly afraid of Michael Jackson's "Thriller" music video. She refused to close the door when she went to the bathroom because she needed to keep eyes on her parents. None of the adults around her worked to get to the root of her fears or saw them as anything other than a kid being dramatic. The daughter of two schoolteachers, she worked hard and got good grades, but couldn't shake the belief that she had to do every single thing right in order to forestall disaster. And though the violence and drug use stayed outside her home, her fears were supported by the messages within. Years after she came of age, she blogged about those lessons: "Growing up as a minority in America, you learn from a very young age that you only have one shot at success. You work twice as hard for half as much. So if you want the whole pie, get ready to work four times as hard."[3]

What does it mean to live your life believing you're always one mistake or problem away from the end of the world?

It meant Toya felt less capable than her peers. On her first day of high school orientation, before she'd set foot in the classroom, she sought out her honors algebra teacher and asked for a tutor. "Because my class was white and I was in the honors class, I just assumed they knew more than me," she said. "I was like, if I'm going to get the grades I need, I need help."

It meant she kept her questions to herself. She went to George Washington University Law School, one of the top programs in the country, where she contended not just with whiteness but overwhelming wealth. Some of her classmates had chauffeurs that drove them to class. "My classmates were more worldly, they'd traveled, they had opportunities that I didn't have," she said. "I felt deficient." She assumed that asking questions would confirm her deficiency. "I didn't want to admit to these people that I don't know what's going on," she said. She barely scraped through her first year of law school.

It meant burying her troubles. After law school, she worked for city government, then as a prosecutor in domestic violence court, then in her own practice in business law. At some point along the path, she started waking up an hour or two early every day to cry before work. "There's pressure to work innumerable hours, not complain, and be the smartest person in the room," she explained. "Your client doesn't want to hear, 'I'm confused. I'm not sure.'"

The weight of trying to be invincible grew heavier and heavier, but Toya couldn't admit it—that would signal weakness to her clients and community. So she refused to acknowledge the issue. "I told myself, 'It's because you're dating and you can't find a guy that you like. You're just not eating healthy. You know what? You just need to drink some more water,'" she said.

From her earliest days in Irvington, she was fighting a set of expectations: the stereotypes our culture places on Black girls from poor neighborhoods. She felt a stifling pressure to prove the negative assumptions—that she wasn't smart enough, worldly enough, or capable enough—wrong. And an equally stifling pressure to prove the positive assumptions right. "'Black girl magic'—that's meant to be inspirational," she said. "But really, what it says to you is if you're not magical, you can forget it." There was no room for vulnerability, playfulness, or anything short of undisputable success. There was certainly no room for quitting.

"I wasn't free. I wasn't looking at an area or a subject and absorbing it because I liked it, or because I wanted to," she said. "It's because I had to prove myself. And if anything showed that I couldn't prove myself the smallest little bit, then I was crumbling."

Her chosen career path didn't help. The stats on lawyers and mental health are grim. A 2016 study in the *Journal of Legal Education* found that 37 percent of law students have an anxiety disorder, a rate nearly three times higher than the general population.[4] In the same year, a separate study found that 27 percent of practicing lawyers experience depression and 21 percent report issues with alcohol.[5] Toya wasn't crying every morning just because she was Black, or just because she was a lawyer, or just because she grew up in Irvington, New Jersey. The same way that I wasn't a people-pleasing perfectionist just because I was a woman. But if you're in a marginalized group, you're contending with extra pressures. The risk factors are higher.

It took a best friend with even more chutzpah than Aunt Patty to help Toya quit. She happened to call one day in the middle of Toya's morning cry.

"I have to go to the office soon and I gotta stop crying and I can't," sobbed Toya.

"I'm gonna call you back in a second," said her friend. A few minutes later, she was back on the line. "This is serious and I'm worried about you," she said. "You're not going into the office."

"I hear you," said Toya. "But can we just do this another day?"

"I called my job and took the day off. Either we do this together and I take you to see a therapist, or I'm going to call the hospital," she said. Then she looked up the number of Toya's employer to tell them she wouldn't be coming in that day. Toya has no idea what she told them.

Her friend drove an hour and a half to meet her. They had lunch, then went to a therapist her friend had found, who Toya ended up seeing for the next few years. "That's how I realized I was going through depression," she said.

Toya's story underlines one of the hardest things about unlearning: It can be extremely difficult to recognize what you need to unlearn. "I didn't know Black people got to be anxious," Toya said to me. The lesson not to show weakness, not to be sad, and not to be vulnerable was so strong she never doubted it. She internalized it to such a degree that it made her blind to any possible solutions. In those situations, community is critical. Friends can see our blind spots better than we can. Great friends don't just tell us about them—they force us to see what we need to see.

Once Toya acknowledged her depression, she realized it was impera-
tive that she take a break from the career that exacerbated it. "All these
things that were a part of my experience built up until my body and my
brain were like, *You haven't been dealing with this shit. And so we're on strike until you do*," she said. She put her practice on pause, moved in with her sister, and augmented her savings with nannying to keep afloat. But mostly,
she focused on therapy, rest, and giving herself the time and space to sort
out what to do next.

In addition to guiding her through this massive change, therapy also
helped her become comfortable enough with vulnerability to do something radical: she wrote about her depression publicly, in a blog post for
Solo Practice University, an online community for solo law practitioners.
"I don't know how mental health and depression fit into the 'one-shot'
equation," she wrote. "Can a Black, female lawyer talk about depression
and still make it?" But she accepted those risks, opening up to the masses
about her despair. "I cried about not being where I 'should' be in life. I
cried about feeling alone, and I cried because I didn't know why I was
crying or felt so bad," she wrote.

The response to this post changed her life. "I got so many responses from
attorneys who were struggling too," she said. "And I realized I want to help
these people. We're good people. We should be able to figure this out."
Toya's coaching practice was born. Over the years, she's expanded her
business from a side hustle to a full-time job and from law professionals to
all women of color. She calls it Woke Up Worthy, and pitches her newslet-
ter with the mantra, "Every week I write to you so that you remember—
every challenge doesn't stem from thoughts that hold you back; some
limitations are just straight-up oppression; you have the power to navigate
both!" She works with her clients on the same struggles that she's faced.
"How do you build a self-concept that allows you to make mistakes, to be
human? To fuck up sometimes, to be good sometimes, to be average most
of the time, and still value yourself as worthy?" she said.

In her transition from lawyer to life coach, Toya connected some important dots. She got started in law because she wanted to help the underdog. "Like, okay, you're trying to take Granny's money? Let's try it now. I'm Granny's lawyer," she said. In her current work, she still advocates for people who need her. Ultimately, her darkest experiences as a lawyer gave her the tools to empathize, and in that way, she brings her past experiences to her current work every day. But more than what she connected, I'm inspired by what she unlearned: the need to orient herself around others' expectations and the instinct to keep her pain inside her. Ultimately, her story is a "no, and" story. Quitting one thing opened the door to a happier, more meaningful path.

Despite the fact that Toya quit practicing law, she's still at risk for depression. Quitting doesn't make you immune to the thought patterns that get you in trouble. But now, she knows how to recognize the signs and address them head on. "If something was nagging in the back of my head, I used to say, 'It's fine. It's not that big a deal,'" she said. "And I would let it go until it was a ten of ten and I was forced to deal with it because there was nothing left." She's also empowered her family to help, telling her husband that if he ever sees her watch more than two episodes of *Gilmore Girls* or *Grey's Anatomy* in a sitting, he should ask her what's up. She's made a rule for herself not to hide from her family when she's upset. "I have to say it. Which is hard, because sometimes I don't want to. But all of that helps to stop a huge depressive episode." Whether you're quitting alcohol or a career, guardrails are important.

* * *

Like me, Toya's career transition started with a sabbatical, a move I highly recommend. But I'm cognizant that a sabbatical is not possible for everyone. I had a CEO and head of strategy who embraced my sabbatical without blinking an eye. I had a financial cushion. I had no student loans or debt. No kids to feed. My parents didn't need physical or financial support.

I once met a life coach who'd made a business out of helping high-earning women rejuvenate themselves by intentionally pausing their work. I asked what she told people who couldn't afford to take a "soulbatical."

"Go get a part-time job that doesn't take all your energy," she said. "Like, go be a barista for three months." But what if you're a breadwinner and part-time work at Starbucks isn't enough? What if you're already juggling two minimum wage jobs just to cobble together enough income to get by? What do you do when everything in your body and soul is telling you to quit, but quitting will put you at serious risk for not being able to fulfill your most basic needs?

· · ·

That question led me to Jen, a single mom born and raised in Back of the Yards, a working class, predominantly Chicano neighborhood of Chicago famous for labor activism, community engagement, and—when the stockyards closed in the early seventies—economic disinvestment. Jen had her son when she was fifteen, during her sophomore year at an all-girls Catholic school. She left for a quarter, then studied double time in summer school and evening classes while her grandmother cared for her infant. After graduating high school with her class, she went immediately to work as a bank teller, then a court reporter, then a temp for a local politician, and, before most of her peers ever set foot into the workforce, as a legal secretary at a prestigious law firm. When she started working at the law firm she was twenty-one, with a high school degree, a six-year-old, and a typing pace of one hundred words per minute from her court reporting stint. "For an administrative role, in terms of skills, I was set at twenty-one," she said.

Jen has spent her life powering through age, education, class, and race hierarchies that would have intimidated the hell out of me. As a teen mom, she dealt with intense judgment at her strict Catholic school. As a twenty-one-year-old Mexican American woman, she supported some of the most venerated lawyers in the city, most of whom were men and none of whom were Latinx. A few years later, when she started working in law recruiting, she was a high school grad schmoozing cream-of-the-crop Harvard Law students. I asked her if she'd ever felt impostor phenomenon.

"My experience was beyond impostor phenomenon," she said. But her self-belief was stronger than her self-doubt. She secretly seethed when senior lawyers complimented her for being "so articulate," reading between the lines their assumptions about how a young Latina woman "should" articulate herself. But she had a young son to support. She didn't have the luxury of acknowledging either the microaggressions or her feelings of inferiority. "I just suppressed it all and thought about my family obligations," she said.

Eleven years after starting at the law office, when Jen was thirty-two and her son was in high school, she had a crisis.

"As I was moving up, I saw there was nowhere else for me to go without a degree," she said. Like me, she had a conversation with her boss about her dissatisfaction. Unlike me, she didn't know exactly what she wanted, and unlike me, she couldn't take a pause or a sabbatical from work—she had a kid in private school. Her boss recommended she take some community college classes to figure out what she wanted to do, so she enrolled in sociology, psychology, and language arts classes at night. A few years later, she started as an undergrad at DePaul University, where she earned her bachelor's degree in psychology—all while continuing to work full time.

She didn't quit her job at the law office until she was accepted to the University of Chicago master's program in social work. And even then, she still worked part time with a medical malpractice lawyer, which she did four mornings a week alongside intense classes and an internship counseling kids with behavioral issues. After graduation, she started working full time as a trauma intervention specialist with Healing Hurt People, a community-based program where she supports people who have sustained injuries from gun violence.

Three things jumped out at me when I heard Jen's story. One, Jen played the long game. Nine years passed between her realization that she was hitting her ceiling at the law office and the day she quit her job and left for grad school. She had fewer safety nets and more responsibility than I did, and so she wove them herself, piling on layers of school and work until she felt stable enough to quit. Two, though she didn't take a sabbatical, she did give herself a test run. She invested time and money in those community college classes to help her figure out what came next. Three, she worked so hard I struggled to comprehend it. Her work ethic is a legacy she traces back to her grandfather, who emigrated from Mexico to work on the railroads. "Family. Work to support that family. Those are the key values that I grew up around," she said. "You are always doing something. There is no time to rest."

I told her about the conversation I'd had with the life coach, who said that if people aren't satisfied, they should take a couple months off to think about what they want to do next. "But what do you do if you can't take a couple months off?" I asked. "What does it actually take?"

"You have to really be strategic," she replied. "Not working never occurred to me. The question was always in the back of my head: How am I going to get the bills paid?" *Strategic* is a good word for working hard *and* smart, and for seeking out mentors and asking them for the right kind of support at the right time, like the law firm bosses who encouraged her to go back to school and the grad school teachers who helped her find the trauma intervention job. *Strategic* also means developing skills and shopping them around where they'll be most valued, like learning to type one hundred words a minute and applying for a law secretary position. It means cultivating a lot of interests, rather than getting consumed by a passion.

"The idea of passion kind of sets you up for failure. You're willing to take a lower wage. You do it unconditionally," she said. "Whereas interests are a bunch of smaller things that you can try on. I have an interest in doing research related to spinal cord injuries and public health. And I also have an interest in doing trauma-informed weightlifting with a group. So I'm able to tap into those things versus having one big passion." It seemed so obvious but also so far from the all-in/no-time-for-dabbling mindset I'd cultivated.

In addition to hard work and strategic choices, Jen also had a lot of assets. First and foremost, she's brilliant and isn't afraid to say it out loud. "I've always been a geek. I've always valued education. I've always been really smart," she said as she set the stage for her story. She shared her accomplishments as matter-of-factly as the weather, neither bragging nor demurring, in a no-nonsense Chicago accent. Her life trajectory would also not have been possible without her family—something she reiterated at every opportunity. She had a grandmother who could take care of her child in his infancy and parents who let her stay rent-free in their basement. Her upbringing instilled confidence in her abilities: "My family support system was like, okay, you're allowed to fall and skin your knee, but you're gonna fix it, and you're getting back up and back out there and figuring it out," she said.

In his book *The Secrets of Happy Families*, author Bruce Feiler reports on illuminating research by psychologists Marshall Duke and Robyn Fivush. The two developed a twenty-question scale to assess how much kids knew about their family histories, with questions like, "Where did your grandparents meet?" and, "Do you know some of the lessons that your parents learned from good or bad experiences?" Over several decades of research, they have found that kids who answer yes to more of these questions have higher self-esteem, better friendships, less anxiety and stress, and fewer behavioral problems.

But the positive impact of family storytelling doesn't end there. Dr.

Duke identifies three predominant "shapes" to family narratives: ascending, which forms around what a family has gained over the years; descending, which forms around what a family has lost over the years; and oscillating, which is a story of ups and downs, advances and setbacks, what Dr. Duke calls "the most healthful narrative." These stories tend to highlight agency, showing kids that hardship is inevitable, but it's possible to work through it. Feiler writes, "Children who know that lives take all different shapes are much better equipped to face life's inevitable disruptions." I can't imagine a better poster child for this insight than Jen.

That said, Jen hasn't worked at 110 percent for her entire life without consequences. The two greatest sacrifices were her mental health and her relationship with her son. "I was always on autopilot mode," she said. "I just needed to go, go, go. And it was extremely, extremely hard." For decades, she felt pressure with no release. Though she provided for her son, their relationship was strained. "As a young mom, I was not very attuned," she said. "I prioritized him, but I also had to prioritize my needs as well." It wasn't until her son was grown and she was starting her master's degree that they started growing closer.

Today she's in her fifties, her son is in his thirties, and they've put in the work to forge a better relationship. But though that particular rift has healed, her life remains enormously stressful. Her job has placed her in close proximity to gunfire. She has lost clients to gun violence. She's aware when she walks a certain block how many shootings have occurred on that corner. Beyond the risk of physical violence, there is the constant frustration of spending each day helping participants navigate a system that isn't serving them, while being part of that system (her organization is funded by a healthcare system). In addition to ongoing therapy, her most important form of self-care is something she calls "radical exercise."

Back in school, she started going to yoga after therapy sessions as a way to physically process her emotional work. When she started at Healing

Hurt People, she switched to boxing and weightlifting. "The fluidity and calmness of yoga wasn't doing it," she said. "I needed something as aggressive as the work was to get it out." One of her burgeoning interests is trauma-informed weightlifting, a practice that unites coaches, physical therapists, and mental health professionals in healing trauma. "I don't even call it exercise. It's just part of what I do on a daily basis," she said. "With the intense trauma work that I do, I will not, I cannot, be effective without it." We are so quick to prioritize our brains and ignore our bodies. We are at our best when we recognize that one can't function well if we neglect the other.

Jen used the phrase "endurance for life" to describe the teenagers and young adults she works with today, many of whom navigated layers of toxic systems—education, healthcare, criminal justice—long before sustaining permanent injuries from violence. I also see endurance for life in every part of Jen's story. At many points, she could have given up, settled, and gotten entrenched in the unfairness of missing so many opportunities to raise a kid. But instead, she kept believing in herself, kept quitting roles that didn't fulfill her, kept cultivating new interests and building them into her life.

On the whole, we don't quit as much as we should. Letting go of naive hopes that we might succeed allows us to view ourselves realistically. Releasing the expectation to keep going spares us the dissonance of pursuits that hurt us, or that we no longer believe in. Culling makes space for priorities. As tidying guru Marie Kondo says, "The best way to find out what we really need is to get rid of what we don't."

Tools for Knowing When to Fold 'Em

Quitting creates space. It's hard to leave something you've invested in, but often (more often than we think) it's the right choice. Do some sort of a test run before you quit something major. When quitting, be strategic about your skills and resources and be patient as you put the pieces into place.

How to Know How You Really Feel

Tell Your Story: Use the 10-10-10 Framework

Imagine that the day has come and you have quit the thing you've been thinking of quitting, whether it's a career, an addiction, a relationship, or a religion. (This framework isn't a machine that takes in your responses and spits out a decision, but it will help you to consider the possibilities.)

- Imagine the future ten minutes after you make the decision. How do you feel? What are the immediate repercussions?

- Now imagine it's ten months later. What are the near-term risks and opportunities?

- Now imagine it's ten years later. What are the long-term risks and opportunities? How might this quit influence your life?

How to De-Risk the Quit

Quit Small (If You Can) Before Quitting Big

If quitting poses serious risks, consider other solutions to help you clarify the decision. Can you take a sabbatical? Take a community college class? Experiment with a new philosophy or practice? What might stem your malaise? What might give you new information about what to do next? Before you move to the other side, go on a reconnaissance mission to see if the grass is actually greener.

- Consider the reasons you want to quit, which may include things you're excited to leave behind (a sixty-hour-a-week job, a stressful environment) and/or things you're excited to gain (creative energy to write, more time to spend on hobbies/people).

- Think of the smallest ways to solve those problems. Can you set an intention to leave by 6 p.m. every night? Can you put certain projects on autopilot to free up more brain space? Can you work double time on work and writing for a finite period? Then expand to larger ways. Can you go part time in your current role? Can you take a sabbatical?

- Go through the list, starting with small interventions. Is it plausible that this will solve your dissatisfaction? If not, embrace that limitation and move on. If so, try it.

- Reevaluate after a month. Did you try the small intervention? How did it go? Do you still want to quit? If so, move on up.

Quit Strategically

Ask yourself the questions Jen asked:

- How will the bills get paid?

- What skills can float me financially while I'm figuring out my next big career move?

How to Maintain Your Relationships

Buttress Your Bridges (Don't Burn Them)

Usually, we don't quit in a vacuum. Whether you're quitting a job, a religion, or a bad habit, use psychologist and peace activist Marshall Rosenberg's method of nonviolent communication to maintain relationships. It can help you resolve conflict of any kind, and is a particularly effective method to shift, change, or quit without burning bridges. Don't skip the early steps! It's important that this person understands why you want what you want.

- Start with a nonjudgmental <u>observation</u>: e.g., "I've observed that no matter how much time I try to carve out to explore this book idea, I can't seem to make any headway."

- Then, share how that observation made you <u>feel</u>: "This makes me feel stifled and stuck."

- Then, identify the <u>underlying need</u> that made you feel that way: "I think I need to make space to pursue this."

- Finally, share your <u>request</u>, what you think the other person might do to address your need: "Would it be possible to take a month of unpaid leave to work on a book proposal?"

Don't Forget

When in Doubt, Quit

Annie Duke writes that by the time a choice appears to be fifty-fifty, it is likely well past that in terms of happiness. But we get wrapped up in our biases. It can be really helpful to talk through your reasoning on exercises like the 10-10-10 framework with a close friend (like Toya's!) who can recognize signals you're missing or burying.

Embrace Your Limitations

Too often, limitations are a source of shame. We see them as something to beat, not heed. But admitting our limitations to ourselves is the first step to living a more authentic, less discordant life. And in certain situations, like Toya's, sharing struggles publicly opens doors we would never have expected.

8.

Redefine Success

Chasing the standard markers of achievement can leave us feeling stressed and unfulfilled. How do we stop worrying about failure and work toward our own best version of success?

For more than a decade, I had stifled my writing dream. On the first day of my sabbatical, I finally brought that dream out into the light. I woke up in the morning, opened my laptop, and sat down at the dining room table. It was late January, and the sky was a cold, dusty gray, but the air felt like spring—that first moment of breath when your lungs don't hurt. I wrote the first pages of what would eventually become this book. The words came in a steady rush. All the ideas I'd been pondering late at night when I couldn't sleep formed themselves into sentences and paragraphs and splashed out onto the page.

During my two months off, I wrote every day. I interviewed a dozen or so other Olympians, geeking out over sports I'd never heard of and comparing notes on the ups and downs of retirement. Every conversation sparked curiosity—someone else to speak to, something else to learn. One word carried me to the next. The flow was like diving when I was diving at my best. My body knew what a great sentence sounded and felt like.

As the weeks passed and the end of my two months off came close, I tried to ignore it. I was not sure what to do after my sabbatical. As far as my day-to-day motivation and happiness were concerned, the break had exceeded all my hopes. Financially, I had saved enough money to spend ten more months paying rent and living on eggs and bananas. But I struggled to let go of the career ladder. After starting my career at twenty-seven, I had spent seven years climbing my way from "far behind" to "somewhat behind" my peers, but I still had so far to go to reach the top.

Late in the evenings, after a day of writing, I'd scroll through LinkedIn, watching an ever-refreshing feed of my classmates from Stanford ascending to VPs or CMOs or founders of million- and billion-dollar companies. I had invested seven years in advertising already. If I leapt now, I'd never reach the top.

It would have been easier if I had another ladder to leap to. Before my sabbatical, I'd plotted out a set of criteria that would prove I was on the right path. Two months, I thought, should easily be enough time to do some initial interviews, whip up a book proposal, attract a literary agent, and get the ball rolling on finding a publisher. In diving, if you place well enough at regionals, you earn the right to compete at zones; if you place well at zones, you earn the right to go to nationals, all the way up until you earn the right to call yourself an Olympian. I was hoping for some sort of medal: an advance, an essay about my diving retirement published in some top literary magazine, or, at the very least, a signed-and-sealed partnership with an agent to earn me forward passage from my sabbatical and the right to call myself a writer.

But I was eye-rollingly, adorably naive. My college creative writing classes had prepared me to draft two fifteen-page essays in a three-month semester, and my brand strategy career had trained me to turn around twenty-slide keynote presentations in a week, but neither of those experiences prepared me for the sheer volume of words and ideas I'd have to produce to write, or even conceptualize, an actual, full-length book.

I was also not prepared for the pace of publishing. When I finally drafted my sixty-page proposal, I emailed it out to a few carefully chosen agency slush piles and received the standard automated response: "If you haven't heard from us within six (or eight or sometimes twelve) weeks, please assume that your project was not a match." Not only was there no medal, but for my entire sabbatical there was no indication of placement, no confirmation of whether I was first or last or had even entered the competition.

I was finally doing the thing I'd always dreamed of doing, and the act of doing it was beating every expectation. The conversations I was having were showing me that I wasn't the only one grappling with questions of purpose and community and "who am I now," and I was starting to see that if I continued exploring transitions for myself, I could help a lot of other people as well. *But*, I had no evidence that pursuing this dream would amount to any sort of financial gain. Aside from the handful of friends who told me what a good idea this was (because what else could they say?) and the positive feedback I got in my continuing studies creative writing classes (from people who were obligated to read my work), I had no external validation that this idea should be a book. I had no guarantee that any of this work would amount to anything.

I don't think I would have made the leap without my partner. Nicholas and I now lived together, and he was a strong safety net should something go off the rails while I was unemployed. But the example he set meant even more than the security he provided. Over the years, I'd watched him choose curiosity over fear time and again, or as Jen would say, interests over passions. He wanted to start riding horses again, so he did, though it was probably New York City's least practical hobby. He wanted to write a children's book, so he did—filming a Kickstarter video, writing the words, finding an illustrator, and getting the book printed and sold on Amazon. He wanted to break free of the social norms of masculinity, so he got a manicure kit and learned to paint his nails. One week, he barely slept because he was teaching himself how to build smart thermostats for our apartment out of circuit board parts he ordered from Amazon. Another time, he called out sick from work because he was inventing a pressure-sensing blanket to map the surface of his horse's back.

The smart thermostats broke after a few months. But now he knew how to solder wires together and build digital hardware out of parts. As for the horse blanket, when he mentioned it offhand to a surgeon at work, she immediately requested a prototype to use in the beds of patients at risk for bed sores. He didn't do these things to be successful, but success came anyway.

Nicholas encouraged me to do what made me happy. But more than that, he demonstrated the good that could come from taking reasonable risks, following curiosity, and allowing projects with uncertain outcomes consume him for a bit. Unlike him, I couldn't figure out how to create that space at my job. So I decided to take the leap. I jumped into the void.

When my sabbatical was nearing its end, I gave my two weeks' notice. I made a plan with the head of strategy to come back into the office the following week to collect my things, return my laptop, and say goodbye. But despite that plan, I never set foot in that office again. There were no hugs, no last conversations, no reminiscent happy hour drinks. I never collected my things, and when I did ship back my laptop a few weeks later, it got lost in the mail because there was no one around to receive it. The day of my planned farewell was the day the office shut down for the COVID-19 pandemic.

· · ·

We rely on many types of ladders to provide our motivation, purpose, and sense of accomplishment. No matter what institution you hold on high, there's a set of steps you're to follow to succeed. In education, you follow the steps that take you from elementary school to college. In sports, you follow the steps that take you from local meets to the Olympics. Our religions define paths to enlightenment and salvation. Our culture reveres a domestic journey that the nonmonogamy community refers to as "the relationship escalator": first comes love, then comes marriage, then comes baby in the baby carriage. Then there's the American dream, a vague but well-marketed route for upward mobility and increasing material wealth.

These systems, ladders, and escalators are so effective, so pervasive, and so woven into our culture that it's hard to question them. They can feel as essential and undeniable as oxygen and sleep. And for many people, they serve their purpose as a framework for how to live. We find happiness and meaning in walking that particular path to that particular version of success. My Olympic dreams brought structure to my days and guided my growth in directions I'm immensely proud of.

But all too often, we adopt the institutional definition of success as our human reason for being. Just because businesses need to make money doesn't mean that making money should be a personal benchmark for a life well lived. Just because schools give grades doesn't mean that an A determines your value as a human. By committing this fallacy, we can break ourselves optimizing for the wrong metrics and still end up dissatisfied, whether we "succeeded" or not. For many of Shelby's clients, the end goal of monogamous marriage led to a lot of cheating and dissatisfaction. For Obhāsī, it was demoralizing to reach graduation without scratching the surface of what he really wanted to learn. For David, putting the podium on a pedestal made it hard to see the good in his fourth-place finish. While I was clinging to the career ladder, I was missing out on the greater satisfaction of writing this book.

We spend a lot of our lives asking the question, "How can I be successful?" In other words: "What will set me up for the next promotion?" "What will it take to get this person to marry me?" "How can I improve my diving enough to win an Olympic medal?" I think we should spend an equal amount of energy asking, "What does success even look like?"

A quick look back through five thousand years of recorded human history reveals how many different ways we've attempted to define a successful life. Should we devote our days to learning what to do (as Socrates argued), or do we also have to do it (as Aristotle argued)? Is life about being equally good to everyone (Mozi) or attributing special respect to your people (Confucius)? Is it up to individuals to create their own purpose (Camus, Nietzsche, Sartre), or is our purpose preordained by a higher power (much of Western religion)?

Humanity seems to nail some questions once and move on. My old co-worker Sam keeps a running list of "finalized" objects throughout antiquity, like the fork, which was invented millennia ago and hasn't evolved much since. How to get food to our mouths—check. But other questions, we keep asking, all over the world, whether our lives are roaring or flickering on their last ember, whether we're fighting to meet our most basic human needs or perched reflectively atop Maslow's pyramid.

· · ·

When I started orienting my interviews around learning what success meant for people, I started realizing how much those ambitions can vary from human to human, both personally and professionally.

Way back in 2012, in the depths of my post-Olympic murk, I was taking my daily doomscroll through social media when I stopped on a post by Jason, a former Stanford gymnast a few years younger than me. He'd founded a company, Ridejoy, a carpooling app that was apparently on the verge of unfathomable success. He'd posted a *Vanity Fair* spread entitled, "Who Wants to Be a Billionaire?" in which he and his cofounders hung out of the windows and front trunk of a Tesla Model S alongside the leaders of a prestigious tech incubator called Y Combinator. Jason and his cofounders had raised $1.3 million and appeared to be the next Silicon Valley wunderkinds. At the time, it reinforced my angst: While

I'd been wiling away the hours at the pool, my peers had been doing *work*. Jason had reached the big time in his career, and I hadn't even started.

Ten years later, another Jason post caught my eye. It was the same *Vanity Fair* photo, now with a different caption: "The highest and lowest moments of my first start-up venture were barely a month apart. . . ." Turns out that right after the *Vanity Fair* article, Jason and his friends had shut the company down and returned all the seed money they had left, nearly $600,000, to their investors. I wondered what Jason's experience with failure had taught him about success and reached out to see if he'd be up for an interview.

As soon as Jason joined the Zoom, life started moving at 1.25-times speed, so fast that afterward I had to play the conversation back in slow-mo to pick everything up. Jason has twenty-one listed jobs on his LinkedIn profile, writes two or three blog posts a week on entrepreneurship, has self-published three books, and is gearing up to write a fourth. His TED Talk on job hunting from a few years ago has nearly five million views. In 2015, he launched the Asian American Man Study, an annual survey to help researchers better understand his cohort. He holds two different Guinness World Records for completing pathological numbers of obscure variations on burpees. His appearance supports the notion that he may well be the most interesting man in the world—his hair cascades long past his shoulders, which are muscular enough to bust the seams on any size off-the-rack button-down. He has branded himself "The Outlier Coach," and his current business is coaching other founders to success.

Jason's not shy about sharing the bad ideas he's had. He regaled me with start-up concepts that didn't make it past the pitch and fledgling companies that rose and fell with the seasons. When he and his friends were in their early twenties, they submitted a pitch to Y Combinator for an app that would resurface articles or posts you'd previously liked. The incubator's leadership hated the idea but invited them for a ten-minute in-person session, where they all brainstormed a new idea on the spot: a program that organized sets of digital photos. Nobody really liked that one either, but Y Combinator accepted them anyway, offering them $20,000 for 7 percent of whatever company they ended up forming, which ended up being Ridejoy. Jason later learned that he and his team had been chosen because they were "super enthusiastic."

A few years after Ridejoy stalled, Jason cofounded a start-up that enabled employers to test a candidate's technical skills. But their technology wasn't gaining traction, so they scrapped everything and launched an esports voice assistant bot. A few years later, the esports business was acquired by Facebook, netting Jason a decent amount of money and a cushy new job developing internal productivity tools. Thus ends this story of start-up success. Not a straight road to epic fortune, but a wild scrabble to moderate financial gain.

I found Jason's story exciting because it flew in the face of so many of the unspoken tenets of success: not just what it is, but how to get there. Back when I'd first registered Jason's start-up career, I'd assumed he succeeded because he'd had a clear goal and managed to squish a decade's worth of discipline into a few years of post-college start-up building. But I'd learned the wrong lesson. He'd succeeded because he would set a moderate bar, work hard for it, recognize if the idea seemed unlikely to reach that bar, and quit without delay. He didn't start Google, Instagram, or Amazon. The website domains for the companies he started went up for sale long ago, and the signboards on their offices have been replaced by several generations of venture-backed start-uplings. Yet he made money and gained the experience that serves him in his current career as start-up coach. It was a different type of success—not a zenith in the sky, but a dot on a journey that keeps moving in the direction of his true goal: a life of personal discovery.

"I don't really fear change," he said. "What I fear more is repetition and boredom." After spending so much time in my own head, wringing my hands about the risks of change and the potential consequences of failure, it was refreshing to hear from someone whose brain worked differently. "Whenever I'm like, 'Oh, I know exactly how this is gonna go,' I'm just not motivated," he said. "If it's unpredictable, it means that there's a chance for me to shape it. If it's predictable, then even if you don't like it, you're stuck with it."

At diving meets, coaches used to perch in their folding chairs and argue with one another about whether athletes were more motivated by loving success or hating failure. Despite his athletic background, Jason seemed to live beyond that binary. A successful life wasn't really about winning, and it wasn't really about not losing. It was about choosing the right dreams at the right time to keep him engaged and excited about what he was learning. I thought of my conversation with Shelby, the relationship therapist, and all the things she worked on with her clients: getting comfy with the unknown, breathing into curiosity. Jason was a natural. Not being too precious about "Will it work?" or "Will it fail?" freed him up to approach opportunities and challenges with a totally different attitude: "Why not try?"

As a culture, the start-up world is built to support this not-too-precious approach. More than once, Jason was given money and support, not for having a solid company but for having optimism and panache. Serial entrepreneurs are accustomed to picking up an idea, working sleeplessly on it, and dropping it if the winds shift. Goals change with the markets; the path to success is utterly mutable. "Move fast and break things," Facebook's founding slogan, was a battle cry in its day, and it supported a culture in which people try new things.

I don't want to make it seem like start-up culture is some sort of utopia, because it's not. "Move fast and break things" has fallen out of favor now that yesterday's start-ups are the primary channels for our social and civic lives, and breaking things risks "ripping apart the social fabric of society," as ex-Facebook employee Chamath Palihapitiya put it. Also, the downside of funding based on fuzzy qualities like "enthusiasm" is that there's no check on ingrained biases. According to the global capital research firm PitchBook, start-ups founded solely by women received only 2.1 percent of US venture capital in 2023.[1] And it isn't just because fewer women pitch (which is true) or they have worse ideas (which is ridiculous). In one experiment, researchers created two recordings of the same pitch, with one voiced by a man and the other voiced by a woman. Listeners were more than twice as likely to back the male recording, deeming it more persuasive, more fact-based, and more logical.[2]

Start-up culture is far from perfect. But there are aspects to it that I wish we could bring into our lives. How much more would we try if all of our bosses celebrated failure at the outset? How much more could we learn if we truly felt the freedom to go after our personal best state—whether that's to feel alive, nourished, curious, or authentically proud—rather than whatever goal our culture has placed on whatever ladder?

• • •

For many of the world class competitors I spoke with, the biggest transition was about retiring from being an elite athlete. Jimmy's was about becoming one.

He was diagnosed with Parkinson's disease at twenty-seven—the same age I retired from diving. Parkinson's is a progressive neurological condition that affects the brain and causes problems with movement, mental health, and sleep. Symptoms generally show up when patients are over sixty and progress slowly. Over time, they intensify to include tremors, painful muscle contractions, difficulty speaking, slow movement, involuntary movement, rigidity, trouble walking, imbalance, and cognitive impairment. "I was told, within fifteen years of my diagnosis, I was going to be relying on my family for everything," said Jimmy. By the time he was forty or forty-five, he should expect to be using a wheelchair, unable to work, with his wife taking care of his daily needs.

Jimmy is about as goal oriented as it gets. His appetite for hard work was ingrained early. His family moved from Taiwan to the US when he was ten. When he got off the plane in Chicago, the only English words he knew were *apple*, because every English book starts with "A is for apple," and *soap*, because he and his brothers had been so bored on the seventeen-hour flight that they stole the soap from the bathrooms and got yelled at by the flight attendants. For the next few years, he spent every summer in language school to learn English, plus phonetic school to learn to speak it without a Mandarin accent. "I learned to be patient, that you can't become good at things overnight. You break things down into smaller goalposts, so to speak, and then move your way through," he said, echoing David's approach to elite rowing.

Jimmy had already set an ambitious career goal: become the chief technology officer of a company by age forty-five. But his diagnosis at twenty-seven caused him to double down, quickly and absolutely. All the other markers of a successful life—how he wanted to raise his family and interact with his kids, for example—disappeared. His only goal was to make enough money to provide for his family's future, then retire at forty-five to a life of inevitable decline.

"The only thing on my mind was to work, work, work, work, work," he said. He organized his life around this goal in a way I related to deeply, but the urgency of his diagnosis caused him to cling to the ladder far more intensely than I did. "I put everything else onto the back burner. Everything except to get that next bonus, to get the next promotion, to find the next client," he said.

Jimmy believed his prognosis was immutable, meaning his health was one of the things on the back burner. He took the drugs the doctor had prescribed, but beyond that, he ignored his diagnosis, so much so that he didn't even tell his wife about it for three months. He didn't do any research, didn't look for ways to slow the progression of the disease, didn't seek out communities or support groups or therapy. Instead, he sat at a desk in front of a computer and flew from city to city working as a consultant, making himself, in his words, "as billable as possible."

Like Toya, the lawyer turned life coach, Jimmy felt immense pressure to hide signs that he wasn't okay. And like Toya, it had tragic repercussions on his mental health. For eight years no one at work knew about his diagnosis, much less the ways it was starting to affect him. "I didn't want them to think, 'Oh, this person is diseased. So I shouldn't work with this person,'" he said. He sat on his hands to keep them from trembling and made up reasons to stay home instead of attending meetings in the office. He also kept it a secret from friends and family, which meant he stopped going to social events. When his kids were born, he shut them out too, refusing to play with them because he was too tired, and on a deeper level, too ashamed that he couldn't move the way he wanted to. "I became angry at the way my body was moving. I became angry at myself for the way I was feeling. I became irritated at every little thing that my family was doing," he said. Unfairness fomented his discontent: This was an old person's illness. It wasn't supposed to attack people like him. With this fatalistic approach, the disease took its course. Within eight years he gained ninety pounds and couldn't walk without a cane.

When Jimmy was thirty-five he attempted to traverse a staircase while holding his ten-month-old son. His leg didn't cooperate, he lost his grip on the handrail, and he and his son tumbled down ten stairs. He managed to twist his body so his son landed on top of him, and both were unhurt. But his wife and toddler daughter witnessed the whole thing. As he was trying to get back on his feet, he looked directly into his daughter's eyes and realized the thing he'd expected wouldn't happen for another five years was already happening. He was becoming a burden to his family and a safety liability to his kids. His illness had progressed to the point that he couldn't hide it, even from his two-year-old. The plan he'd had of chasing financial success at all costs wasn't working. "I could do two things," he said. "I could continue the path I was on and continue to put the burden on my wife and be a danger to my family, or I could, at least at a minimum, try to make some changes."

But what could he do? He'd spent the past eight years stoking his de-nial. At the time of his diagnosis, he had torpedoed through the murk so quickly and so blindly that he'd left uncertainty in the dust. Now it caught up with him. "What's next?" he said. "You just fell down the stairs. You're 250 pounds. You still need a cane to walk. What can you do?"

For the first time, he opened that pamphlet that the doctor had given him at his diagnosis. He started searching online. After wading past an abundance of predatory supplement companies offering cures, he saw that there were a lot of clinical trials in the works for his disease. He piv-oted his formidable work ethic toward gaining access to this leading-edge research, signing up for every clinical trial he could find, sometimes flying to different cities for different treatments. One of them, a "forced exercise" study, involved manipulating his limbs and engaging his mus-cles every other week. The day after his first session he was utterly de-pleted, but the day after that, he moved with a little more fluidity than he had before. He decided to start exercising more often.

What follows is the kind of story that shows how day-to-day choices be-come legend; the kind of story that makes you believe in miracles. He started walking around the block with his cane, then found that he didn't need the cane anymore. He walked, then ran, longer and longer dis-tances. Two years after his first forced exercise session, he completed his first 5K, a proud feat given he'd never run more than a mile before his diagnosis. Six months later he ran his first marathon, and over the next decade, he ran fifteen more. He began using his marathons to raise money for the Michael J. Fox Foundation to support Parkinson's research, which meant going public with his diagnosis. Now that his friends and family knew, he no longer had to hide from them. As his health improved, so did his mood. He wasn't angry all the time; he started playing with his kids. He also realized—if running was good, wouldn't a more full-body workout be better? He started parkour training, eventually competing on the obstacle course game show *American Ninja Warrior* five times. And in between all the running, training, family time, and raising $800,000 and counting for Parkinson's research, he still found time to become a chief technology officer by age forty-four.

All this became possible when Jimmy changed his definition of success from a sole focus on financial security to a broader goal to live better, longer. Denial and acceptance are at opposite ends of the Kübler-Ross stages of grief, but Jimmy's story illustrates how muddy the waters can get. Jimmy in his workaholic era might have said, "I've accepted my diagnosis and I'm doing what it takes to set my family up for the future." But in hindsight, he sees it differently. "I was hiding," he said. Acceptance predicated on not reading the pamphlet the doctor gives you is not really acceptance.

It would be nice to say Jimmy embraced his diagnosis, discovered exercise, reconnected with his people, and lived happily ever after. But there are no happily ever after stories in this book. Whether you achieve your success or you don't, you keep navigating life. If you're a climber, you reach one goal and keep climbing. Jimmy's lesson: You can climb multiple mountains at the same time.

In 2022, eighteen years after his diagnosis, Jimmy ran his final Ninja Warrior course. He competed alongside his thirteen-year-old daughter, the one who'd watched her father fall down the stairs holding her brother more than a decade before. In his farewell interview, he looked like one of the fittest forty-seven-year-olds I've ever seen: lean, muscled, smiling confidently, his shoulders straight, his gaze direct, and his body swaying slightly side to side. "Even though I'm strong and I'm fit, my window of movement on any given day is getting smaller and smaller," he said. The video cut to a closeup of Jimmy's trembling fingers struggling to do a set of shirt buttons. The small things that give him trouble are piling up: getting a credit card into a slot, getting the right number of his tiny pills out of the bottle. He bites his tongue almost every meal, can't hear out of his right ear, and lost his sense of smell years ago. And yet, he's a few months shy of fifty now and is in better shape than all but the strongest thirty-year-olds. Talking with Jimmy, you start to see the parallels between a devastating prognosis and plain old time.

He's run his last marathon, muscled through his final obstacle course. He's one of the most driven people I've ever met. I was curious what was next for Jimmy.

"You had your work era, your marathon era, your ninja era," I said. "What era are you in now?"

"My goal right now is just to get my kids off to school and get them the best start I can give them in life," he said. His daughter is fifteen and already being heavily recruited by collegiate softball programs; he had a lot of questions about my time at Stanford. His son would like to become a pilot someday. He wants to set them up for their own version of success.

Though he's done trying to beat Ninja Warrior courses, there's no choice about whether to keep working out or not. Intense exercise is holding back the tremors like a dam. When he got COVID in 2020 and stopped exercising for three weeks, his symptoms exploded. "What three weeks did to my body, it took almost a year to get it back," he said.

When he recovered from COVID, all the parkour gyms were still closed for the pandemic lockdown, so he started looking into what it would take to break a world record. He liked burpees as a way of falling and getting back up safely; he took that to the extreme and ended up earning two Guinness World Records, one for the most chest-to-ground burpees in one minute, and the other for most chest-to-ground plyometric lateral push-ups in one minute. (If this is sounding oddly familiar, this is because these are extremely similar exercises to Jason's world records in Aztec push-ups and burpee pull-ups. Jason and Jimmy hold the unique distinction of being adjacent in both the Guinness Book of World Records and the book you're reading.)

"I always joke with the kids, once you guys are off to college, then I can just sit in my corner and just kind of whittle away," he said, with a smile. Then he shook his head. "But they know that I'll find something to keep me busy."

But it's hard. It's hard for the Olympic athletes I've interviewed. It's hard for my parents. It's hard for anyone I've spoken to about aging, injury, or illness. It's hard to know that doors are closing, that you are not physically capable in the same way you used to be. "I don't know what I'm doing next. My training, my daily routine in the gym, is all over the place. There's no consistency because there's no plan," he said. "But it's as important as eating and breathing for me. So I have to do it." I sensed a moment of fear then, but he immediately circled back to optimism. "Life is always going to throw obstacles at you. There's usually a way around them that everybody takes and everybody knows. But when you're unable to take that, if you're willing to invest the time in finding what that new route is around this obstacle, then it can be done." It might have sounded trite, a bright Band-Aid on an age-old fear, except that I know he's living those words. He's practiced the skill of finding his own way around obstacles as intensively as any dive or feat of strength. He's faced uncertainty in more than one transition and has inevitably found something to keep him going.

· · ·

Jimmy's story illustrates how important redefining success can be in guiding you through a life worth living. But there's actually no wrong time to shift your perspective. Reevaluating your transition mid-stream, or after the fact, can change how you see yourself in a way that's just as impactful.

Back when I interviewed Stanley about his time behind bars, he described a powerful set of conversations he'd had with a psychologist. When he was forty years old and had been in prison for fifteen years, he was denied parole for the second time. He had allowed himself to hope they'd find him suitable for release, and when the verdict came back that he'd have to remain in prison indefinitely, he sunk to his lowest. "I didn't know when I was gonna get out," he said. "I had no wife, had no kids, had no money." It wasn't just the prospect of a longer sentence, but the fact that by every measure in his mind, he was a failure.

No release date, no wife, no kids, no money were facts, and as long as he was in prison, there was no way to change them. Instead, the psychologist helped him question whether those things really were the *only* measures of a successful life.

Stanley started reflecting on what he had accomplished over the past fifteen years. He'd become active in the prison church and self-help groups. He'd faced the trauma of his past and learned to neutralize the anger that used to overtake him. As a group leader, he'd guided other prisoners to better understand themselves. "Even though I wasn't getting out at the time, I was able to help people who *were* getting out to get out with a better chance of succeeding," he said. "I started redefining success not by the things I had but more about the impact I had on peoples' lives, whether it was good or negative."

This effort to redefine success has had a lasting impact on his psyche, even years after his release. "Even now, I'm out, and people are like, 'When you gonna get married? You gonna have some kids?'" he said, laughing. "And I'm like, 'Do I need to get married? Do I need kids?'" He can laugh about it now, because he's done the work to be okay with himself regardless. "You have to be okay that you don't fit into the norm," he said.

. . .

Stanley's story about redefining success reminded me that I'd also redefined success for myself. Back at the London Olympics, immediately after my incomprehensibly bad last dive, I was shuffled toward a gauntlet of news writers. I'd worked for NBC in 2004, so I knew the drill. Tears get ratings. They were going to try to make me cry. The commentator that I'd helped with name pronunciations and crowd spotting eight years earlier made professionally sad eyes at me. She wanted my story to fit a TV formula: the thrill of the hunt, the agony of defeat. But I could not—would not—accept this narrative as story. So I smiled back at her. I would not cry. Then I moved on to the next reporter and did the same.

The last reporter in the row tried extra hard. "But aren't you even a little upset?" he asked. I talked about the joy of competing, the rush of the crowd, the fickleness of sports and how this was a moment I was lucky to have had. I was mortified when he later wrote about a tear I know I didn't shed until later:

> I had to ask upon watching that smile still there, still hard at work: How was she doing it?
>
> "I *am* sad," she finally conceded, a tear streaming down the right cheek and her lip trembling. "A little bit."[3]

His story was not my story. When I look back on my career, I am proud of the pursuit. I started out a terrified competitor with a tendency to get so frazzled that my muscles shook as I walked down the board. I became a steady performer, calm and elevated by the butterflies. I started out with strong legs and zero precision, hitting the water like a windshield wiper—sometimes vertical, sometimes horizontal. In the prelims, semifinals, and finals of Olympic Trials, and later in the prelims, semifinals, and finals of the Olympics, I missed one dive out of thirty. I hate that it was my last one. But I love that that dive was totally absent of fear.

Often, the only difference between success and failure is how you define success. Consider what really matters to you, what you've learned, how you've grown, and what's made you feel proud. Make sure, when you tell your story, that you're not devaluing those wins just because they're internal.

Tools for Redefining Success

The dreams society expects of you may not, in fact, be yours. In that case, design your own. Failure's not an end, and success is not an end-all-be-all. Look beyond the status quo binaries, ladders, and mandates and set goals that make you feel alive.

How to Find Success in Failure

Tell Your Story: Curate a Wall of Fame and Fail

In an ideal world, we'd all be a lot quicker to celebrate the small stuff, both good ("I did it!") and bad ("I learned!"). Instead, we often ignore small successful steps and beat ourselves up for small unsuccessful steps. That's why I recommend making your own Wall of Fame and Fail. Set aside thirty minutes at the end of each week to write down one success you've had and one mistake you've made. Give yourself a pat on the back for each. Each small success—and small mistake—is a step toward your goals.

How to Reframe Failure

Fix It in Post

No matter how much you try to desensitize yourself to failure, it can still stick with you. Particularly if it had lasting or permanent consequences. You can't undo a bad decision or a painful moment, but you can reevaluate what it means and how much it matters. When you're hit by shame or disappointment, reflect on the following:

- Failure is a thing that happened, not a part of my identity.

- Failure is an opportunity to learn, not a dead end.

- Failure is not more valid, more impactful, or more definitive than success.

- What have I done that I'm genuinely proud of?

How to Open Your Eyes to Other Definitions

Ask the Question

One of the cool things we did in my agency job was start every project by asking, "What does success look like for your company . . . for this project . . . for your career . . . for you, personally?" Occasionally, people from the same company would align on some of the answers, but never all four. It was *personally* exciting to see how far-ranging everyone's definitions were (although it caused me work trouble when leaders disagreed). If you want to see this for yourself, ask the people around you: your coworkers, your fellow niche hobbyists, your spouse, your kids. Not only will it open your eyes to all the flavors in the world; it will help you better support them in reaching their own goals.

How to Make Your Success More Real than the Ladder

Shout the Answer

At first, it was hard to come out and say, "I have this idea and I don't know where it's going to go but I want to write a book about transitions." But the more I said it, the more real it became. People introduced me to friends and family members with interesting stories and gave me podcasts to listen to and books to read and documentaries to watch. My sabbatical was the tipping point, not just because I had created time to write, but because I had shouted my goal out loud and gone out on a limb for it. Say your dreams out loud. It will make you accountable and inspire others to support you in very real ways.

Don't Forget

Don't Skip the Murk

Try things. Learn things. Sit with tough emotions. Seek education and advice and therapy. Don't hitch your wagon to the first definition of success that comes along and roll with it for the next eight years. Tune your peripheral vision to pick up opportunities and be ready to redirect to different goals.

9.

Build Your World

Living outside the status quo isn't easy. What happens after we've made the choice to leave the stability and assuredness of society's norms? How do we design a more authentic life?

Within a few weeks of lockdown, all my family members—my parents, my brother, Nicholas, and I—were hunkered down at my childhood home in the suburbs of Pittsburgh. I had pictured myself jetting around the country, visiting Olympians, having deep conversations over bottles of wine. Instead, I hosted Zoom calls from my old bedroom, sheepishly explaining posters on the wall I'd put up as a child. My writing didn't stall, but it certainly slowed.

The world was fighting a war against an enemy no one imagined. We were afraid for our friends, afraid to go to the grocery store, afraid for our neighborhood back in New York where sirens blended into one another and makeshift morgues closed streets.

The silver lining was getting to spend more time with my family. My brother and I were both in our thirties. We could easily have gone the rest of our lives without spending more than a few days under the same roof with our parents. Now we were living a strange sitcom version of our high school days. Nicholas and I adopted Dad's favorite beverage—boxed wine, Cherry Pepsi, and a splash of tonic water—which we'd drink from Tervis tumblers over late-night card games of cribbage and oh hell. My brother, who came home later than the rest of us, quarantined in a hammock in the basement for his first two weeks, emerging to eat and pee when the coast was clear. We all took up disc golf, one of the few outings that seemed to follow social distancing protocols, driving out to a hilly course a half an hour away to throw things and tromp through the underbrush.

I had conversations with them that I never would have had otherwise. Two years before the pandemic, at age seventy, my dad had retired after thirty-eight years of coaching diving at the University of Pittsburgh. For the next year, he sat in his worn recliner, doing Kakuro puzzles, watching MSNBC, and thinking about getting older. He fixated on the time it took him to finish a puzzle and the number of figures he used to be able to hold in his head. He despaired at the news: an environment out of control, a president he couldn't comprehend, freedoms under attack, the divide between rich and poor growing larger. He sat in that chair for a year before, thank God, someone offered him another coaching position. During our time in Pittsburgh, he and my mom were preparing to sell the house and move out to California for his new gig. Despite the fear and frustration of lockdown, he was upbeat about his upcoming life transition.

I asked him over wine-and-Pepsi coolers what had changed. "You have got to have a purpose," he said, enunciating each word. Then he gave me the only book recommendation I've ever gotten from him, *Man's Search for Meaning* by Viktor Frankl. In his memoir, Frankl describes how his sense of purpose—his *why*—helped him survive the Holocaust. "A purpose can get you through anything," my dad said. "For my whole life, coaching has been my *why*. It was harder than I expected to find a new one."

My conversation with Dad was surprisingly similar to the conversations I'd been having with athletes. Many had experienced a comparable murky malaise after their own retirements. I wondered: What could Dad have learned from the people I was interviewing? What could they have learned from him? Up until that point, I'd been focused only on interviewing Olympians for my book. I realized then that I should be interviewing people from all walks of life, because transitions are universal. We all can learn from one another about how to navigate the big before-and-afters of our lives.

· · ·

As the world emerged from the pandemic, Nicholas and I left Pittsburgh and returned to a shaken New York City, battered by months of fear and death. The omnipresent sirens had slowed, the mobile morgues had emptied, and the tourists had started trickling back to Times Square. Many people had died. Many people had left. Many people who remained were coping with the acute psychological impact of months stuck in a tiny apartment afraid to go out, or months working on the front lines unable to stay in.

But witnessing New York after the peak of the pandemic was like witnessing a blade of grass forcing its way through a sidewalk crack. By late summer, the parks were full and music and conversation drifted in the streets. That summer, millions of protesters marched, chanting the names of Eric Garner, George Floyd, and others killed by police, in what *The New York Times* said "may be the largest movement in US history." There was a shared sense of responsibility to build a better world in which to live our tenuous lives.

One night in August, Nicholas took me on a meandering walk around Central Park, and finally, when dusk hit and the fireflies came out and my stomach was grumbling, he proposed. I said yes.

The circus school also reopened that summer. Over the years, I had become so immersed in trapeze that I not only practiced at the school—I also taught occasionally. Now I ramped up both teaching and training. We practiced outdoors, and though we were masked and seated in chairs spaced six feet apart, we felt immense gratitude to be able to resume something resembling a normal activity. Pandemic restrictions caused this particular community to blossom: so many activities were still on hold, so many jobs hadn't come back, so many outlets were still shut down that we doubled down on our dedication to our weird circus passions and our friendships with one another.

I'd been around sports my entire life, but I don't think I fully realized how important they were until the pandemic. One of the disciplines I taught at the circus school was trampoline, where I helped people to safely learn aerial awareness: how to control—and when to give up control—of their bodies as they hurtled through the air. My clientele were mostly women in their forties and fifties who had been cooped up in apartments, existing as disembodied heads on Zoom calls for half a year. I guided them through the steps of increasingly complex skills and watched them discover the same joy as I felt in physical repetition, in small notches of incremental progress. It echoed the lesson I'd learned from Jen, who saw boxing and weightlifting as critical forms of therapy. Humans are built to use our minds and bodies together, but our culture prioritizes mental over physical, living at a desk over living on our feet. What, other than sports, can make us feel so wholly human?

In my writing life, I was having deep, soul-affirming conversations, connecting dots between stories and weaving chapters out of them. Five months after beginning my sabbatical, I had finally connected with a literary agent who loved my writing and agreed to represent me, giving me the bump of professional validation I'd been craving. In my social life, I was investing in friendships in a way that I'd never done before and building a forever partnership with my best friend. In my acrobatic life, I was discovering how to learn and grow for myself, without a coach pushing and prodding me toward success. I had figured out how to follow my creative dreams and sate my athlete soul, with time left for the people who made life worth living.

There was just one problem. I was nearly out of money.

I needed to start making money again—a few hours a week teaching at the circus school wasn't making a dent in my expenses, and working with a literary agent was no guarantee that I'd ever make a dime from my writing.

It had felt like a major accomplishment to land an agent, and it was. Harry Bingham, founder of the writer support organization Jericho Writers, estimates that the typical agent receives about two thousand submissions a year from new writers and accepts two or three of them.[1] That might be too rosy—an agent/friend told me she receives closer to three thousand submissions a year and some years accepts only one. But getting an agent on board still doesn't mean the book will sell. Bingham estimates that a "good agent at a top-class agency" might sell two of every three books they pitch to publishing houses.

My own agent had shared a lot of constructive notes and edits, which prompted several rounds of revisions to my proposal. My savings ran out before we'd finalized it, and before she'd sent it to a single publisher.

I *wanted* to keep writing my book, whether or not some publisher eventually found it worthy. But I didn't know how I'd do both: write a book and work. I had a mental model for workaholic: how to cut back my relationship, my hobbies, and my social life to make sure my number one thing was number one. I was afraid that the moment I started working again, work would become number one again and I'd allow everything else to slide. What if I found myself looking up from my work again in seven more years, maybe from a higher rung of the corporate ladder, with an even starker view of everything I'd left behind?

. . .

Around this time, a freelance advertising opportunity came my way. I hemmed and hawed over whether to take it. As usual, Aunt Patty guided me in the right direction. "You know . . ." she said, in the practiced way of someone who knows the right answer but appears to help you come to it on your own. "You probably have enough experience to be able to do the job in fewer hours than most." This hadn't occurred to me.

I calculated and recalculated my budget, envisioning the pros and cons of less travel, less takeout, and—the real crux—less self-reliance. I'd been paying my own bills since I left Stanford, and when Nicholas and I first moved in together, I'd made a big deal about paying exactly half. I had grown up in the years of Sheryl Sandberg's *Lean In*, and it felt antithetical to my own ideas about independence to willingly earn less than my partner. But Nicholas encouraged me to chase my dream, and the fact was that we could live comfortably even if I was earning less money. Nicholas's support offered me the opportunity to build the life I wanted for myself and I (gratefully) took it.

With a good deal of trepidation, I negotiated my terms: twenty-five hours a week, max. Somehow, negotiating was more nerve-racking than just saying no. But I did, and they accepted—another win in the "asking for what I need" category. As a full-time employee, I had been overly generous with my time, but now I became anal-retentive about tracking my hours down to the minute. "They're going to fire me," I'd moan to Nicholas every time I hit a hiccup or chose to save something for tomorrow rather than trying to fix it on the spot. But they didn't. I did good work; I got a good paycheck. It was amazing how freeing it was to release the idea that I needed to constantly keep pushing for more responsibility and a bigger title.

This freelance job certainly wasn't a world-encompassing passion, but I enjoyed it, and as a slice of pie, it went down well. I worked, with time to write and do trapeze and teach for the circus school and overindulge in TV shows every once in a while and plan my wedding. I built an à la carte life, focused on many passions and activities, not one monolithic goal.

Some things were harder. As a more-than-full-time worker, I'd taken a lot for granted. Money came in and money went out. I was all set with insurance, vacation time, a 401(k), and more broadly, on the size and slices of my pie: I worked, and worked, and worked, and jammed in trapeze and boyfriend time when it fit. As a part-time freelancer, I felt pangs of inadequacy when I saw peers rise on the career ladder I'd left. I didn't earn as much money as I would have keeping my nose to the grindstone. I missed the thrill of guiding clients toward bigger, better swings, but did not miss the stress of being constantly in pitch mode. If there was an area of my work where I devoted extra energy, it was in mentorship. I was a sucker for overworked, underconfident, stressed-out juniors. I wanted to show them that there was another way to live.

. . .

There's a constant hum in the background of our staunchly capitalist, increasingly individualistic society: *more is better.* More work, more experiences, more things, more followers, more technology, more advancement, more power, more growth. But in the process of reimagining my life, not as a single ladder, but as an à la carte set of choices, I stopped asking, "How can I make more?" and started asking, "What is enough?"

It bears emphasizing that this is a privileged question to be able to ask oneself. Below a certain income, the answer is more about math: What does it take to cover basic needs and provide basic levels of security? But as income rises, the answer is more about personal values: How much do you value comfort, security, and financial freedom, and what does it take for you, personally, to feel comfortable, secure, and free? How much does it take for you to live your own version of the American dream? Which Joneses are you trying to keep up with?

I'm one of many who have opted out of the traditional full-time workforce post-pandemic. There were nearly half a million more Americans incorporated as "self-employed" in 2023 than there were in 2019.[2] Between 2019 and 2023, part-time jobs also increased and the average work week got shorter, particularly for workers with higher incomes, according to analysis of thirteen million jobs by payroll service ADP.[3] Culturally, the phrase "quiet quitting," had a major social media moment in 2022, when thousands of employees lit their ring lights and addressed their TikTok audiences to share (from one point of view) their decision to assert healthy boundaries around corporations that didn't have their backs and (from another) their infuriating refusal to do anything beyond the bare minimum at work.

Anecdotally, I've spoken to a number of professionals finding more fulfillment in à la carte lives: an OB-GYN who drastically limits her patients so she can have more control over her schedule, a supply chain manager who switched to consulting so he could spend more time with his daughter, a Broadway stagehand who said no to a coveted full-time job so he could avoid the burnout and high divorce rate that plagues his evenings-and-weekends industry. It takes effort, planning, and a salary significantly above minimum wage to build a life more evenly divided among its pieces. But for me, it's been worth it.

Going freelance in the hopes of living a more balanced life is not exactly radical. But it did force me to think critically about my time, money, responsibilities, and ambitions, explain those choices to others who didn't necessarily understand them, and advocate for myself in situations like job negotiations. Making choices that ran against the current caused friction, both within myself and in my interactions with the external world.

If you want to opt out of the status quo, then you will need to do some building on your own. This applies just as much to social ladders (relationships, kids, and building a "successful" family life) as it does to career ladders, as illustrated by my friend Katrina's unique path to motherhood.

. . .

Katrina has spent most of her life rocketing up various ladders to success. She was a soccer player at Penn, powered straight from college to Wall Street investment banking, attended business school, and spent sixteen years working her way up the chain of command at the company that sells Planters Peanuts and RITZ Crackers. Along the way, her ambition spilled out into other hobbies: choreographing the Kellogg School of Management student musical, skiing, climbing, hiking, and trapeze. She's compassionate, fun, reliable, and a little intimidating. All this makes her a surprising poster child for life off the ladder. But sometimes, building a world outside of the status quo is the result of careful consideration. And sometimes life tosses a boulder and you leap out of the way to somewhere surprising.

For Katrina, kids weren't a consideration until they were. As an athlete, her body wasn't something she wanted to mess with. As a workaholic, her career came first. A doctor once asked if she wanted to start a family and she said, "When I'm running out of time, I will make the decision." True to her word, she didn't start thinking about having children until her early forties, right around the time her relationship with her husband hit the rocks. Their marriage ended, and before the smoke had cleared, she knew one thing: She *really* wanted to have a baby.

What's an ambitious unpartnered woman in her forties to do? Her first instinct was to get pregnant on her own. She attempted several cycles of IUI, a process that boosts your chances by placing specially prepared sperm directly into the uterus. But her body didn't cooperate. Then, the pandemic hit pause.

In May of 2020, just as the world was starting to think about reopening, she met a man—let's call him Thomas—on one of the dating apps. They had great conversations. He shared her love for skiing, hiking, and working out, and more importantly, he shared her perspectives on the value of family, self-improvement, and career ambition. Six months later, she met Thomas's six-year-old daughter and eight-year-old son. She approached cautiously. "Show up for a few hours, do something fun with them, and then leave," recommended her therapist, and that's what she did, coming over occasionally to bake cookies or play soccer in the park. She was good with kids, already lovingly referred to as "Super Auntie" by both of her siblings and many of her closest friends. She built their trust, demonstrating that she could listen, have fun, admit mistakes, and show up for them. She didn't start spending the night with Thomas until they were sure both kids were excited about her, a full year into the relationship. By that time, she had fallen in love with them, just as much as she had with Thomas.

Katrina thrives on definition. But it was a hell of a thing trying to define her relationship with those kids. In the fairy tale canon, stepmothers are the only group more maligned than quitters. Also, that word simply didn't describe the relationship. "The kids have two parents . . . and I'm not their parent . . ." she said, stopping after each step in the logic sequence like she was telling a riddle. "We have not gotten married . . . but all of a sudden they have a third adult who loves them and cares about them . . . and is responsible for them . . .

". . . and that's how I became a bonus mom." She erupted in a goofy grin, like a toddler sharing a prized scribble. "Isn't that awesome?" It was clear how deeply Katrina cared about these children and also how tickled she was to have found a label for this part of her identity. Katrina first heard it on a podcast with soccer star Abby Wambach, who calls herself Bonus Mom to her partner's three kids. Katrina cried the first time she heard Abby describe their blended family. Finally, someone else had put into words what she had been struggling to articulate.

Just because becoming a bonus mom was awesome, doesn't mean it was easy. A few months after she first slept at Thomas's house, Thomas needed to go on his first overnight work trip since the start of the pandemic. He had planned for a family member to stay with the kids, but when the family member refused to get vaccinated, Katrina offered to watch them. Katrina was thrust into the role of twenty-four-hour care-giver, first for a night, then two nights, and eventually, for weeks at a time. She wore different hats on different days. Sometimes, she lived alone in her own condo. Some days, Thomas handled all the childcare and she just got to be Dad's girlfriend. And some days, she was primary parent, rolling one kid out of bed, getting him dressed, making him breakfast, schlepping him to middle school, and coming back to repeat the process for the elementary schooler.

It's a big transition, going from single to partnered and at the same time, going from child-free to Bonus Mom of two. Katrina found man-aging a portfolio of million-dollar snack brands was nothing compared to managing calendars for two children. "It was really hard for me," she said. "I couldn't remember, and then he'd get frustrated with me that I couldn't remember. We had to have a Google Doc with all these col-umns: Where's Katrina? Where are the kids? Where's the cat?"

It was also challenging to play the role of parent without being a deci-sion maker. Whenever Thomas was away on business, Katrina spent an hour and a half each morning driving the kids around because Thomas had made the choice to live out of bussing range. "Maybe if we're mar-ried or decide to buy a house together, I have a leg to stand on," she said. "But until then, I have no way to influence it or change it."

And then there are the institutional challenges. At one point, Katrina took a kid to the dentist. The kid unexpectedly needed X-rays, so Ka-trina texted Thomas, then his ex-wife, trying to find someone to tell her whether to do them or not. Finally, the ex-wife texted written approval. Only then did the receptionist inform Katrina that a parent needed to be present. Meanwhile, the kid was getting anxious because he'd been in the dentist's office for ages and his bonus mom was having frantic conversa-tions with his parents and doctors. When all was said and done, Thomas was dumbfounded that she hadn't just forgone the X-rays in the first place. "But I've never taken a kid to the dentist before," she said. "I can't be thinking ahead and asking the questions, because I don't know what the situation is going to be. How am I supposed to know?"

The lack of relatable parental role models has made a substantial contribution to these difficulties. The standard templates for motherhood weren't built for someone who meets her children as half-grown kids, for someone whose relationship and responsibilities don't check any of the standard guardianship boxes. Not that traditional parenting isn't hard, but when you're playing the role of "mother" or "father" there are billions of cultural models to identify with, commiserate with, laugh with, cry with, and help you understand and become the kind of parent you want to be. The same cannot be said for stepparents, bonus moms, blended families, foster families, and all types of alternative structures. "In my family, there are no good examples of this," she said.

It's a lot of pressure to put on a fledgling relationship. Three years after she and Thomas started dating, Katrina asked for a break. "The stuff in the 'us' bucket was good. The stuff in the 'kids' bucket was good too. All the issues that he and I had came out of the 'us with the kids' bucket," she said. She assumed that taking a break meant not getting to see his children and was devastated about it. But then he surprised her by asking her to remain in their lives. Most of her friends thought this was a terrible idea. "They were like, 'He's trying to use the kids as a hook to keep you around,'" she said. But one friend shared a story about how she'd broken up with a long-term partner but maintained a loving relationship with his adult children. It wasn't the same, but it was close enough to give Katrina hope. After a couple months of separation, she went over to Thomas's house for dinner, toting along half a cake she'd made. It was a lovely evening.

They started dating again. But this time, instead of focusing on climbing the rungs of the traditional relationship ladder—moving in together, getting married, etc.—they've decided to step off the ladder and just take it day by day. Katrina has been surprised to find she's actually pretty okay with that. Now in her late forties, she's given up on the idea of biological children. As a result, the pressure she used to feel to move the relationship "forward" has dissipated. "We're not all the way in it, but we're not all the way out of it," she said. "And that's okay." I commented on how much of a relief it seemed to be, to have given up on that particular view of success, and she nodded. "Maybe we'll do the work and decide to commit more deeply," she said. "But if we spend another couple of years together and it doesn't work out, I'm not gonna feel like I wasted [this time]. Whereas previously, there had to be this end in sight."

The kids are ten and twelve now and it's a version of the good life she never would have imagined for herself. The four have traveled together a couple of times during this new evolution in their family relationship and the kids fight over who gets to sit with Katrina. They confide in her when something goes down at school or their dad does something annoying or they can't get their hair to look right under the ski helmet. "It's given me a different kind of empathy, being responsible for little humans who I didn't fully raise but I came into their life and had a role in helping to shape them," she said.

I learned two things from my conversation with Katrina. First, the value of forging a different kind of family. Katrina did not have to follow the whole dating-to-marriage-to-kids trajectory in order to be happy. In fact, getting to help raise two full-fledged children for the past few years has been one of the most rewarding things she's done. Similarly, letting go of rigid expectations for how a relationship should progress has enabled her to appreciate her current relationship with Thomas without stressing about whether to make a lifelong commitment. The ladder comes with an incredible amount of pressure, and it doesn't need to be that way. It is a construction, and you can deconstruct it. You can take what you need from it, leave what you don't, and build your own world.

I also noticed that a lot of the stress of building Katrina's bonus mom world came from practicing a lifestyle that was uncommon. If there were more Abby Wambachs in the world ranting on podcasts about how all of a sudden, you acquire three kids and everyone is stealing your stuff and trying to climb you all the time, Katrina would have felt less alone. If she had a community of friends navigating the strange power imbalance of coraising a partner's children, maybe she would have felt more prepared. If more people were parenting in nontraditional ways, maybe the dentist would have known how to gracefully handle a caregiver who wasn't Mom or Dad. In that way, simply by living authentically and opening her heart to a possibility outside of traditional expectations, she is part of the solution for other bonus moms like her.

In her book *Quit*, Annie Duke writes about the dangers of telling only one type of story. Who cares if the stories we read are all about grit rather than quit, or if they all show just one type of family? We all should. Stories show us what's possible for ourselves.

. . .

For Katrina, being a bonus mom has been hard, but mostly it's been the good kind of hard. I am reminded of one of Rick's Sports Psychology 101 slides: "Stress occurs when there is a substantial imbalance between the physical and psychological demands placed on an individual and the person's ability to respond under conditions in which failure has important consequences." For Katrina, there was some stress, but for the most part she had the tools necessary to respond. When she met Thomas and his kids, she already had a ton of experience as an aunt, plus four decades of navigating the complexities of human relationships more broadly. She entered into being a bonus mom together with a partner whom she respected and who was motivated to sort through the difficulties with her. There was some stigma around what she was doing, some cultural beliefs about kids needing rock-solid adult relationships in their lives, but most of her friends and family got it when she explained it to them. She had Abby Wambach to help her conceive what a bonus mom was and what it was like to be one.

That point led me to wonder—what does it feel like to build your world in a way that's further from the beaten path than freelancing or bonus momming? What do you do when fate puts you in a situation that people respond to not with mild misunderstanding but with vitriol and hate?

. . .

Daya is a sixty-year-old actress with a warm, midwestern matriarch vibe. She looks a bit like Meryl Streep and speaks with the unmistakable vocal range of a thespian. "I'm, like, musical theater corny," she told me. "Very optimistic about life." Her optimism is impressive, given the amount of pain it's taken just to exist in the world as herself.

Daya was born in 1963 in the town of Eastpointe, Michigan, a Detroit suburb she describes as having a cloying pride in being "the picture of what a typical American family town should be." As far back as age three or four, she sensed she was different, and so did the other kids, who bullied her. "I always knew that there was a feminine desire in me, but I didn't really have any words for it," she said. When she was twelve, she saw an episode of the TV series *Medical Center* in which the dad from *The Brady Bunch* played a trans doctor. "I kind of knew in my heart of hearts that that's what I wanted to be," she said. "But I was just as convinced that it could never happen." She came out as gay at age fifteen—which was, in itself, a pretty courageous move in 1970s family town America— in the hopes that that would sate her discomfort. "I knew that I liked boys," she said. "I was already bullied for being effeminate. Eventually I was like, 'Can we just get this out in the open, so I can take a breath?'" But while effeminate was always at the surface, she kept her desire to be *feminine* deeply hidden. "I never pushed away being gay," she said. "But I was always trying to push away the feminine part, the desire to cross-dress."

Transness was also much harder to conceptualize than gayness. In Eastpointe, Michigan, in the seventies, there was no internet to search, no books on gender or sexuality to read, no teachers or friends or family members to confide in, no trans people out and about to observe in passing. "It wasn't like I could say, like a young person can today, 'Oh, I'm in touch with these people and I think I might be transgender,'" she said. And yet, somehow, she always knew. "Since I was a teenager, my transness was like a beast that would surface every now and then, climb on my back and get its claws into me. And I would get depressed. And I would fight against it. And I wouldn't understand how I was feeling. And then I would get beyond it and it would be gone again for a little while," she said.

Imagine feeling so wrong in your own skin, and knowing, instinctively, what would feel right. Imagine that "right" feeling being so encased in shame and judgment and impossibility that you hate yourself for wanting it. Caught between that rock and that hard place, there was no world in which Daya could envision herself being happy. "It prevented me from having any interest in building my life because I didn't feel like I had much of a future," she said. "I didn't see beyond whatever pain and confusion I was in." She hated school and barely made it to high school graduation. She'd always dreamed of performing but was too insecure to try. Instead, through high school and the year that followed, she partied, drank, and did drugs.

In 1987, when Daya was in her mid-twenties, she moved to San Francisco, where she lived and worked in the Castro District, then the most openly queer place in the world. "It was still a very, very queer-male place," she said. "You just didn't see a lot of trans women running around. And if you did, the people were made fun of." Nonetheless, she felt free enough to try. She found a therapist and began the process of transitioning.

But one year into the process, she gave up. The daunting part, she'd realized, wasn't the physical process of transitioning. It was building a world for herself as a trans person.

She worried about how she'd make money, how she'd look, and what it would be like when she could no longer hide her otherness, not for a minute, not from anyone. Her friends were supportive, but would they continue to be? After spending her entire childhood being bullied, she was afraid that even here, in the heart of the gay and lesbian world, she would lose the safety she'd found among the masses. "I was fearful of being ostracized and othered when all I had to do was just try to fit in, and I wouldn't have to deal with that," she said. Bolstering these fears were an overwhelming number of daily decisions. "What am I going to do, just like, choose a female name and start wearing a dress out of nowhere?" she said. "I didn't know how to do that. It was too much of a leap for me to take by myself."

It didn't help that doctors and therapists guarded the gate to medically transitioning like Fort Knox. "Back then, there was one path," said Daya. "You started seeing a therapist, you got to the point where the therapist took you seriously enough to prescribe you hormones, you got electrolysis, you started living the real-life test where you lived in that gender for a certain amount of time, and then you got surgery." At every stage, it was critical to reassure the therapist that you were still 100 percent in—to "perform the gender they expected of you, in order to get the permission from the gatekeeper to do your thing"—making it seem like the inevitable anxieties and vulnerabilities were signs of unfitness. All this had to be paid for out of pocket and totaled tens of thousands of dollars, money that Daya didn't have.

Today, it's possible to find entire communities, online or IRL, that have deconstructed the scaffolding around "male" and "female" enough to be precise about these terms. They share a belief in basic principles: There is, for example, a difference between sexuality and gender—you can be attracted to gay men, straight men, or women and separately identify as a trans woman. Also, gender is a spectrum, not a binary, and the expression of that gender is fluid and multifaceted. Today, Facebook offers more than fifty terms for gender on user profiles. Eight percent of eighteen-to-twenty-two-year-olds identify as transgender or nonbinary, according to the US Census Bureau's 2022 Household Pulse Survey.[4] Kids these days are growing up with the framework, language, and support to envision gender differently. But in the late eighties, there was no such shared understanding. And at this point in Daya's life, she had still not had a single conversation with another trans person.

The final straw? She had developed a crush on a gay man, disrupting the fragile logic she'd built around her instincts. "My brain said to me, 'Okay, well, part of why you're doing this is you say you can't find love with someone who's gay, because you only have crushes on straight men. But if you're actually able to have a crush on this person, then that means you're wrong,'" she said. "'So you need to stop.'"

The tires screeched; the breaks burned. A year after writing her parents a letter announcing she was trans, she stopped the hormones, cut her hair, grew mutton chops, got tattoos, and became, in her words, "a Castro clone." She stopped going to therapy—"Why am I spending the money to go see a therapist? I don't need it anymore," she said—and dove headlong into drug use. By 1994, she'd also become a right-wing conservative. "When I listened to right-wing talk radio, the vitriol and the negativity matched what I had going on inside my spirit," she said. "I hated myself so much because I had failed that gender transition. I was ashamed that I started it. And I was ashamed that I had failed."

Musical theater probably saved her life. She started taking singing lessons and loved them so much that a few years later, in 2000, she worked up the courage to get headshots and try out for acting roles. Though she was in her late thirties and had never acted before, she was cast right away. She went professional almost immediately, met her future husband, Mark, on one of her first shows, and performed full time for the next seven years. "I thought I'd found home," she said. "It was the community and home I'd always sought." She paused. "Except, I never forgot about being trans." Once the glow of being a new performer wore off, the desire came back just as insistent as before.

In October of 2006, well into her forties, Daya decided to try again. Personally, she had more to lose now than she did the first time around. Transitioning meant she could kiss her theater career goodbye. "I was successful because I was of a certain age, I was male, I could sing, and I could act," she said. "But there was no way I could transition and keep acting."

Culturally, not much had improved since her first attempt fifteen years prior. The early 2000s were the Jerry Springer years; talk shows depicted transness as a grotesque spectacle, the camera panning frequently to the live studio audience's jeering faces. The "unexpected trans woman" gag had also become popular, where cis men, from Ace Ventura to Peter from *Family Guy* to the boneheads in *Dude, Where's My Car?*, retched at close encounters with trans intimacy. When they weren't the butts of such jokes, trans women were victims on procedural shows.

But she did have one thing that she hadn't before: a supportive partner. When she and Mark had first started dating, she'd decided to tell him the truth. "I've had questions about my gender identity," she'd said. "And I'm just sort of seeing my therapist to kind of talk it through and see what's up with that." He looked directly at her and said, "I think I would enjoy you as a woman. But I think I like you better as a man right now." Five years later, he backed her unconditionally. "I had a safety net—emotionally, financially, whatever—that I never had in the past," she said. "And I was able to say, 'Okay, I can try this now.'" I could relate. When you're contemplating a move that scares you, to a life where much is uncertain, the value of one person who truly knows and supports you is inestimable. Daya reached out to all the casting directors and told them she was retiring from performing.

After her transition, old friends showed up for her in ways she hadn't expected. Years ago, in her musical theater days, she had performed in a production of *Fiddler on the Roof*. The hair and makeup stylist for the show was none other than Karie, the salon owner from chapter 1, and they'd become friends through the course of the production. Two years after Daya started transitioning the second time, she got a call from Karie. "She's like, *'How dare you'*"—Daya mock-roared this with all the drama one might hope for from a professional stage performer—"'How dare you transition and not reach out to me. Get your ass in here and let's figure you out!'" Daya is grateful, not just for the help with her look, but for the invitation to her community. "She invited me into a sanctum that was particular to women that I hadn't had any way of encroaching before," said Daya. "I felt really accepted there. And that really helped me over the coming years to solidify who I was."

It's been nearly twenty years since Daya transitioned, and in that time she has had the peculiar experience of watching the mainstream world catch up to hers. She and Mark moved back to suburban Detroit over the pandemic and she's been shocked to see so many trans people, a bit like Dorothy returning from Kansas to learn that someone has managed to turn their world technicolor without all the trouble of going to Oz. "Here I was thinking I had to run full force from where I lived in order to get away, and maybe I did in 1987. But they didn't. They stayed, and they did it anyway. I have a lot of respect for that," she said.

The greater joy is the way that her theater career has restarted. In 2018, she returned to the stage, playing a character named Stu Rasmussen based on America's first openly transgender mayor. Back when she had started performing as a man, it changed her life because it showed her she could love and be successful at something. But she was always anxious to hide the parts of her that didn't fit the role. "I hear old recordings and I can hear myself hiding my sibilant S, because I didn't want to come off as gay on stage. So onstage, as a man, I always felt like a phony," she said. This post-transition return has been her true homecoming. "It was the first time I've ever felt what it felt like to perform in front of people without that anxiety layered on to it," she said. "And it was complete liberation."

But though trans visibility has brought unexpected opportunities, it's also brought pain. Back when Daya transitioned, a lot of people were thoughtless, but not hateful. Today, many of those who used to be ignorant are now aggressive. They call to ban trans peoples' rights to affirm their genders, perform, participate in sports, use public restrooms, and more. "It's way more open, which has given me more opportunities," she said. "But also I just want to crawl back under a rock and not know that all these people, including family members, would rather I not exist."

"You've done a lot of brave things," I said. "I think a lot of people feel fear and then just stop." I was thinking not just of her trans transition but of all the others: I thought it was brave to even consider transitioning in the eighties, with no support and no community. I thought it was brave to launch a professional stage acting career from scratch at thirty-eight, brave to leave it behind in order to become herself, and brave to start auditioning again years later, performing with a changed voice and body.

"I let myself be paralyzed for most of my life," Daya said. "I was convinced I would never be able to get outside of myself and my fear to quit smoking, quit drugs, quit drinking, start performing, transition . . . to do something that would be better for me on the other side of it. And I punished myself instead of doing the scary work." But the shame she once felt now feeds her bravery. "I still get to points where I'm like, 'Oh, no, I can't.' But I know I have to, because of what I've gone through," she said.

She hopes people read this story and understand that more is possible than they think. "I just . . . I want people to not be afraid of themselves," she said.

A great many people hide things about themselves in order to fit in. We bury our passions, hold our tongues, question our instincts, and deny core truths about ourselves. We get stuck in bad jobs. We lash ourselves to bad relationships. We see the ways that the world is not set up for us—the stigma, the confusion, the financial and institutional and career hurdles we might face—and are overwhelmed by everything we will have to build, explain, forgo, endure, and defend just to swim against that tide. It takes tenacity to see the world as it is, and also to be yourself within it, without succumbing to the gravitational pull of the status quo. But it is worth it, and not just for yourself. It's hard to know how many people you influence just by building your world.

Tools for Building Your World

You don't always realize how many cultural templates are guiding you until you start opting out of them. But the upside is the chance to live an authentic life and break free of the stress and restriction of societal norms. Find your people and hold tight. If you have conviction in your beliefs, you will help others to have conviction in theirs.

How to Build Your World in Community with Others

Seek Support

Daya didn't have the internet. You do! You can search for Instagram and TikTok influencers, nonprofit organizations, Reddit and Quora communities. There are so many ways to find community. Granted, you may need to do some filtering. In addition to genuine people looking for connection, there are also predators and trolls. But know you're not alone.

Tell Your Story: Interview a Kindred Spirit

Connect with someone who's working to build their world in the same way you are: a fellow freelancer, bonus mom, or trans person. Maybe it's a friend, maybe it's someone you've found on social media or through a support group.

- Connect with this person and ask if they have time for coffee or a quick video conversation.

- Write down a list of questions you have and things you're struggling with in your transition. Use that list to guide your conversation.

- Remember: This person is (probably) not an expert! The point is not to get answers. The point is to connect and compare notes. Also remember: Just because this person is also freelancing, bonus momming, or trans, doesn't mean you'll agree on everything. Everyone's experience is different. That's one of the things that makes connecting so rewarding.

- Afterward, write about your experience. What surprised you? What intrigued you? How did it feel? What did you learn?

How to Focus on Those Who Matter, Not Those Who Mind

Trust in Your People

One reason we're often afraid to swim against the tide is that we're afraid of what "they" will say. We think the world will judge us, bully us, misunderstand and fear us. But break apart your definition of "they" and you will likely find a handful of true bullies in a sea of neutral-to-positive forces. One person who truly understands and cares about you can overcome an entire ocean of "theys."

How to Create a Multifaceted Vision of Success

Do What Centenarians Do

Writers Héctor García and Francesc Miralles went to one of Japan's "blue zones"—a term used to describe communities with a high percentage of people who've lived past one hundred—and learned about the Japanese concept of "ikigai," which translates to something like "reason for being." On the tiny island of Okinawa, they found robust communities of people in their eighties, nineties, and one hundreds waking at dawn and devoting themselves to their daily tasks. They visualized ikigai as a framework of four overlapping circles.

- What you love

- What you're good at

- What you can get paid for

- What the world (or your particular community) needs

I don't interpret ikigai as one thing at the center of those four circles. I think it's more useful to see it as a combination of things that total up to your purpose.

- First, brainstorm a few items in each circle. Overlap is great! The ideal is to have two or three meaningful activities that each cover multiple circles.

- Reflect on whether your life, in total, is fulfilling all of these circles. Which circles are harder to fill in? How can you invest more of your time, energy, and learning in this area?

Don't Forget

Take Pride in Your Differences

The fact that you are figuring things out will help those around you more than you know.

Allow Contradictions

You may not know how you feel because you haven't figured out how to put words to it yet. You are capable of more as you expand. Things that feel scary at first will become old hat. You can change your opinions and decisions as you learn and grow.

Just Because You Share an Experience Does Not Mean You Are Part of a Monolith

Respect similarities and differences. Embrace the challenges of being supportive and intersectional while recognizing you are also a unique human with your own values, viewpoints, and life priorities.

10.

Start Over

There's no such thing as happily ever after. What do we do when everything we've built shifts? At the end of the day, what really matters?

I finally felt like I had figured it out. I was in a groove with work, writing, and trapeze. I was a better partner and a better friend. I had successfully created an à la carte life. Then, I got pregnant.

She was conceived in Hawaii, maybe on New Year's Eve, maybe a day before or after. We were low-key trying. I'd had my IUD removed in November right after the wedding, and it was our second month of living dangerously. It wasn't a surprise and it wasn't an accident. It also wasn't a result of some deep hunger. Some people imagine themselves as parents from the beginning. When they close their eyes at age ten, they dream of pushing babies around in strollers and spoon-feeding them small piles of peas. When I closed my eyes, I felt myself ripping the perfect dive or seeing my name in print. It's not that family wasn't in the cards; it just wasn't a clear part of my vision.

But then I hit my late thirties and the now or never alarms started ringing with urgency. "I want to be a mom someday, or rather, I don't not want to be a mom someday," I wrote in my journal a few weeks before I got pregnant.

That first positive pregnancy test ignited a roiling ball of anticipation that shot out feelings as random and powerful as solar flares. Joy flashed, with dreamy visions of tiny fingers squeezing mine, the weight of a too-large head at peace on my shoulder. Curiosity sent out tendrils: Would she be more of a thinker or a feeler? Would she be active? Artistic? Imaginative? Empathetic? Fears erupted: What if she was born with challenges we couldn't anticipate? What if we ruined her somehow? Every once in a while, I shook with giddiness: Nicholas and I had signed up to do one of the hardest things I could imagine, together. I couldn't wait to see how we'd grow.

But the most consistent feeling was foreboding. I spiraled through metaphors in my journal, trying to make sense of what was coming: "I feel like I'm rapidly getting sucked into a black hole . . . on the way up a roller coaster . . . on a spaceship to Mars," I wrote. It's a fact of most anticipated transitions that it's much easier to imagine what you're losing than what you're gaining. I was keenly aware that bringing a child into the world meant less freedom, less sleep, less money. And not temporarily. It meant leaving behind a lot of things I loved—my body, my lifestyle, my autonomy—for responsibility that lasts forever.

I'd only attempted to change one diaper in my life and it was an epic failure. Over a decade ago, in the house of seven stories, my ex-boyfriend, a random musician, and I had been put in charge of a robust eighteen-month-old. I held her shoulders while the musician held her legs and my ex managed the changing. Still, she managed to flip over and escape, dragging the dirty diaper behind her. Would I ever learn? I'd hardly held a baby, bringing on the all-too-familiar athletic holdover: *I haven't practiced enough to be a good mom.*

A handful of my trampoline students were moms. "I worry that my body will never be the same again," I threw out in class one day, hoping someone would refute me. The moms chimed in, almost in unison, "Oh, it won't." My heart sank. Of course it wouldn't.

Most of my friends were childless, and I had a hard time picturing what life looked like with kids underfoot. Would I be able to bring the baby to the trapeze rig and stow her in a Pack 'n Play like my mom used to do with me at the pool? Would I need to make more money? At this point, my agent and I were compiling a list of editors at publishing houses to pitch. What if none of them wanted to acquire my book? What if one of them did acquire my book, but I was too incapacitated by motherhood to finish writing it?

I intellectually understood that grief is an inevitable part of change, that the unknown is full of both risk and opportunity, that it's possible to choose curiosity over fear. I had spoken to friends and strangers about their most immense pivots and witnessed how the act of transition, whether good or bad, anticipated or unanticipated, increased their capacity for life.

Yet even with all that knowledge, I was still afraid.

I tried to research my way past this fear of the unknown. But motherhood is so wrapped in expectations, the actual experience is often obscured. Pop culture has created a false dichotomy: Some moms keep their passions; others cave to "just" being moms. In my rage to predict my own future, I ate that dichotomy up.

On the one hand were stories about super moms: comedian Mindy Kaling, who had two children on her own in 2017 and 2020 while at the same time creating, producing, writing, and acting in two television series and a handful of movies; Olympic runner Allyson Felix, who spent her first pregnancy battling preeclampsia and fighting Nike for a contract that didn't penalize her for being pregnant, then won Olympic gold in Tokyo in 2020 while raising a sleep-resisting two-year-old; Jen, from chapter 7, who juggled single motherhood, graduate school, and full-time work so she could continue her own education *and* send her kid to private school.

On the other hand, I found a pile of research that showed Mindy, Allyson, and Jen to be outliers, highlighting how hard it is for women to keep nurturing their other identities when they become mothers. Many relinquish their careers: The wage gap between men and women, which currently has women making an average of eighty-four cents to every dollar earned by a man, doesn't really appear until they have kids, according to a 2020 study in Social Science Research.[1] They relinquish their sex lives: Around 9 percent of women experience some sort of sexual dysfunction, but for new mothers, that number rises to 40 percent, according to a 2021 study in a Polish medical journal.[2] They relinquish their happiness: "When a child is born, parents experience a decrease in happiness that doesn't go away for a long time, in addition to a drop in marital satisfaction that doesn't usually recover until the children leave the house," reported a 2021 article in *The Atlantic*.[3] Women in America, more than women in other relatively progressive countries, are pressured to lean fully into motherhood. A whopping 41 percent of Americans in 2017 agreed "the role of women in society is to be good mothers and wives"—nearly twice the percent of participants in Sweden, Spain, or Great Britain.[4] I wanted to be a Mindy, an Allyson, or a Jen, but I couldn't imagine how I'd do it. I didn't want to lose my autonomy, my identity, or my sexuality to motherhood, but I couldn't imagine how I'd avoid it.

· · ·

During my pregnancy, I spent a lot of time thinking about a conversation I'd had years before with Olympian Amy Chow. She was one of the first retired athletes I'd reached out to with my nascent book idea. She was also my childhood hero. I was an eleven-year-old gymnast during the 1996 Atlanta Olympics, when Amy and her "Magnificent Seven" gymnastics team won the all-around gold. In a sport whose default was total home-schooled dedication, Amy was an athlete-nerd like me, balancing gymnastics with national piano competitions and a full school day. While the rest of her team was living it up on the post-Olympic arena tour, Amy was flying back and forth to Palo Alto for her freshman year at Stanford.

The accomplishment train didn't stop chugging when Amy retired from gymnastics after the 2000 Olympics. She graduated college with a GPA that somehow ended up above a 4.0 (4.02). She started medical school, but soon grew bored with "just" being a med student and took up pole vaulting. With weekly instruction from a friendly neighbor who happened to also be a pole-vaulting coach, she cleared thirteen feet, four inches—not quite Olympic height, but totally respectable in, say, an NCAA national championship final. She began her residency at Stanford's Lucile Packard Children's Hospital and a year later, decided that diving would be her new hobby.

On a rainy Wednesday in 2011, I arrived at diving practice to find someone new stretching on the mat, her head buried between her knees like a crisply folded paper. She looked up. At that point she was nearly twice the age she was at the 1996 Olympics, but she looked exactly the same as she did then. I played it cool, like I had not spent sixth grade jamming my school papers into a folder with her face on it. For the next six months, we dove together. I was starstruck, and Rick was too. We'd watch this thirty-three-year-old doctor hang from the stall bars, her legs rising to meet her face in endless sets of impeccable pike-ups. "She beats the shit out of you on abs," Rick would say gleefully. Typically, an elite tower diver limits herself to ten or fifteen dives off the ten-meter platform in a day—any more and fatigue sets in. Amy was logging twenty. She had carved out four precious hours a week—two on Wednesdays and two on Saturdays—to be the best diver she could be, and she wasn't wasting time.

Amy showed me a side of passion I hadn't recognized before. Passionate people have a reputation for being fiery, flamboyant, and all or nothing. Obsessed with greatness, like Rick. Burning with feeling, like Fabio.

Awash in suffering, like Christ. But Amy was quiet and pragmatic. Rick used to question my dedication. "You're too even," he'd say. I thought it was a shortcoming to be as even-keeled as I was. Diving with Amy showed me a different side of passion.

I lost touch with Amy between 2012, when we both stopped diving, and 2020, when I drove to her house in the East Bay to interview her. It was week two of my sabbatical. I was curious to find out what great things she was achieving now, what was next on the accomplishment train. But she surprised me.

"So you're a pediatrician now?" I asked.

"Well, I did that for four years, and then when my second was born, I went out for maternity leave, and I didn't go back."

Amy had worked full time for a few years before having her first kid, and part time between kids number one and two. It wasn't a fulfilling compromise. "I felt like I was missing a lot of my kid's life," she said. "I just wanted to be with him. I wanted to see all the firsts that I missed." When her second was born, she decided to lean all the way into motherhood. I did quick math. Her youngest was five.

"So now you . . . take care of two kids?" I asked. I didn't know what else to say.

"Yeah, it's so cool to see them learning stuff and enjoying what they're doing," she said. She paused, sensing I needed more explanation. "I kept thinking: 'What if I want to go to this mommy and me gymnastics class? Or what if my kid has a performance? Then I have to take a special day off of work just to see it . . .'" she trailed off, leaving the conclusion unsaid.

"And . . . what do you do on the side?" I asked.

"I don't really do anything on the side," she replied. She went on to explain that her kids were still only in school part time, and she needed to drop them off and pick them up, and that her old job kept calling back to hire her again, but she kept deferring. Work wasn't worth it.

I'd left that interview feeling disoriented. I appreciated that you don't really get do-overs in motherhood—that the milestones pass at blink-and-you'll-miss-it speed. But it was hard to square what I'd learned about Amy with the leaned-in heroes of modern feminism. Amy, my hero. Amy, the encyclopedia definition of *high achieving*. She was "just" a mom.

· · ·

When I got pregnant, I remembered my interview with Amy. Knowing I had a child on the way cast parts of our conversation in a new light.

I called Amy back to ask her more about stopping work. I resolved to listen more carefully this time. In our first interview, I'd failed to learn something critical: Was she happy?

To my chagrin, she was fully aware of inspiring the type of reaction that I'd had at first. "I've gotten a couple interview requests over the last couple years, people saying, 'We want to interview you because of your success as a doctor.' And I have to write back and say, 'I'm not practicing anymore. Do you understand that? Do you still want to interview me?'" she said. "How come being a mom doesn't have that same clout? Why is it that we feel like our success is defined by our careers so much?" I blushed, my present self cringing at my former self's narrow-mindedness. I now felt frustrated right along with her. I thought about all the facets of motherhood that panicked me and also all the facets that I looked for-ward to. Who was I to judge someone for devoting themselves to this grand adventure?

"What do you think success means?" I asked Amy.

"I always believed it was something very tangible," she said. "Like, 'I want to go to the Olympics' or 'I want to be a doctor.' But now I don't have to be the 100 percent best anymore."

"You seem . . . happy," I said.

"Definitely," she replied.

The idea that I'd have a child myself—a daughter, someday soon—gave me not just empathy, but gratitude, for Amy's path. She had made the choice that enabled her to spend her time the way she wanted, with her kids. It wasn't an easy choice. Decisions of that much magnitude rarely are. But Amy helped me realize that there were women I respected at both poles: mothers who were deeply dedicated to professional goals and passions, and mothers who were embracing stay-at-home parenting. Most exist somewhere in between.

Amy had allowed her definition of success to evolve. Too often, we cling to the model that's worked in the past, like I had, replacing grades and medals with pay raises and promotions. Life is short. Give yourself the grace to shift paradigms. And recognize that most seasons don't last forever. Kids grow, interests shift, energy ebbs and flows, you change, your people change, the world changes.

Many people aren't lucky enough to choose whether and how much they work. They work a job or two or three to survive, or they live in cultures or relationships where the decision is made for them: the man is the breadwinner, the woman stays at home. But I, like Amy, was living a life of privilege, which is to say, a life of choice. How much of my pie did I want to go to writing, to working, to trapeze, to my husband, to my child, to myself?

. . .

My mom, my husband, and I were two-thirds of the way through making dinner when my water broke. We turned off the burner under the chicken coconut curry, unplugged the rice cooker, hustled into the cab, and sped to the hospital, where I spent the next thirty-one hours trying in vain to get the baby to come out. About eight hours in, I had to ask a nurse if I was in labor. She laughed at me and said, "Honey, if you have to ask, you're not." Eventually, we got to the point where it was dangerous for the baby to remain inside me. The doctors came in, notified me that I needed an emergency C-section, halted the contraction drugs, and wheeled me into the operating room. Some combination of drug withdrawal, sleep deprivation, and intensity caused my arms and shoulders to shake so wildly that they had to strap my entire body down to the table, and when I vomited, someone had to turn my head so I didn't throw up straight in the air like a geyser. Aside from the final thirty minutes, my most prevalent emotion was "bored." I've never heard anyone use that word for a birth story before, so here it is, added to the canon.

From the moment the surgeon pulled out the baby, gooey and screaming, life was not boring. She did not keep us waiting but rather started exercising her tiny lungs the moment they touched the air. By the time they'd brought her around the curtain to place her body against the only skin I had available, my cheek, she'd stopped crying and was simply blinking, craning her head left and right in what I interpreted as wonder. Most newborns seem to keep their eyes squeezed shut, but hers were wide open. Deep, black eyes. Ocean eyes. We named her Ocean.

Before birth, moms-to-be are encouraged to take naps, give into their cravings, pamper themselves, and use their hormones as an excuse to indulge. The tone is so upbeat, it's dorky. "Take care of yourself, Mama. You're cookin' a baby!" The books focus on your changing body and how much energy it's exerting but never come out and say the full truth: "Sleep now, because once you have a newborn, you can kiss time to care for yourself goodbye." After Ocean was clean and swaddled, we rolled to a cramped recovery room for a few hours. I was wavering so completely between asleep and awake that I couldn't hold a thought long enough to make it come out as words. Mom kept trying to feed me—I remember her saying something about spaghetti—but all I wanted to do was sleep. But I couldn't sleep because there was this baby that needed me. But I couldn't lift her out of her bassinet because I'd been torn asunder and was still numb from the waist down, couldn't feed her because my milk hadn't come in, and could hardly look at her because my eyes were crossing with the exertion of keeping them open.

The first few days were far more difficult than I'd imagined. I somehow expected there would be a nursery where infants could go so their mothers could get three hours of uninterrupted rest at some point in the forty-eight hours after sustaining a six-inch slice through their abdominal muscles and uterus. It turned out there was, but only after my husband literally begged a nurse to take the baby away. I tensed every Olympic muscle trying to hold Ocean to my breast in a way that she'd latch. Feeding her left me so drenched with sweat that the surgical tape holding the IV to my hand curled up and needed to be replaced after every session. My husband is a data scientist, meaning he tracks every metric. So I know with absolute precision that on day two of Ocean's life, I spent eight hours and thirty-five minutes actively trying to feed her. Still, she lost 11 percent of her body weight in her first four days. In movies, a woman gives birth, the screen fades to black, and next you know she's cuddling at home in a sunlit bedroom. More than four out of five US women give birth at some point in their lives, but somehow this particular transition was still totally opaque.

At the end of day one, I couldn't imagine how we'd last a week, but somehow we did—and by that time, the baby had started gaining weight and I was changing diapers like I'd been doing it all my life. At the end of week one, I couldn't imagine how we'd make it to a month, but somehow we did—and by that time, the baby was sleeping four-to-five-hour stretches and sucking down milk like a pro. At the end of a month, I finally had the wherewithal to write down a few things, but I couldn't imagine how anyone with a child spent more than fifteen minutes a day on anything other than basic necessities. At the end of two months, my husband and I moved across the country from New York to California. By six months, we were both working new jobs with more responsibility than we'd had before the baby. And within a year after my daughter's birth, I had the thing I'd been working toward since before the pandemic: a book deal. A publisher wanted to publish my book.

. . .

Ocean is a year and a half as I'm writing this. If you'd handed me this squirming, tantrum-prone toddler on day one, I would have been traumatized. But we evolved together. A little after she turned a year old, she started resisting diaper changes, twisting her body around like Rulon Gardner on the wrestling mat. I learned to distract her with fake sneezes and let her hold the wipes for me, and when that failed, to pin her right shoulder to the changing table with my elbow while holding both legs in one hand and managing the diaper business with the other. Holding an infant for fifteen minutes used to leave me utterly exhausted. But now I can spend all day with this twenty-six-pound kid on my hip. Back in my agency days, I'd found it impossible to force myself to write in the mornings or weekends. Now I wake up at 5:30 a.m. five mornings a week so I can work when my brain is fresh. It has become the proudest part of my day.

The law of inertia applies to transitions: The longer you stay in one place, the harder it is to move. And the more you keep moving—the more you keep swimming with change instead of against it—the more prepared you feel for whatever might come your way. A baby learns and grows at a pace that is magnificent and terrifying. That I expected. But what I didn't anticipate was that I would learn almost as quickly as she did.

We cause ourselves a lot of stress by trying to skip straight to the end of a transition. There are things that seem unfathomable looking forward. The secret is that you don't know how capable you'll be by the time you reach them.

There's an old saw about New York, that at one point the city was growing so fast and people were taking so many horse-drawn carriages that it would be impossible to clear the manure piles, which would reach third-story windows by 1930. But then, of course, the automobile was invented and the old fears were nullified and replaced with entirely different ones. I needn't have worried so much about motherhood being the end of the road. I still miss the spontaneity of life without kids, and I don't devote as much time to trapeze as I did in my heyday, but those things are less important to me than they used to be. For the things that matter, like writing, I have accomplished far more than I did before I became a mother. I've learned this is true of most transitions: There's always something to grieve and something to gain. I grieve my fancy-free life. But I have gained a child who scatters cracker crumbs of joy across each day, a deep source of purpose in raising her right, and a new level of appreciation for the most important parts of my pie.

. . .

When I was Ocean's age my home was the natatorium where my parents coached, my bed was a Pack 'n Play a few feet from the pool, and my family was the diving team. I was a child of the diving village, steeped since birth in the chlorine air. My mom scoffed at maternity leave, bringing me to my first competition at one week old. When she needed her hands free, she passed me off to whatever high school diver was nearest.

Heather was fifteen when I was born, a ringleader of the cooler-than-cool posse of teenagers that ruled my parents' team in the mid-to-late eighties. While other teams were getting in trouble for drinking in their hotel rooms, these kids were stealing signs from restaurants and jumping off hotel balconies. They were also helping to raise me. "You were the first baby that any of us had ever seen," Heather said. While my parents were coaching, these gold-hearted hooligans held me, shushed me, and fed me. When I pulled myself up the ladder, they spotted from behind, and when I threw myself into the deep end, they were there in case my early swimming skills failed. When I started speaking, they worked with me for hours on my vocabulary, teaching me to yell "Rock your skull!" and punch an open palm, and to answer the phone by announcing that I had "rig-a-mort-is."

I was barely out of diapers when Heather left Pittsburgh. As I grew up, she was a faraway auntie who swooped back in when I needed her. When I was in fourth grade, she cleaned out her childhood bedroom and gave me all her old books, inspiring my lifelong love of Roald Dahl. She was there when I was graduating high school and contemplating college, and much later, when I was considering advertising as a career and New York as the place to do it. She organized my dad's retirement party and would call my mom to gab for hours a couple times a year. She was one of the first people to look at an early proposal for this book. I don't think she ever anticipated being part of it.

My mom was the one who got Heather's text, asking if there was a time we could all talk together. That's when she gave us the news.

Pancreatic cancer. Stage 4. Inoperable. It had spread to her liver, lungs, and gallbladder. No medicine. No surgery. No treatment. All they could do was patch things up as best they could, turning her digestive system into a game of Chutes and Ladders, a stent here and a stent there to bypass all the blocks and backups. Then they sent her home with an aggressive collection of painkillers to sort out how to die with dignity.

The doctor gave her twelve weeks, best possible scenario, then told her all the things that could go wrong—heart attacks, strokes, the failure of any one of the bypasses they'd jerry-rigged to keep her digestive system puttering along. She could feel the cancer growing inside her. "Personally, like inside, I feel like I probably have another month from right now," she said. Not four thousand weeks, but four. Maybe. "If anything goes wrong, it goes wrong. And, you know, they give me a bunch of morphine and push me out to sea," she said.

Mom immediately asked if she could visit. Heather equivocated. "Part of me would really love that, but . . . I've got to think about it," she said. She explained that it was tricky—she never knew when the pain would be too much, when she'd have to go full ham on the drugs and get too loopy for visitors. "I've tried to keep it very low-key in terms of who I tell, because every conversation with someone that I haven't talked to becomes really draining," she said. "I have to protect my time and protect my family by not draining myself."

I gave her an update on the book and slowly, haltingly worked my way around to the question I wanted to ask. She responded immediately. "Of course you can interview me." The gift was so heavy I almost dropped it. "Are you sure?" I asked. "I don't want to take another hour away."

"All those other conversations are just conversations," she said. "But words last, you know?"

I called her back the next day.

Heather's voice sounded exactly the same as it always had, a wicked Pittsburgh rasp. I don't know what she looked like—she asked to do our interview off camera. "Sorry about the Zoom thing, but you know, there are days," she said.

Her husband, Bill, has always had a culinary streak, and he's showing his love by finding ways around all the restrictions caused by Heather's digestive chutes and ladders. His personal mission is to make her the world's best stent-friendly morsels, shaving off tiny shreds of filet mignon with a razor and experimenting to find exactly the right type of acid to poach a Chilean sea bass down into its most tender form. Her parents and sister spend all the time they can at her condo on the lake outside Charlotte, North Carolina, and while they leave the cooking to Bill, they have also embraced the best-possible-moment philosophy. "It comes down to these little day-to-day things, like, 'What's the best bite she can have today?' 'How are we going to get her to have the best nap of the day?' And someone's like, standing there with a clipboard and a timer saying, 'Hey, how can I improve this?'" Heather said.

I almost laughed. "That sounds . . . athletic."

"It's hilariously athletic," she said. "Honestly, it's like when you're at Olympic Trials and you're like, 'How can I do the best in this moment that I can? Maybe I can, maybe I can't, but I'm gonna try.'"

Heather wasn't an Olympian. She stopped diving three decades ago. But here and now, at the end of it all, in the single hour we had to talk before we both knew her energy would wane and she'd need to go nap or take her pain meds or be with her family, she returned time and again to the gratitude she felt for sports. Not for the medals she won or the skills she learned, but for what they taught her. She recognizes diving as the setting where she learned how to be a good competitor and a good human. "It teaches you to give your friend the best hug you can give them," she said. "How to find the good in people that you don't like, how to compete side by side with them and hope that they do well." Gratitude is contagious. I felt the truth in her words, and they left me swelling with thanks for the village that raised me, the parents who taught me that doing hard things is fun, the teammates who shared my love, fear, and triumphs, and the coach who pushed me to learn what I was capable of.

She is rapidly approaching the moment when her worst fear comes to fruition: not death, but pain. "I'm afraid of that overwhelming, all-over pain that can't be ignored," she said. "But the bigger fear is, how do I handle it? Can I be the badass that I've always been?" Sports give her the tiniest spark of confidence that she'll know how to cope. "Physical pain is something that I've done," she said. "I spent a good deal of my life relegating pain to a place where I acknowledge it's there, and as long as I'm not further damaging it, I'm going to be okay with it." The old sports lessons didn't just teach her how to live. They are also helping her grasp how to die.

Regarding the afterlife, she has hopes. "I'd very much like to fly," she said. "In my prayers I'm always like, 'Before whatever else happens, just let me take a little zoom around.'"

After seeing her shadow-pocked digestive system on the CT scan slides, she knew it was bad. Google result number one confirmed that no one gets out of stage 4 pancreatic cancer alive. More than a week passed between getting the scan results and learning that there was nothing anyone could do about them. She spent that week agonizing over what treatment decisions she might need to make. It's a morbid thought experiment turned all too real for terminal cancer patients: How much are you willing to suffer for an extra month of life? But when the team of surgeons and oncologists filed in to deliver the verdict, someone said, "If we removed everything that needs to be removed, you'd have nothing left." Chemo and radiation would have killed her much faster than they would have cured her. "They just took that right out of my hands," she said. "I was thrilled about that."

Some of her friends have not been able to relate to this. They wonder how she can be so resigned; why she's refusing to spend all day and all night chasing down clinical trials. This taxes her patience. "This has been decided, by whatever authority, God, planetary energy, whatever," she said. "I'm now going to be going somewhere else. And I'm on that train. So trying to get me off that train or onto a different train, that's unproductive."

There are similarities between her situation and Jimmy's, who made his life miserable by refusing to question his doctors' Parkinson's prognosis. And there are differences. Infinitely more is possible in decades than in days. Beyond that, Heather's peace has stemmed from a pragmatic acceptance of her circumstances. Jimmy describes his early decline as a period of denial. Heather is not in denial. On the contrary, she's facing what comes and choosing to live her life fully focused on the present, rather than distracted by moon shots. She doesn't want to die. If there was a chance chemo could significantly add to her time, she'd do it. But may we all be able to recognize a silver lining when we see one: In a life full of murk and uncertainty, a sure thing can be a blessing.

I'm reminded of the serenity prayer: *God grant me the serenity to accept the things I cannot change, the courage to change the things I can, and the wisdom to know the difference.* Heather is living this prayer, and it has brought a peace to her life that I wouldn't have expected. Naps alternate with patches and pills. She's dived into the administration of pain meds like a general strategizing in battle mode. She has drugs to ease the daily peaks and valleys, drugs for expected and unexpected barrages, drugs for specific attacks, like Lorazepam for cramping. "I'm playing around with things like . . . can I take the painkillers and not the Lorazepam?" she said. "I don't wanna get too cute with it. But when I have to take all of it, then I become really stupid." She'll start telling a story out loud, then notice her voice is taking a different track than her brain, thinking one thing while hearing entirely different words come out of her mouth. In those moments, hovering on the edge between terrifying and hilarious, it's critical that the mood tips in the right direction. "My sister will be like, 'Say that again?' and then I won't even be able to do it and we'll just laugh until my stomach hurts and I have to take more Lorazepam," she said. I thought, *If Heather can do this, I can.* We don't have to just let emotions run roughshod over us. Scary or funny? With the right people around us, we can choose how to react.

There's no rushing to accomplish bucket list items, no grand plans for a last big trip. Heather doesn't have time for one last conversation with everyone who played a role in her life. A lot of the stories in this book have been about prioritization, or reprioritization, and Heather has had to prioritize more aggressively than anyone.

This begs the question: What matters to Heather?

Not accomplishments. "Who cares that I traveled the world or was on a national team? None of that matters, it just doesn't," she said.

Not self-improvement. "What else am I going to fix about me right now? Not a damn thing," she said. "There are four weeks, I'm sure I could put together a little program and work on that. But like, is it really me that needs to be worked on now? No."

Not trying to change one single thing about the past. "When I look at all the things I have done, it's such a big, long, happy checklist of everything I wanted to do. I was lucky to be surrounded by my parents, my friends, my coaches, my teams, my husband, my sister, and all of it has been just such a good experience," she said. "I hope for people to look at their lives that way when they're not dying, you know?"

What matters for the next however many minutes is family, both born and chosen. "They're the ones who deserve my time and have a right to it," she said.

Few of us consider our legacies; they are woven by others from scraps of the life we've led. But Heather has considered hers, and she is living it. "I can't think about anything better to represent me than to have been a good friend, that friend that they needed," she said. "It matters that I made someone's life better for a minute at any particular point in time. That's what matters to me." Instead of a bucket list, she's been working on a gift list. For one of her old teammates, she's made a bracelet that says, *'Til we meet again,* in morse code. It's not a promise, exactly. It's more a symbol, an ever-present reminder that in her last days, their friendship mattered. For her godchild and her stepson, she's trying to find a memento that reminds them that she loves them and that, whatever they run into in the future, "It's all gravy, baby."

"You seem so . . . at peace with this," I said. "Has that been hard for you? Or is that just a perspective that's been sort of natural?"

I couldn't see her through the phone, but I imagined her shrugging. "Natural," she said. "I have to credit a big part of that to my husband, who is one of the calmest people that I know. And to my dad, who has always just been like, 'Hey, things are what they are. You can rail against them, or you can find the solution.' And in this case, the solution is to be calm." Beneath the surface of that calm lies something powerful: *radical acceptance.* Heather showed me how much is possible when we don't hide from what is.

Every single evening since they learned about her diagnosis, Heather's neighbors in the condo upstairs have turned on a bubble machine to show her that she is loved. She spends those evenings surrounded by family, watching bubbles dance on her balcony and leaves drift out on the lake. "There's this feeling that this is me blowing back and forth day-to-day, and it's okay. It's what the world does," she said.

Heather gave me hope that when it comes time to die, there's a chance I will find myself prepared, the same way that I was prepared for the unfathomable task of motherhood. My life isn't shaped like a ladder, with even rungs and a continuous progression of skills. With each transition, there are lessons to keep and lessons to leave behind. But our capabilities do add up. Transitions give us the tools we need to face the next one, and the next one, and the next one, on to the last one.

My last question for Heather was the same as my last question for everyone. "What advice do you have for others going through a major transition?"

"That's a tough one," she grumbled. "Actually, that's the toughest one."

"I know, sorry," I said. "I ask that of everybody and nobody likes it." No one likes being put on the spot with advice—it's easier to tease it out of a story in post than get it all at once in a pithy sound bite. Still, I always ask.

"Let it happen," she said eventually. "If you know it's gonna happen, you just gotta ride with it." She gained steam, conviction stoking the fire. "The angrier you get, the more minutes you lose off your life. And now that we're talking about minutes in my life, literally, those minutes are precious. Anger is like smoking a cigarette. You're wasting your time. Don't fight change. Be at peace with it."

With that, we said our goodbyes.

"You're one of my heroes, dude," she said.

"And you're one of mine," I replied. I hope I've done her justice.

. . .

Always the same last question. Nearly always the same answer.

Nora the cancer survivor's advice: "Everything goes in phases. And they're always going to change again, for better or worse." *Change is inevitable.*

Shelby, the queer relationship therapist, said: "Once you've transformed, you can't go back into the cocoon. You have changed, and you have no other choice but to fly." *We were not meant to huddle in a cocoon forever.*

Emma, who fought through her depression, answered: "Instead of thinking about what comes next, think, 'I just have to get through today. I don't need to know who I am, or figure out an identity, I just need to not go back to that [old] one.'" *Trust change to bring you through uncertainty.*

Stanley, who transitioned into and out of prison, responded, "Sometimes, you can only discover the answer as you go. I think that's part of the transition. Being okay with not having it all figured out." *Control what you can, and beyond that, let change do its work.*

What matters is different to each of us. What jobs we choose or dreams we chase, the hang-ups we fight and the best selves we work to become. There's no one right way to live; the answer is as personal as our identities. There really is only one sure thing. Boil this book down until there are only two words left, take the lid off the pot, let the steam clear, and what you get is: *Accept change.*

Change is a boulder rolling down a hill. Whether you tipped it off yourself or some butterfly flapped its wings and started it rolling; whether you anticipated it or it caught you unaware; whether it resulted in a major event or a major nonevent, one thing is true: You can't control the boulder. You can't stop it, and you can't roll it back up the hill, and you can't blink yourself to a future where you don't have to deal with it. You can only control how you react in this moment.

A large part of our suffering around navigating transitions is our resistance to being in this state. It's powerful to accept the feeling of living in the unknown, and to recognize that until we cross over in our last great adventure, the only constant is change. Let it carry you.

Tools for Starting Over

So you've reached the end, only to find it's a middle in disguise. As long as you're alive, you'll likely be rewriting your story. In fact, life is a constant process of rebuilding, relearning, and re-evaluating. Change is inevitable. Trust the process.

How to See Yourself as a Change Agent

Tell Your Story: Reflect on Your Narrative

When anticipating a scary transition, remember that you may find you're capable in ways you didn't anticipate. Think back to your story and focus on the biggest transitions. What self-doubts did you have before the transition? What was the worst possible scenario? How did you avoid it? What happened instead?

How to Live Your Minutes Right

Practice Gratitude

"All of it has been just such a good experience," said Heather. "I hope for people to look at their lives that way when they're not dying, you know?" We can get so focused on the things we *don't* have that we forget to notice everything we *do* have. In her book *The Stress Prescription*, well-being expert Elissa Epel calls for "bliss bookends":

- When you wake up, sit up, stretch, put your phone down, take three mindful breaths, and spend five minutes considering:

- What am I looking forward to today?

- What am I grateful for?

- Before you go to sleep, sit down, get under the covers, put your phone down, take three mindful breaths, and spend five minutes considering:

  - What am I grateful for today?

  - Was there something that happened that went better than expected?

  - What made me smile or feel good today? Did I make someone else smile?

How to Reframe Anger (Or Sadness, Or Fear, Or . . .)

Mindful Metaphor

Undesired change can bring up a whole lot of negatives—negatives that have the potential to swallow up precious minutes, hours, and days. Mindfulness calms the part of your brain that erupts in emotion, strengthens the part of your brain that controls executive function, and interrupts the rumination cycle that keeps bringing up negative thoughts and ideas. This prompt is grounded in Buddhist mindfulness.

- Name the emotion. Say (in your head or out loud), "Anger is here."

- Take three mindful breaths, focusing on the sensations of air going into and out of your lungs.

- Notice how the anger is affecting your body. Are your shoulders tense? Shake them out. Is your heart racing? Take a couple more deep breaths.

- Imagine yourself on a riverbank, watching thoughts flow by. You are not in the water, just observing it. Your anger is a current or eddy; the thoughts that fuel it are bubbles that rise and dissipate. Let them come and go. There's nothing right or wrong about feeling anger, it just *is*. But you, your actions, and your sense of self don't have to be wrapped up in it. You can observe it without being in the water.

Don't Forget

Live

You can set your intentions and plot your course and interrogate your definitions of success all day long. But if you keep following your interests and savoring the people you love, you can't be too far off the mark.

Epilogue

I almost didn't go to the 2024 Olympic Trials. I hadn't been to one since I stopped competing; in fact, I'd barely watched them on TV. I'd spent most of the preceding years steering clear of diving. By 2024, I'd come to realize how special my old sport would always be to me. But I still had serious reservations about flying across the country for a diving meet I wasn't competing in. *I've been away too long,* I thought. *I'm not going to know anyone anymore.* But as the Trials began and I started seeing photos on Instagram of old friends in attendance, I realized how badly I wanted to go. I scrambled to sort out my schedule so my family could survive without me for the weekend, and then I was on a flight to Knoxville, Tennessee.

It had been twelve years since my final dive. A handful—maybe four or five—of the divers in the meet were still hanging on from my competition days. The fresh-faced babies who had been eighteen and nineteen back then were now in their early thirties and groaning like jaded boomers about their aching shoulders and bandaged backs. Once upon a time, I had retired at twenty-seven, not because my body had broken down but because the pool felt small and the world felt big. More recently, I'd been wondering if I still had it. What if I did ab workouts every day and stopped eating chocolate chips out of the bag—could I still come back for an Olympic medal? But now, watching the old guard continue to jump

and spin, their bodies held together by prayers and KT Tape, I knew that
the moment I let that spark touch the air it would burn through the
dream like cotton. The only reason I could imagine a comeback was that
I had gone out before my body hit thirty.

I needn't have worried about not knowing anyone. There were scores
of retired divers in the stands at Olympic Trials, all hailing from different eras and teams and levels of success. Some were old friends and
Olympic teammates; some I'd never met. One recognized me as the two-
year-old who stalled an international diving contest by leaping into the
water under the board he was about to dive from. Every single one of us
had experienced the euphoria of diving success and the gut punch of failure, and we were called back to the gathering like moths to a flame.
They say "game recognize game," but that's just the tip of the iceberg. It
was love recognizing love, grit recognizing grit, loss recognizing loss.
Yes, we must go where change leads us; yes, we moved on. But we'd all
come back for this one weekend to form a vibrant community. Moving
forward doesn't have to mean never looking back.

Several of Heather's old teammates were at Olympic Trials, the hench-
men that taught me "Rock your skull" and "Rigamortis." Heather, too,
had planned to be there—she'd booked her trip in the weeks before she
learned that the yellow tint of her skin revealed more than just a lack of
sun. She passed away five days before Trials began. We swapped Heather
stories in the stands.

"I was 'Good Heather' and she was 'Bad Heather.' That's how she's in
my phone," said one, before launching into a saga about one of the hi-
jinks she and Heather had gotten up to back in the day.

"She was always there when you needed her. She was one of the most
caring people I've ever met," said another.

"I think this is what she would have wanted. For us to share stories of
the good times and what a good friend she was," said someone else.

I was able to add—with the certainty of having asked her myself—that

that was exactly the legacy she had wanted to leave. It was a reminder to ask questions, learn what your people have to say about themselves, and understand their stories. Heather's legacy was not made in an eleventh-hour conversation with a kid she used to babysit. She loved her people well in all the big and small moments of her life, and they will always remember her for it. Still, with all the possible layers of interpretation and memory, it felt good to have asked for hers.

. . .

Rick and I watched my event from the top row of the stands, sweating in the cloud of humidity trapped by the roof. Someone did an inward two-and-one-half, cut off at the top and backed too far away from the board, then squeezed it around to vertical through force of will. "My inward was pretty good," I said. "Best in the world," Rick replied, as matter-of-fact as the heat. We spent the contest bantering back and forth like those old Muppets in the theater box.

Soon after I'd stopped diving, he'd retired from Stanford, only to be lured away from retirement by the head of the Australian national team. It was what he'd always wanted: a job that allowed him to focus 100 percent on achieving best-in-the-world greatness, making eights into nines and nines into tens. But by the 2024 Trials, he was in his seventies and newly retired again. He no longer had the energy to be a 24-7 coach. He wanted to fish in the summers and read by a lake and spend time with his big Boston family. But what do you do when you've spent your last five decades igniting and sustaining visions of best-in-the-world great-ness? How do you learn to live differently? "I just have one question," he said, batting me on the shoulder so I turned to face him. "How do I spend the next ten years?"

When I was a diver, Rick's voice had been *the* voice, narrating my goals and interpreting my actions. I'd spent the decade since my retirement cobbling together a new life that carried me beyond the external narrator, beyond the Olympic dream, beyond that one-choice vision of a life well lived. It was strange to find our roles reversed. His journey was just beginning.

My advice for Rick was the same advice I would have given myself ten years ago, the same advice that came up, in one way or another, across all the transitions in this book:

Try things. Find pursuits that you love and invest in them. Maybe it's trapeze. Maybe it's fishing. Commit to those things. Enjoy them. Fully appreciate the moments you spend doing them, even if you are just starting out and are painfully aware of how much you don't know yet.

Actively work on building relationships. They don't build themselves. Take care of your people, and more importantly, let them take care of you.

Know that you don't have to have it all figured out. That desire for certainty, for one all-encompassing pursuit that gives you everything you need forever? Let it go. It's okay to be passionate about something and not give 100 percent of your time to it. It's okay to love your family and also bar them from participating in your favorite hobby. It's okay to devote time and care to something with an uncertain outcome. It's okay to change your mind.

Life, if you're truly living it, brings you to periods of uncertainty, anxiety, and out-of-control change. It's okay to not know what's next.

Above all: Know that transitions are an opportunity to expand your heart past its former boundaries.

• • •

There's a grainy home movie of me at the age Ocean is now, back in the days when Heather was my favorite babysitter. I climb a bench on the back porch, bend my little legs, and leap to the ground. I'm trying to stick it like the gymnasts on TV, but instead I fall to my lumpy butt. *Again.* I lurch forward, giggling. *Again.* I bounce sideways. Family lore says I was at this for hours over days over months.

I give thanks to my parents, who nurtured that little girl's spirit, to my teammates, who shared her love, and to Rick, who helped her push further and love more deeply.

That little girl continues to flap her hands in excitement when her daughter learns a new word, when she catches a trick in trapeze, or when she makes her husband smile. She loves the incremental progress of creation, of struggling toward something better.

There are times when I've applied her spirit to the wrong things. Not everything in life merits her approach. But she continues to guide my heart to invest hard work into the right things. She reminds me that I'm not scared to fall, I'm excited to fly. I'm not here for the judges, I'm here for me. I didn't just crash, I learned. I feel her most when I write. She giggles at the adrenaline and mystery of hucking out a new idea. "Again, again," she says as I reread my paragraphs, shaving off words and molding sentences, making the shape more beautiful.

As satisfying as happily-ever-after endings are, they preclude life's real work: the daily choices that bring us happiness and meaning. So I'm ending, not with a happily ever after, but with a renewed commitment to living a creative and multifaceted life.

My world will continue to change. As will yours. Life is nothing other than a series of transitions. Embrace change, trust that you'll be capable of handling whatever comes your way, and keep searching for what makes you happy, engaged, and purposeful. Again. And again. And again.

A Tool for Deeper Friendships and Better Transitions

The before-and-after questions

Major life transitions are the stars in our constellations; the chapter breaks in our novels; the liminal spaces where we stage our personal revolutions. They represent the times when we've felt most afraid, most sad, most hopeful, and most excited. These periods of time have an outsize impact on who we are, and who we *are not*. By asking your loved ones to tell you about their biggest transitions, you are asking them to tell you what has mattered most in their lives.

The questions below are not answerable between pickleball points or in the five minutes before your next meeting or while you're cooking dinner (unless you, unlike me, are exceedingly good at conversing and cooking at the same time). They are not small talk. They are big talk. Schedule time in which your attention won't be divided—a long walk, a coffee date, a drink at an uncrowded bar—to focus on asking, sharing, and listening.

Prompt 1: What are the biggest transitions of your life?

- For some people, a death, marriage, or graduation is earth-shattering; for others, not so major. Let people tell you what transitions have had the most impact on them.

- Prompt 1 is often an overview—you'll get a pivot-by-pivot summary of your friend's life, with a smattering of details here and there. They might tell you about one huge transition; they might share five or six. Author Bruce Feiler estimates that people experience three to five "lifequakes" (his term for those big before-and-afters) in their lifetimes, but notes there's a lot of variation.

Prompt 2: What happened? Tell me the story.

- This is where things get juicy. Start with one particular transition, the one with the most emotional heat, the one they seem most interested in telling you about.

- Ask your loved one to dive into the details. What was life like before that particular transition? What changed? How did they react to that change? What scenes or moments stand out to them from that period of time, and why? What emotions rose to the surface? What do they know now that they wish they knew then?

- Listen well, and let curiosity be your guide. If they make a point or share a feeling that you deeply relate to, don't be afraid to mention it. But try to spend 80–90 percent of the conversation listening. You can offer to let them interview you next time.

Prompt 3: How has that shaped who you are today?

- What about this particular transition has stuck with them? What did they learn—or unlearn—that has an impact on who they are today? What did they lose during this transition, and do they miss it? How did their goals, priorities, and outlook on life change?

- We make so many guesses and judgments about who people are, from our closest friends to our newest acquaintances. This is a chance to actually ask them.

After prompt 3, assess the levels of energy, curiosity, and focus in the room. How are you and your loved one feeling? If you're excited to take on another of their transition stories together, proceed! If you're feeling drained and ready for a change of pace, there's no shame in wrapping up and giving your hearts and minds a break.

Finish with gratitude. Sharing big transitions can feel quite vulnerable. Ask how the experience was for your loved one, and whether they have any questions for you. Mention a point or insight they shared that really floored you, if one comes to mind. Offer to let them turn the tables at a later date. Make sure they know how thankful you are for the privilege of learning their story.

Acknowledgments

It takes a village to raise a book, particularly this one.

Aemilia Phillips, thank you for seeing a small spark in my proposal, rescuing it from the slush pile, and patiently helping to evolve this concept from a disjointed collection of athlete retirement bios to its final form. Since the beginning you've been the kindest advisor and the most powerful champion of this work. Many thanks to you, Chandler Wickers, and everyone at SKLA for your perspectives and support.

Amy Sun, you recognized all that this book could be before I did. Thanks for convincing me to take a leap and guiding me as I flew. You've been a phenomenal creative partner, cultivating a bolder vision, clearer stories, and better words. I'm so grateful and proud of where we've landed.

Nora Feely, thanks for reading every word (and helping me to remove many of them). You've made every chapter better, expanding my perspective, revealing my blind spots, and connecting me to a broader range of stories. Danny O'Neil and Xingjian Li, your encouragement helped me see myself as a writer, and your feedback made me a better one. Plus, writing is so much more fun with friends.

This journey started with Sarah Robb O'Hagan, whose Extreme You workshop helped me name this goal and get out of line, and Ivan Kaiser and Liesje Hodgeson, who probably knew I wasn't coming back after my sabbatical and supported me anyway.

It continued with coffee chats, late-night beers, and Zoom conversations with forty Olympians. It was an honor to compare notes (and loves, and scars) with each of you. Your insights showed me the shape of a transition and laid the foundation for this manuscript.

I honed my idea, and my craft, with a series of sharp-eyed, encouraging teachers, particularly Sarah Perry, Lydia Danziger, Gabrielle Bellot, and Terry Wolverton.

The dream became real thanks to the Penguin Life team. Meg Leder, Brian Tart, and Kate Stark shepherded this work into the world. Isabelle Alexander shared keen observations. Nick Michal, Logan Hill, Tess Espinoza, Katelyn MacKenzie, and Alexis Farabaugh turned a raggedy Word doc into a gorgeous book. Jessica DiDonato polished away all the weird phrases and ambiguous citations. Extra kudos to Jason Ramirez, Elizabeth Yaffe, and the cover design team for going above and beyond.

The best and most anxiety-filled thing about this book is that many of the people closest to my heart are in it.

Mom, thanks for always believing I'd find my way, and for teaching me how to meet people where they are. Dad, you demonstrated how to live a life of purpose. Kyle, you showed how unimportant all the "shoulds" are. Patty, you opened doors I didn't even know were there. Mikey, you showed me the power of genuine enthusiasm and curiosity. Rick, you inspired me to dream the dream. I wouldn't be who I am, and my story wouldn't be what it is, without you. I love you all and am grateful for the roles you've played in my life and in this book.

Nicholas, thanks for inspiring me to be not just brave, but bold. Thanks also for telling me every draft was fantastic, for reminding me to go on a run when I got antsy, and for cajoling me into shutting my laptop when I couldn't see through the postdinner haze.

And finally, thank you to everyone who told me their tales (including the many whose stories aren't written in these pages, and the several who let me interview them under the condition that their words would never, ever, be published). Thank you for being brave, open, and vulnerable in revealing your biggest before-and-afters. Your stories are a gift to everyone who will read this, and a message that none of us are ever truly alone.

Notes

CHAPTER 1: RECOGNIZE THE END

1. Redelmeier, Donald A., Joel Katz, and Daniel Kahneman. 2003. "Memories of Colonoscopy: A Randomized Trial." *Pain* 104 (1): 187–94. https://doi.org/10.1016/s0304-3959(03)00003-4.

2. Powdthavee, Nick. 2010. *The Happiness Equation: The Surprising Economics of Our Most Valuable Asset.* London: Icon.

3. Feely, Nora. "The Script Characters with Cancer Are Told to Follow." Catapult.co. October 25, 2021. http://magazine.catapult.co/column/stories/the-script-character-with-cancer-are-told-to-follow_nora_feely_jane_the_virgin_parenthood_survivor.

CHAPTER 2: HONOR GRIEF

1. Selassie, Sebene. "Pain X Resistance = Suffering." Happier App. October 28, 2023. https://www.happierapp.com/meditationblog/the-difference-between-pain-and-suffering.

2. Mills, Kim. "Speaking of Psychology: How Grieving Changes the Brain, with Mary-Frances O'Connor, PhD." American Psychological Association. March 30, 2022. https://www.apa.org/news/podcasts/speaking-of-psychology/grieving-changes-brain.

3. "Dr. Robert Neimeyer: The Three R's of Processing Grief." Open to Hope. YouTube video. June 20, 2017. https://www.youtube.com/watch?v=G7Lm-Fo2UGw.

4. Neimeyer, Robert A. 2019. "Meaning Reconstruction in Bereavement: Development of a Research Program." *Death Studies* 43 (2): 79–91. doi:10.1080/07481187.2018.1456620.

5. Neimeyer, Robert A. "Grief Therapy Masterclass Volume 4: Reinventing the Self After Loss." Psychotherapy.net. Accessed November 13, 2024. https://www.psychotherapy.net/video/grief-therapy-course-v4-resilience -informed.

CHAPTER 3: EMBRACE THE MURK

1. Manson, Mark. 2018. *The Subtle Art of Not Giving a F*ck: A Counterintuitive Approach to Living a Good Life.* New York: Harperluxe.
2. "For Gen Z, (Location) Sharing Is Caring." Life360. August 24, 2023. https://www.life360.com/blog/gen-z-location-sharing-study/.
3. Gallup, Walton Family Foundation. "Walton Family Foundation-Gallup Voices of Gen Z Study." Gallup. 2024. https://www.gallup.com/analytics /506663/american-youth-research.aspx.
4. American Psychological Association. "APA Dictionary of Psychology: Identity." 2014. https://dictionary.apa.org/identity.
5. Jackson, Maggie. "How to Thrive in an Uncertain World." *The New York Times*, sec. Opinion. January 13, 2024. https://www.nytimes.com/2024/01 /13/opinion/uncertainty-anxiety-psychology.html.
6. Hanh, Thich Nhat. 2011. *Your True Home: The Everyday Wisdom of Thich Nhat Hanh.* Shambhala Publications.

CHAPTER 4: ASK FOR HELP AND SEEK COMMUNITY

1. Grant, Adam M., and David A. Hofmann. 2011. "Role Expansion as a Persuasion Process: The Interpersonal Influence Dynamics of Role Redefinition." *Organizational Psychology Review* 1 (1): 9–31. https://doi.org/10.1177 /2041386610377228.
2. Bohns, Vanessa K. 2016. "(Mis)Understanding Our Influence over Others." *Current Directions in Psychological Science* 25 (2): 119–23. https://doi.org/10.1177 /0963721415628011.
3. Winton, Richard, Jack Harris, and Joe Mozingo. "Kobe Bryant's Death in Helicopter Crash Stuns the World, Leaves L.A. Grieving." *Los Angeles Times.* January 27, 2020. https://www.latimes.com/california/story/2020-01-27/kobe -bryant-killed-helicopter-crash.
4. Brown, Brené. 2010. "The Power of Vulnerability." TED Talk. December 23, 2010. https://www.ted.com/talks/brene_brown_the_power_of_vulner ability?.
5. Setiya, Kieran. 2017. *Midlife: A Philosophical Guide.* Princeton, NJ: Princeton University Press.

6. Junger, Sebastian. 2016. *Tribe: On Homecoming and Belonging.* New York: Twelve.

7. Mineo, Liz. "Good Genes Are Nice, but Joy Is Better." *Harvard Gazette.* April 11, 2017. https://news.harvard.edu/gazette/story/2017/04/over-nearly-80 -years-harvard-study-has-been-showing-how-to-live-a-healthy-and-happy -life/.

8. Santos, Henri C., Michael E. W. Varnum, and Igor Grossmann. 2017. "Global Increases in Individualism." *Psychological Science* 28 (9): 1228–39. https://doi.org/10.1177/0956797617700622.

9. Greenfield, Patricia M. 2013. "The Changing Psychology of Culture from 1800 through 2000." *Psychological Science* 24 (9): 1722–31. https://doi.org/10 .1177/0956797613479387.

CHAPTER 5: CONNECT YOUR DOTS

1. Little, Brian R. 2016. *Me, Myself, and Us: The Science of Personality and the Art of Well-Being.* New York: PublicAffairs.

2. Ahmed, Afran, Tatyana Cruz, Aarushi Kaushal, Yusuke Kobuse, and Kristen Wang. 2020. "Why Is There a Higher Rate of Impostor Syndrome among BIPOC?" *International Socioeconomics Laboratory* 1 (2). https://doi.org/10 .5281/zenodo.4310477.

3. Cooper, Anderson. "Effort to Get Help to Haiti; Stories of Survival Against the Odds; Haitian Field Hospitals Struggle to Fill Void." CNN. Aired January 18, 2010. https://transcripts.cnn.com/show/cnr/date/2010-01-18/seg ment/04.

4. Martschenko, Daphne, and Tymir Green-Ellis. "David Banks: Two-Time Olympic Rower and Role Model Talks Importance of Diversity." *Rowing in Color.* June 18, 2020. https://www.buzzsprout.com/866344/episodes/4227848 -david-banks-two-time-olympic-rower-and-role-model-talks-importance-of -diversity-with-daphne-martschenko-and-tymir-green-ellis.

CHAPTER 6: LEAVE YOUR BAGGAGE

1. Lieberman, Gabrielle, and Tom Handcock. "Gender Diversity in the C-Suite." Russell Reynolds. January 24, 2023. https://www.russellreynolds.com/en /insights/articles/gender-diversity-in-the-c-suite.

2. Damour, Lisa. "Why Girls Beat Boys at School and Lose to Them at the Office." *The New York Times*, sec. Opinion. February 7, 2019. https://www .nytimes.com/2019/02/07/opinion/sunday/girls-school-confidence.html.

3. Dondi, Marco, Julia Klier, Frédéric Panier, and Jörg Schubert. "Defining

the Skills Citizens Will Need in the Future World of Work." McKinsey & Company. June 25, 2021. https://www.mckinsey.com/industries/public-sector /our-insights/defining-the-skills-citizens-will-need-in-the-future-world -of-work.

4. Brassey, Jacqueline, and Aaron De Smet. "How to Become More Adaptable in Challenging Situations." *Harvard Business Review*. March 3, 2023. https:// hbr.org/2023/03/how-to-become-more-adaptable-in-challenging -situations.

5. Esfandiary, Jessica. "Pleasure, Kink, and BDSM With Shelby Terrell." *Open Late*. August 30, 2023. https://www.openlatepodcast.com/episodes/112.

CHAPTER 7: KNOW WHEN TO FOLD 'EM

1. O'Neil, Danny. "The Power of Quitting." *Seattle*. March 6, 2024. https:// seattlemag.com/love-and-wisdom/the-power-of-quitting/.

2. Duke, Annie. 2022. *Quit: The Power of Knowing When to Walk Away*. New York: Portfolio.

3. Gavin, Toya. "A Conversation about Lawyers and Depression." Solo Practice University. October 17, 2017. https://solopracticeuniversity.com/2017/10 /17/a-conversation-about-lawyers-and-depression/.

4. Organ, Jerome, David Jaffe, and Katherine Bender. 2016. "Suffering in Silence: The Survey of Law Student Well-Being and the Reluctance of Law Students to Seek Help for Substance Use and Mental Health Concerns." *Journal of Legal Education* 66 (1): 116. https://jle.aals.org/home/vol66/iss1/13/.

5. Krill, Patrick R., Ryan Johnson, and Linda Albert. 2016. "The Prevalence of Substance Use and Other Mental Health Concerns among American Attorneys." *Journal of Addiction Medicine* 10 (1): 46–52. https://doi.org/10.1097 /adm.0000000000000182.

CHAPTER 8: REDEFINE SUCCESS

1. "US VC Female Founders Dashboard." PitchBook. Accessed June 1, 2024. https://pitchbook.com/news/articles/the-vc-female-founders-dashboard.

2. Brooks, A. W., L. Huang, S. W. Kearney, and F. E. Murray. 2014. "Investors Prefer Entrepreneurial Ventures Pitched by Attractive Men." *Proceedings of the National Academy of Sciences* 111 (12): 4427–31. https://doi.org/10.1073 /pnas.1321202111.

3. Kovacevic, Dejan. "Kovacevic: A Dive like No Other for Krug." TribLIVE .com. August 5, 2012. https://archive.triblive.com/news/kovacevic-a-dive -like-no-other-for-krug/.

CHAPTER 9: BUILD YOUR WORLD

1. Bingham, Harry. 2020. "If an Agent Accepts Your Work, What Are Chances of Getting Published?" Jericho Writers. November 26, 2020. https://jerichowriters.com/if-an-agent-accepts-your-work-what-are-chances-of-getting-published-2/.

2. Cai, Julie Y., and Dean Baker. "The Pandemic and Self-Employment: An Update." Center for Economic and Policy Research. October 11, 2023. https://cepr.net/the-pandemic-and-self-employment-an-update/.

3. Wang, Liv. "People Are Working Less. Who— and Why?" ADP Research Institute (ADPRI). February 22, 2024. https://www.adpri.org/people-are-working-less-who-and-why/.

4. "Household Pulse Survey Data Tables." United States Census Bureau. 2022. https://www.census.gov/programs-surveys/household-pulse-survey/data.html.

CHAPTER 10: START OVER

1. Cukrowska-Torzewska, Ewa, and Anna Matysiak. 2020. "The Motherhood Wage Penalty: A Meta-Analysis." *Social Science Research* 88–89. https://doi.org/10.1016/j.ssresearch.2020.102416.

2. Fuchs, Anna, Iwona Czech, Agnieszka Dulska, and Agnieszka Drosdzol-Cop. 2021. "The Impact of Motherhood on Sexuality." *Ginekologia Polska* 92 (1): 1–6. https://doi.org/10.5603/gp.a2020.0162.

3. Bloom, Paul. "What Becoming a Parent Really Does to Your Happiness." *The Atlantic*. November 2, 2021. https://www.theatlantic.com/family/archive/2021/11/does-having-kids-make-you-happy/620576/.

4. Jackson, Chris. "Four in Ten Americans Believe Women's Role Is as Mothers and Wives." Ipsos. April 25, 2017. https://www.ipsos.com/en-us/news-polls/womens-role-as-mothers.